D0445170

For Cubs Fans Only

There's No Expiration Date on Dreams

By Rich Wolfe

Published by Lone Wolfe Press

ISBN: 0-9729249-6-5

Cover Photo presented and photographed by Don Marquess, Marquess Gallery, St. Louis, Missouri
Cover Design: The Flag of the Cubs Nation conceived by Dick Fox based on a concept and photograph from Mr. Don Marquess
Photo Editor: Dick Fox
Cover Copywriter: Dick Fox
Some chapter photos from the Marquess Gallery in St. Louis
Interior Design: The Printed Page, Phoenix, AZ

www.marquessgallery.com
www.baseballfineart.com

5-11-10   24-95

The author, Rich Wolfe, can be reached at 602-738-5889 or at www.fandemonium.net.

Page Two. In 1941, the news director at a small radio station in Kalamazoo, Michigan hired Harry Caray away from a station in Joliet, Illinois. The news director's name was Paul Harvey. Yes, that Paul Harvey! "And now, you have the rest of the story......

DEDICATION

To

Dickie Walters, Mr. Walter B. Planner
and Jim Hancock

World famous all over Davenport

ACKNOWLEDGMENTS

Wonderful people helped make this book a reality, starting with Ellen Brewer in Edmond, Oklahoma and Lisa Liddy at The Printed Page in Phoenix—wonder women who have been indispensable sidekicks for many years. Ditto for Special K in Falmouth, Massachusetts. A big thanks to Barry Friedland and Eric Lefkowsky for Lone Wolfe Press and the good guys over at Wolfegang Marketing Systems, Ltd.—But Not Very like Jon Spoelstra, John Counsell, and Jim Murray.

How about Travis Seibert in Madison; T. Roy Gaul in Bettendorf; Dave Morris, still the smartest person in Smithton, Illinois; Joe Liddy, Phoenix; and the Tower of Power in Ladue, my good friend Don Marquess. Speaking of good friends, gracias to Dale Ratermann, Rhonda "What Have I Created" Sonnenberg, the always enjoyable Peter Golenbock, and the knock-down gorgeous Carol Reddy in Phoenix-town.

Certainly, we will not forget Mike Jones and Susan Jeep; Michael "Stanford" Deuser; Stephanie Leathers at the Bleacher Banter; Panama Farlow, the King of Cubbie Fans in Osceola, Iowa. Ditto for Joe Hutchinson in Phoenix; Jim "Boo" Bradley in Wrigleyville; George Castle, Curt Smith, and Rick Wolff at Time-Warner; and Matt Fulks in Kansas City.

A tip of the hat to all those interviewed who missed the final cut—we just flat ran out of time. Three chapters were cut indiscriminately due to space limitations. It was close and we're gonna do it again next year. Thanks everyone!

PREFACE

What a year. They "cowboy-ed up" in Boston and promptly fell off the horse, "The Rocket" had his last glare waxing and waning under a Moon over Miami, and the Cards—minus aces—folded in St. Louis. But in Chicago, the Cubs fought the good fight, the Marlins finished the race, and the Cubs fans have kept the faith. It's right there in the Bible… way in the back somewhere.

Chicago is a pain in the neck…horrible traffic, lousy parking, miserable winters. I love Chicago…because it is the best sports town in America, with the best ball park in America with the most beautiful spring and fall seasons in America, but most of all, it simply has the best people of any major city in this country—particularly, the sports fans. The fans are knowledgeable, passionate, loyal, and most of all, enjoyable. Thus, it was with great anticipation that I set off to do this book…because it means I'll get to see many good friends again in Chicago and slip down to see the Irish play in South Bend…where "Win one for the Gipper" has been replaced by "Just win one."

For Cubs Fans Only is part of an 81-book series to be released in the next 15 months. From Green Bay to Austin, from Notre Dame to Boston, and 76 other places, loyal followers will trumpet their neatest stories about their favorite teams. No other team's fans will have the heartbreak nor the undying belief or the fun that characterizes all Cubs fans.

For some of us, baseball recalls broken glass, broken bats and broken dreams of lingering reflections of a simpler, more innocent time.

For many of us, baseball defined our youth, still overly-impacts our adulthood and is one of the few things, that can make you feel young and old at the same time.

And for all of us, it is—most of all—a game of memories: the transistor under the pillow, sitting outside a small store feverishly opening newly purchased baseball cards, our first uniform, learning to keep score, the dew and mosquitoes, the sounds of the radio or our first big league game. Little did many of us know that baseball would be the best math and geography teacher we would ever have…and none of us knew the vibrant green of the field during our first major league game would be the lushest green, the greenest green and the most memorable green that we would ever see in our entire lifetime.

Now is a good time to answer a few questions that always arise. The most often asked is, "Why isn't your name on the book cover, like other authors?" The answer is simple: I'm not Stephen King. No one knows who I am, no one cares. My name on the cover will not sell an additional book. On the other hand, it allows for "cleaner" and more dramatic covers that the readers appreciate….and the books are more visible at the point of sale.

The second most frequent query is, "You sell tons of books. Why don't they show up on the best seller list?" Here's how the book business works: Of the next 170 completed manuscripts, 16 will eventually be published, and only one will ever return a profit. To make the *New York Times* Bestseller List, you need to sell about 30,000 copies nationally at certain stores, at big book chains, a few selected independent bookstores, etc. My last eight books have averaged well over 60,000 units sold, but less than 15,000 in bookstores. Most are sold regionally, another deterrent to national rankings. While I'm very grateful to have sold so many books to the "Big Boys," I'm a minority of one in feeling that a bookstore is the worst place to sell a book. Publishers cringe when they hear that statement. A large bookstore will stock over 150,000 different titles. That means the odds of someone buying my book are 150,000-1. Those aren't good odds; I'm not that good of a writer. For the most part, people that like Mike Ditka or Dale Earnhardt—previous book subjects of mine—don't hang around bookstores. I would rather be the only book at a hardware chain than in hundreds of bookstores.

Example: My *Remembering Dale Earnhardt* hardcover sold several hundred thousand copies, mostly at Walgreens and grocery chains; places not monitored for the "best selling" lists. I sold the paperback rights to Triumph Books, Chicago. They printed 97,000 paperbacks, all sold through traditional channels. My hardcover did not appear on any bestseller list. Meanwhile, Triumph had a paperback on Earnhardt that made number one on the *New York Times* non-fiction trade list. Go figure. Also, I never offer my books directly to Amazon.com because I can't type, I've never turned on a computer and I keep thinking that Amazon is going out of business soon. For years, the more customers they recruited, the more money they lost…so sooner or later, when the venture capital is gone, the bookkeeping shenanigans are recognized, and the stock plummets, look out. Meanwhile, maybe I should call them.

Since the age of ten, I've been a serious collector of sports books. During that time—for the sake of argument, let's call it 30 years—my favorite book style is the eavesdropping type where the subject talks in his or her own words—without the "then he said" or "the air was so thick you could cut it with a butter knife" waste of verbiage that makes it so hard to get to the meat of the matter. Books such as Lawrence Ritter's *Glory of Their Times* and Donald Honig's *Baseball When the Grass Was Real.* Thus, I adopted that style when I started compiling oral histories of the Mike Ditkas and Harry Carays of the world. I'm a sports fan first and foremost—I don't even pretend to be an author. This book is designed solely for other sports fans. I really don't care what the publisher, editors or critics think. I'm only interested in Cubs fans having an enjoyable read and getting their money's worth. Sometimes a person being interviewed will drift off the subject but if the feeling is that baseball fans would enjoy the digression, it stays in the book.

In an effort to get more material into the book, the editor decided to merge some paragraphs and omit some of the commas, which will allow for the reader to receive an additional 20,000 words, the equivalent of 50 pages. More bang for your buck…more fodder for English teachers…fewer dead trees.

As stated on the dust jacket, there have been hundreds of books written about the Cubs but not a single one about Cubs fans— until now. From one baseball fan to another, I sincerely wish that you enjoy this unique format.

Hopefully, the stories you are about to read will bring back wonderful memories of your youth and growing allegiance to the Cubs. Wouldn't it be nice to have a do-over? It just seems that sometimes, as you get older, the things that you want most are the things that you once had.

Go now.

Rich Wolfe
Celebration, Florida

CHAT ROOMS

Chapter 1

Fandemonium

An Eclectic Sampling

ROOTIN' FOR THE CUBS IS LIKE FLYING SOUTHWEST FOR THE FOOD

Joe Bartenhagen

After growing up in the Midwest, namely Muscatine, Iowa, Joe Bartenhagen, 35, moved to Salt Lake City, Utah, where he insists everything is "fine." His job in advertising has afforded him many luxuries—chief among them, his wife Kristen.

No one chooses to grow up a Cub. How could you choose something like this? Who would choose something like this? All fumbling, fit-inducing and completely painful Tim McCarverisms aside, choosing to grow up being a Cubs fan would be like choosing to have a brain embolism, or choosing to have a comically minute penis, or choosing to listen to **Tim McCarver**—no one in his or her right mind would do it…

…Unless he or she were cursed.

The curse comes in the form of hope—though you don't know this when you're young, and older Cubs fans won't explain this to you. When you're young, it feels like certainty. But, older Cubs fans know this as pathological, unending, malignant, stupid, stupid, stupid, never-to-be-paid-off hope. By the time you begin to suspect the truth, say in 1984, back when you were fairly sure that Keith Moreland was a legitimate everyday player and that Gary Matthews' lunging, plunging coverage of left field was merely, ahem, unorthodox, it's too late.

Growing up, all the other kids were Cowboys fans, or Lakers fans, or Yankees fans. They were all reasonably well-adjusted—except for Allen Steckman, an ardent Thurman Munson devotee who threatened

> Brent Musberger was the home plate umpire when Tim McCarver made his pro-baseball debut for Keokuk (IA) in the Midwest League in 1959.

to break all of my pencils if I didn't call him Wild Man—and good-looking kids. I was, even though I didn't realize it at the time, already a mess. I was a bad dresser. My hairstyle never progressed much beyond simply being combed. Oh, and I was hopelessly, hopelessly chunky. Looking back, I realize this. At the time, I thought I was fairly cool. By no means a "Fonzie" but certainly a steady, if not periodically flashy, Richie Cunningham.

The reality that I was actually one hundred percent Ralph Malph—only chunkier—dawned on me about the same time that I realized that being a Cub fan indicated some unfortunate things about myself:

1. Being a young Cub fan meant that I was comfortable with under-achievement. Losing didn't really faze me—in fact, it felt like home.

2. "Wait 'til next year"—wasn't just the mantra of my team; it was the ethos that guided my personal development. While young Yankees, Dodgers and Cardinals fans were winning spelling bees and kissing Katie Reardon, I found myself biding my time, waiting for the right moment and telling myself that Katie Reardon wasn't worth kissing anyway—though she was totally and undeniably the Hottest Thing to ever walk the halls of Hayes Elementary; not only was she worth kissing—she was worth some sort of coerced marriage.

3. Like my favorite Cub, Dave Kingman, I had little range, streaky power, an amorphous strike zone and a penchant for, when faced with one of life's little, rolling groundballs, falling down for no reason and watching remotely as the ball trickled down the line and into the bullpen—as my cap slipped down over my eyes, a little.

My first real girlfriend was a Cardinal fan. She had no patience or sense of humor, though the Cubs—and I—amused her a little. Her dad—the source of her Cardinal fandom—was a dour little troll who spent his evenings parading around in his sagging JC Penney briefs and hating me, not necessarily for being a Cub fan, but for exhibiting the qualities of my team. He was no prize, ensconced in his not-as-tightie-as-one-might-likey-whiteys, but he made his admiration of the Cardinals seem like the result of an elegant though completely rational and obvious algebraic equation. Lou Brock was the symbol of all that was right with his team and all that was wrong with mine.

Invariably, I would counter with my theory that, while Ryne Sandberg was my generation's symbol of grace and power, Tommy Herr was my generation's symbol of why grown men should never, ever get a curly perm.

The relationship—with my girlfriend and her badgerish father—did not end well. Which is fitting since it neither started nor continued well.

In the end, I wonder: Do I have any advice for the young Cub fans of today? Yes—yes, I do…It is this: Cherish every moment you spend in Wrigley Field as a child—it is the most special place in all of sports. It will never change. And when you visit it 30 years from now, you will remember the very first time you walked in—how it smelled, how old it seemed… It is the best reason for being not a Cubs fan, but a fan of anything.

Most importantly, and in addition to all these things, work as hard as you possibly can to become interested in **soccer** or something else. Because being a Cub fan is the worst thing in the world—worse, even than being forced to listen to Tim McCarver trying so speak English.

That brings me to the incredible 2003 season. I'm watching the 2003 NLCS Game 6 and Steve Bartman commits what will forever be known as "The Act." It probably won't be forever known as that. I'm still working on what it will forever be known as. Frankly, I doubt my power to make something be known forever as something unless it is something minor and intensely personal like the time my wife caught me looking down the checkout girl's blouse and gave me what will forever be known as The Awful Look of Rebukement.

So, Bartman commits "The Act"—reaching for a foul ball and interfering with **Moises Alou's** ability to put another nail in the Marlins' figurative, post-season coffin…who would've thought that they would have won the World Series the way they did! And, comically, I scream. I scream "Ahhhhhh!" My wife says, "It's no big deal, it's just a foul ball." And I—again, comically—say, "You don't know! You

> More U. S. kids play soccer today than any organized sport, including youth football. The reason so many kids play soccer is so they don't have to watch it.

weren't there in 1984 when Leon "Bull" Durham let the ball roll between his legs, helping to finalize three straight Padre wins! You weren't there in 1989 when the Pacific Sock Exchange hit .800 versus Cub pitching! You weren't there when the Cubs were righteously paddled by the Braves and actually nothing particularly unexpected happened! This is a tide-turner! This is a momentum-shifter! The Cubs have lost the pennant!"

I really need to stress that I said this all very comically, even though the frequent use of exclamation points and complete absence of traditionally "funny" words, phrases or sentiments might suggest something less comical—more like ranting or whining.

As it turns out, I am right. Soon after, the Marlins score eight runs in an inexplicable torrent of offense. An incomprehensible beating as if God Himself has descended from on high and administered it Himself. The Cubs' World Series hopes? In tatters. Blood-speckled, tear-ridden tatters. But where am I? Watching it on TV? No. Listening to it on the radio? No? Again, *comically*, I am driving around in my car, numb to all feeling, a whirring in my ears. It is the whirring of the Universe exposing itself to me, opening up and showing its innerworkings that somehow involve the Cubs never making it to the World Series. Innerworkings that, while consigning the Cubs to eons of nothing, involve giving the Yankees everything; ensuring that Yankees fans will go through their stunted, ursine lives with a profound, chronic, sense of entitlement. By the way, all Yankee fans are terrible, terrible louts; blathering scum; they know nothing of baseball—only that they win constantly. No Yankee fan ever has won an argument of any kind and yet, I believe, walks around under the distinct impression that they have never lost—anything! I have never

Graffiti seen in a Nebraska truck stop, 1973:	
(Written on wall)	*The answer is Jesus.*
(Written below)	*What is the question?*
(Written below)	*The question is: What is the name of Matty Alou's brother?*

ever, not even by mistake, made friends with a Yankee fan, because they are all, to a person, *Everything That is Wrong in America!* They're easy to spot in a crowd, but they're easier still to uncover in casual conversation—in that they invariably reveal how genetically weak and adverse to pain they are. They are awful, awful people.

Later, I am home again, throwing my two Cubs hats into the garbage and my wife is watching me. This post-season has tired her out, too. My Tourette's-like bouts of swearing, my furniture-kicking, my obsessive, superstition-following—though I didn't—couldn't—watch Game 7, I did burn an old Cubs ticket stub and rub its ashes on the TV—to no avail… It's all been too much. And she has, what will forever be known as, *Had It With Me.* "Won't you need those next year?" she asks. And I shake my head, a little comically, but probably not very. "No," I say. "Never." And this time, I mean it.

On "Late Night with David Letterman" nightly the host has a Top 10 List. Following are some of the "messages left on Steve Bartman's answering machine" after the NLCS:

- "You owe me $7.50 for the beer I threw at you."

- "I'm with Century 21—heard you might be moving."

- "Hey, I just got back in the country—how was the game?"

- "Don't worry, I'm sure we'll get another shot at the World Series in 2098."

- "Hey, it's Don Zimmer. Thanks for taking the heat off me."

- "Hi, this is Mike from Hasbro. I'm calling to verify some information for your Trivial Pursuit question."

- "Hey, it's Bill Buckner. Want to hang out?"

C.B.S.
HEY, THAT'S WHAT HAPPENS
WHEN WE WATCH BUD SELIG

Harry Smith

Harry Smith grew up in Lansing, Illinois, in Cook County, straight south of Chicago. The 52-year-old now lives in Manhattan and is the anchor of The Early Show *on CBS.*

Baseball was not at all important in our family. Neither of my parents nor my siblings were fans. Kenny Borgman, my best friend who was a good baseball player, and I would sit and watch day baseball. We used to play on the street in front of our house. The manhole cover was home plate, and I got knocked out by foul tips. It was hardball. It was real life.

Nobody in our town wore a white shirt to work. Nobody went to the South Shore to get on a railroad train to go to work. Everybody in our town worked in the steel mills or oil refineries or chemical plants in south Chicago and in northeast Indiana. My dad drove a milk truck and then worked part-time as a cop.

Baseball was pretty much the deal back then. It's about geography, and it's about class. Since we were South Side guys, we were not part of that yuppie whatever-it-was. The bond didn't even exist. All we knew was that they played in this very green place that seemed extra far away.

I didn't understand the "white collar—Cub fans," "blue collar—Sox fans" until much later in life. I didn't understand that in an organic sense until years later. As a kid, we saw both. We were all crazy about the Cubs and the Go-Go White Sox in '59 and '60— Luis Aparicio and Nellie Fox and Early Wynn and Minoso and all those guys.

The first game I ever went to was in Comiskey Park. I didn't go to Wrigley Field to see a game until I was an adult.

WGN used to broadcast both the Sox and Cubs. Jack Brickhouse was the broadcaster, and that's what we did. The Cub team of memory for me is 1969. It was the summer I graduated from high school. I was working six days a week on a truck farm, loading trucks all day, outside of town. My one solace the whole summer was the Cubs. We'd have transistor radios and turn them on during lunch break at three o'clock. Sunday was my only day off. I would be so completely exhausted. I was getting ready to go to college and play football. I would go to church on Sunday. I'd come home from church, go work out by running the stadium stairs, and I would sit there in this exhausted heap, in a trance-like dream, watching the Cubs. Back then, they also played **doubleheaders** on Sunday, too. It was this nirvana, this amazing, perfect place to go. And, of course the Cubs ruined it in the end—just couldn't keep it together!

I was initially attracted to them because of Leo Durocher. Leo Durocher was this character. He was part of baseball history. He was so salty and acerbic and growly. If you'd opened up a book that showed what a baseball manager is supposed to be like, there would be Leo Durocher's mug. That was the thing that attracted me first. and then I fell in love with them.

As a Chicagoan, you always had to respect Ernie Banks, because he played on these crappy teams and won the National League MVP twice.

He was followed on his heels by Billy Williams, who was another phenomenal player, once again playing for one of these teams that were never going to go to the post-season. There was something emotionally attractive about the Cubs, about having a great player who was destined to never go to the post-season—the best player nobody knew about because he played in Chicago.

Not being a baseball player, I only went to a handful of major league sporting events before I became an adult. It never occurred to me that

In 1943, the Chicago White Sox played 44 doubleheaders.

you could actually just jump in the car and go to Wrigley Field. I seem to remember that Fergie Jenkins was out on the mound every Sunday. He was unbelievable. Every Cub fan lived and died with every single pitch. They were so sterling and amazing and absolutely unbelievable. Here was this place—this stadium—absolutely packed to the gills with people. The Cubs had been beaten on for so long that it was electric. Jenkins was phenomenal. With every strikeout, the place just erupted with these cascades of applause and elation and adulation. I was about eighteen years old and I remember sitting there thinking, "This is baseball perfection."

To me, the Cubs have always been on a noble quest. My relationship with baseball is very complicated. I grew up as an American League fan, originally, a White Sox fan. I forsook them that year, 1969, for the Cubs and what I've realized since is that, without question, the National League game is a superior game. I don't think there's any comparison. There's no reason for there to be a designated hitter in baseball. It actually requires there to be a manager if there's no designated hitter. It's just my being in touch with what I first fell in love with, which was going to Comiskey Park, an exploding scoreboard and the Go-Go White Sox. That was my first understanding of what baseball was.

In 1969, I was going off to college. The world was in turmoil with the Vietnam war still going strong. That was the last year to get a student deferment, one of the great inequities in all of American history. I left to go play football in college, to worry about a war, and to wonder about what the future of America was going to be like. I remember picking up a paper in September and seeing that the one gleam of light, the amazing pure thing of that summer, was being wasted, as well. It just fit in with all the turmoil.

Then I realized that in truth I had made an error, made a mistake, because by birth and by lineage, by where I was from and who I was, that I was actually a White Sox fan. I absolutely would not have thought or said, "I'm not rooting for these Cubs anymore."

I drive my children crazy because I love all of baseball. They want to have clear definitions and rivalries—these guys are good guys and these guys are bad guys. I don't allow for that. If a guy is a good player, then I'm adamant and don't allow the children to trash him.

If you go back to WGN, you go back to a kid without a family loyalty to a particular baseball team. Here, both teams were on television all the time. I grew up in a bizarre, schizophrenia of baseball. No one made me claim one team or the other. So I was in baseball no-man's land. I was caught between second and third.

I was on the speech team in high school and my friend, Jack, and I used to bring a huge tape recorder to high school basketball games. We would pretend we were Red Rush, who used to broadcast the Loyola basketball games on WCFL in Chicago. We'd broadcast the games into the tape recorder…and make up commercials for Gonnella bread.

During the Marlins-Yankees World Series, I'm listening to Jack Buck's kid. I'm thinking that I'm so old. I used to listen to Harry Caray in St. Louis on KMOX." I'm so old I never got used to the idea that Harry Caray was the Cubs announcer. I always thought of him as "the guy from St. Louis." I know he really was the iconic figure in Chicago, but if you're as old as I am, you remember certain cultural contacts. I always remember Harry Caray as the St. Louis guy.

The 2003 season, you almost thought that the planets were aligning in a way for all baseball romantics to have this baseball orgasm—to have the Cubs and the Red Sox in the Series at the same time. It sure looked good for this to happen.

I have a huge family still back there on the South Side, and I'm sure they're all Cubs fans, but what they really are—are Bear fans. I do a lot of promotions with the CBS station in Chicago, and they were always asking for my loyalty, and I had to 'fess up. The easy thing to do would be to say you're a Cub fan, but I'm a Sox fan, and I actually brought my Sox hat in one day. It's easier to be a Cubs fan—they're cute. Cute.

DOC WOULD BE BUSIER, AND HOCKEY MORE FUN, IF THE PUCK WERE TRANSPARENT

Jerry Wachs

Dr. Jerry Wachs, a dermatologist and cosmetic surgeon, grew up in Chicago but now resides in New York City. He has also been the team physician for the NHL's New Jersey Devils and the NBA's New Jersey Nets.

My father was not a Cubs fan, but I was very fortunate. I had two uncles who were major, major sports fans and major influences on my life. They both played, what we in Chicago called, Windy City Softball. It's a totally different game than anywhere else in the United States. The ball is a sixteen-inch ball. Although it's called a soft ball, it's rock hard. You play with no gloves. It's underhand pitching. It's made of the same material as a big-league fast ball. Every single Sunday for my entire youth I went to the games with my two uncles who both, coincidentally, were named Morrie. One of them played semi-pro ball. He was a big man, nicknamed "Tarzan." The other one played third base and they tried to be on the same team as often as possible. I would go there and would be the water boy and watch them play. I grew up with Windy City Softball.

My earliest memory of being a Cubs fan was probably in September of 1945 when I heard everybody talking about the Cubs winning the pennant. I didn't really know what that meant, but I remember running around screaming in happiness, "The Cubs won the pennant. The Cubs won the pennant." This was the war period, but as young as I was, the war meant nothing to me, so I was caught up in Cubs baseball. I do remember my parents talking about the atomic bomb, and that's about as much as I remember for that.

The first time I went to Wrigley Field, it was with my father. I remember the Cubs won, and Phil Cavarretta hit a home run. My Uncle

Morrie, "Tarzan," would bring me to the games. As I got older, I remember sitting in the bleachers for doubleheaders, which was a lot of fun. I would take the *Chicago Sun-Times* with me, go into the bleachers, without a sunscreen, without a hat, and watch games. In between games and innings, I would read the newspaper. It was just a whole afternoon you got to spend. It was just a fun way of spending time.

My first memory of the Cubs is outfielder, "Peanuts" Lowrey, and his number was 47, so that became my lucky number. I remember once Hal Jeffcoat came to speak before our temple so I became a Hal Jeffcoat fan. He was an outfielder who became a pitcher, a very unusual combination. My early days, the Cubs had a weird outfield because it consisted of Ralph Kiner and Hank Sauer in left and right and poor Frankie Baumholtz in center field running around like crazy 'cause Kiner and Sauer couldn't move. He had to play three outfield positions defensively. It was a fun time. The Cubs never did well, although Hank Sauer did win the MVP award.

Growing up in Chicago, there was a tremendous rivalry between the Cubs and the White Sox. "Tarzan" was a White Sox fan. I had to be careful in my rooting for the Cubs and against the White Sox, but indeed I did. He was always very mature, and he was very careful in front of me not to root against the Cubs. I was a North Sider, and he was a teacher who taught on the South Side so he had a natural inclination that way. Everybody else I knew, everybody, was a Cubs fan, so it was the simple way to go.

The problem was that if you were a Cubs fan and you hated the White Sox, you had to pick an American League team to root for. In 1945, when this happened to me, I was given the option of who to root for. Arbitrarily, for no reason that I can ever think of, I chose the Yankees. If I would have chosen a winning team, I would have chosen the Tigers, or I could have chosen the Red Sox, the 1946 pennant winner, but I didn't. I just chose the Yankees. Ever since then, I've also rooted for the Yankees. So if I was listening to a World Series while at synagogue, most of the time I'd be listening to the Yankees. Then, of course, I would come back and tease my uncle about the fact that the Yankees consistently beat the White Sox. He didn't really come back to me about the Cubs—he was much more polite than I was.

If I had been asked before the 2003 NLCS, what has been my favorite time with the Cubs, I would have said this year. All four of my children and friends called me after the Cubs lost to the Marlins. After fifty-eight years, I thought 2003 was our year. I realized it wasn't going to be in the eighth inning of the sixth game—it wasn't really truly interference—when the fan diverted the ball, and the next batter walked. You could see that Prior was losing it. Gonzalez made the error. I just knew there was no way on Earth the Cubs were going to win the seventh game. When your emotions are up like that, you have five outs to go, and you think you are going to win, and you lose, somehow you don't come back again.

I think about the Red Sox and the Mets, the time Billy Buckner made the error, the time in the sixth game in Kansas City versus St. Louis when the umpire blew the call, when that happens the team is just so deflated that it's just really difficult to come back. Even though we had Kerry Wood, I was very, very discouraged. I did not think we were going to do it. I thought before the Prior game that we had a fabulous chance to win one of the two games.

After the Cubs were eliminated, I was depressed all day. I got on a lot of baseball chat lines. I spent the whole day reading baseball messages. When the Cubs do well, I read *CBS Sportsline* and the *Chicago Tribune*, and I read *The Sporting News*. I read nothing that sad October day.

One of my hobbies is that I'm a collector of books. Although I have a very, very serious collection of poetry, my other collection is the Cubs. I collect baseball books and have more than a hundred on the Cubs.

There's a man named Eddie Gold, who wrote for the *Chicago Sun Times*. He was one of the most knowledgeable sports people ever. Eddie died in December, and it was very sad because he was a wonderful guy. I belong to the Society for American Baseball Research (SABRE), and he was extremely active there and was the trivia champion many, many years. I have all of his books. He divided the Cubs up into three eras. He talks about the Golden Era Cubs and the New Era Cubs and the Renewal Era Cubs, with nice little stories about individual players.

Eddie was unbelievably knowledgeable. He knew trivia. If you go to a SABRE meeting and listen to the trivia contest, the knowledge of the people there is astounding. You cannot believe people can be able to remember things they do. You'll say to them "1889 Cleveland Spiders—give me the names of the umpires of a certain game." Someone can do it. They have the deepest knowledge of the most unbelievable things.

The highlight of my collection is a book by Warren Brown called *The Chicago Cubs*. The copy I have was signed by every single player from the 1947 Cubs. I'm looking at it right now—Bill Jurges, Bill Nicholson, Harry "Peanuts" Lowrey, **Andy Pafko**.

Nothing in my life will be fulfilled until the Cubs win the World Series. Our mother was born in 1908, and she's no longer alive, but I often think of the fact that she was alive when the Cubs won the first one, but she was never able to see them win one again.

We've won so little. I have one brother and we were together on the day the Cubs clinched the Eastern Division in '84. I was out in California with him two weeks ago, when the Cubs won the doubleheader clinching the Central Division now.

My all-time favorite Cub player has to be Ernie Banks, just because of his enthusiasm. There has been a program on television the last couple of days and I saw somebody say, "Let's play two." I'm sure the author had no idea who he was quoting, but Banks was such an effervescent, enthusiastic person with huge talent. Leaving Chicago, as I did, in 1963, I didn't follow the day-to-day Cub news. When I lived in San Francisco, the papers didn't carry much Cub news. Although I physically left the Chicago area, I never emotionally left the Cubs. I never became a San Francisco Giants fan. I hate the Mets. I've always rooted for the Cubs. I am completely and totally impassioned.

Being a Cubs fan is just a part of my being me. If you're a Yankee fan, you just go in every year expecting to win. Now, if you're a Cubs fan,

> In the very first set of Topps baseball cards, the first card (#1) was Andy Pafko.

you go in thinking, "How do you find a way to lose?" I remember someone was asking me, at the beginning of the Marlin series, what I thought the Cubs would do. I said, "Oh, I'm still waiting for there to be a replay of the Braves series. They're going to find a mistake was made in the fifth game, and we have to replay that game." You're always waiting for something bad to happen, for a fan to reach over and take a ball out of Alou's glove—things like that.

Cubs fans and Red Sox fans feel the same way, but Cubs fans are more even-tempered about it. We're so used to the fact that it's going to happen. We've never been to the World Series since '45. The Red Sox have been in the World Series four times since our last appearance, and they keep losing. They've lost several seventh games like we lost to the Marlins. I think it's worse for them than it has been for us.

One of the biggest problems the Cubs have—the reason the Cubs have done so poorly for the last forty years—is that management needs an incentive. A typical incentive is empty seats. If there are empty seats, management says, "What can I do to fill those seats? I'll get better ball players." If you have thirty-six thousand people at every single game in a ballpark that holds thirty-nine thousand, why spend an extra ten million dollars for another player if you're not going to make it back. So, the fact that we're such good fans that you can't get into a game hurts us because management does not have to do everything in their power to improve.

Joe Torre was player/manager of the Mets for 18 days in 1977. Since 1962, there have been four player/managers with Pete Rose (1984-1986) being the last....In 1935, there were nine player/managers.

ROOTIN' FOR THE CUBS IS LIKE PLAYIN' HOOKY FROM LIFE

Carol Haddon

In her late fifties, Carol Haddon is a retired teacher of developmentally disabled children. She lives in Glencoe, Illinois.

Although I was on the South Side of Chicago, I became a Cubs fan because of day baseball and Wrigley Field and the policy to be fair to the fans by providing something called Ladies Day. My mother and her girlfriends started taking me on the "L" when I was three years old. I don't remember that, but one thing I do remember is making it to the seventh-inning stretch the first time without wanting to eat more. In the beginning, the focus was food and the excitement, of course. I loved the adventure.

I went to my boyfriend's senior prom when I was a sophomore. Instead of going the next day to the picnic to get drunk and all that, he and I had tickets in the upper deck for a Memorial Day doubleheader. I laugh when I look at my high school yearbook because I have all these remarks from friends. Usually students write things like, "Good luck in your future. Wish you the best. You'll be good at this or that," the usual things people sign. I would say ninety percent of the things in my book have the Cubs mentioned in them. This would have been my senior year in Niles Township High School in Skokie.

In college, **University of Illinois**, I had a hard time picking up Cub telecasts, but I had my radio on trying to get the games. I was always

> The Bears' season ticket holders live in 46 different states…the Bears have the same colors as the University of Illinois because their founder, George Halas, was once a star player for the Illini.

reading box scores. The Cubs were always so bad—they really were bad. I lived in a sorority and nobody else cared about the games. I have been friends with men since my youth because I was a real tomboy. Then there were no female athletic programs, and I played football with the boys until the principal told my mother it was no longer a good idea.

At Wrigley, there was a much older woman, a grizzled old woman with a baseball cap—I think she had a drinking problem, but you didn't know it—and a very ornery nature who sat where I now sit behind the on-deck circle. She would get really irate when a ball player would stand in front of her, and she would yell at him, things like, "You're not glass. You're like wood. I can't see through you. You're not a glass door." Later on, one of the ball players—I can't remember which one—asked about her and if I knew what happened to her.

A lot of people "dis" baseball because it's not violent and it's not fast. That's what they like is all that action. I, on the other hand, enjoy the serenity of baseball and don't find it boring at all because each individual player is seen separately and you can appreciate the skills. Being a Cub fan, unfortunately, a lot of the people I admired were often on the opposition.

I don't usually keep score when they're away. But sometimes like Opening Day, wherever they're at, or the All-Star game, which is a challenge to do, I do score the game. I don't look at them, but somewhere in my house there's a huge collection of scorecards, because I've saved them for the last twenty years. For many years, I used a book, but now I'm back to scorecards. I'm going to have to go back to a book because scorecards are getting too expensive.

Wrigley Field is home for me. I have been in every nook and cranny of that ballpark. I'm just so comfortable in that neighborhood. By now I know the people from security and the ushers, and there are just so many different wonderful people there. I used to want to bring a friend all the time, but if I'm there by myself—I'm never by myself. Because of my seat, I remain in good contact with a former ball girl,

Marla Collins, who is now a divorced mother of two. She was the **Playboy** centerfold that Harry Caray used to go crazy over.

Bill Madlock did something so wonderful for me. When my daughter was nine years old and celebrating her birthday, I brought her with friends to the ballpark. I actually was able to get a bunch of seats right around me there above the dugout. Bill Madlock, knowing this, came over before the game began and visited with this little group of children and gave each one of them an 8x10 picture of himself which he autographed for them. It would be very unlikely for that to be allowed to happen today.

I have two children, and my children are now thirty-five and thirty-three years old, they're only fifteen months apart. I started taking them to games when they were infants. I would carry one in what was then a jerry-built carrier, like a sling, and the other would be walking along. In the beginning, I was just taking one and then I finally got lucky with some day-care during the game. I would take them on the train. To this day, they have a moderate, not a fanatical, interest in the game. I probably overdid it.

Now that I'm a birdwatcher, it's added so much more to my life 'cause Arizona birds are so different. At Wrigley, there are common nighthawks visiting and flying overhead. I have a routine—I bring a scorecard, radio, baseball glove and towel to sit on. My Tom Glavine glove has been signed by him three different times because I keep wearing the signature off. I don't wear the glove because I aspire to catch anything, but I have a fear for my life. There have been ten people hurt around me. I've been told by many players that I don't have a chance if its coming at me anyway.

I'm not a big collector. I get maybe three or four baseballs a year from people I admire. I don't go asking for a lot of autographs. I do

In 1968, Bo Belinsky married 1965 *Playboy* Playmate of the Year, Jo Collins. In 1973 they divorced. Belinsky died in Las Vegas in 2002. Tennis ace, Jimmy Connors married the 1977 Playmate of the Year, Patti McGuire in 1978. They are still married.

have over the years a fantastic collection of Cubs and some baseball memorabilia, which includes a baseball signed by both Barry and Bobby Bonds. I have early Dusty Baker autographs.

I don't wear anything special to the ballpark, but I do own a "blue mink." The Cubs had a fund-raising event. It was Cub wives and Cub Charities and they raffled a one-of-a-kind short blouson-type mink jacket. It's Cubbie blue with a small "C" in red on the chest. It doesn't have anything emblazoned across it. I knew when I saw it I had to have it. I took my own money, my face-lift fund, and spent it on that coat—two thousand dollars. I still have it, and I wore it one game of the series. Aside from that, I don't dress in Cub things all the time. I usually wear jeans and whatever shirt, but I don't make a point of wearing Cub things.

In summation, I guess my Cub fandom has always been a separate life that I can't share with people in my social life. I'm pretty low key. I'm not as extreme. I don't usually run onto the field, but I did do that in Pittsburgh in '84. I sit in a spot that gets a lot of attention, and I don't want to draw unnecessary attention to myself.

Seated from left to right in the right field bleachers are Adam Magdziarz, Jason Yurechko (before his days as Chug-Chug, the Comeback Clown), and Mike Dickerson

FIRST, CARDINAL FANS LOOK AT MARK PRIOR AND KERRY WOOD. THEN, THEY WEEP FOR THE FUTURE.

Marc Stoff

Marc Stoff, 29, has lived his entire life in St. Louis...as a Chicago Cubs fan. He works for the city in the license collector's department.

My earliest recollection of being a Cubs fan is being at Six Flags. My father was a union man who loved St. Louis and loved the Cardinals. He picked out a St. Louis Cardinals hat to give to me. At some point in the exchange of money, I got a Chicago Cubs hat. The vendor thought my father knew that, and that's what I walked off with.

I didn't go to Wrigley Field for the first time until I was in my twenties. We had always planned baseball trips with my father and my grandfather and my brother and a couple of buddies. We would never go up to Chicago, because that would break my father's heart. We went up on a "stadium tour," so that made it more palatable for my dad. But we couldn't go up for a Cardinals-Cubs series; that was forbidden. It was a series against the Dodgers. It was the middle of the June, and it was about 42 degrees in the ballpark. My dad—a shorts kind of guy—absolutely refused to buy any sweatshirt that said CUBS on it, even though he was freezing. It was everything that I dreamed of. If it hadn't been a freezing cold day, I would have been disappointed. It was a doubleheader. It went twelve innings and it ended exactly the way I thought it would go: Chan Ho Park got walked in for the winning run by a Cubs pitcher. But my father never used a Cubs loss against me: he never had a bad word to say after a loss.

My dad collected a lot of Stan Musial memorabilia. I've bought him Stan Musial, Ken Boyer, **Mark McGwire** stuff, pictures of old Sportsman's Park. I was allowed to wear my Cubs hat in certain situations. It wasn't a matter of making my dad feel bad, it was just an issue of supporting my team. I couldn't wear it if company was in the house. If we were up at Charlie Gitto's house—he's a famous restaurant owner and his restaurants are hang-outs for the Cardinals. Charlie and Tommy Lasorda are great friends, and my dad was great friends with him, so wearing it then was a bad idea, too. All of my friends except for my one friend, Elliott Reed, was a Cardinals fan. He was a Twins fan, so he sided with me for the Cubs whenever there was a dispute. The one thing being a Cubs fan in St. Louis teaches you early on is to get a feeling of self-worth, because if you don't have it, they'll beat it out of you. Being a Cubs fan builds character. It's like having kids—it's unconditional love. You may not always like them, you may not always want to be around them, but you always love them. I always wanted to brag on behalf of the Cubs, but it's hard.

All of my co-workers are Cardinals fans. My friend, Dave Schmidt came in with red Cardinal shoes, red Cardinal pants, red Cardinal belt, red Cardinal shirt, red Cardinal tie, and red Cardinal hat. Dave will let me know exactly what the standings are, whether the Cubs have done anything bad recently. It has always been enjoyable. He was the first person to give his congratulations when the Cubs got into the playoffs, and he was the first to give his condolences when they lost. My fiancée is a Cardinals fan. She already has a son. She gave me a Cubs hat for Christmas the first year when we were together, and her son took to the Cubs hat right away. The next day her dad came in with two Cardinals hats, the old "You've got to root for the Cardinals" trick. There was a weekend game in the playoffs, and I said to her son, "Who do you want to win?" And he said, "The

Mark McGwire's brother, Dan McGwire, once a starting quarterback for the Iowa Hawkeyes and a former #1 pick of the Seahawks, is the tallest NFL QB ever at 6' 8". Former NBA star and Toronto Blue Jay, Danny Ainge, is the tallest major league second baseman ever.

Cardinals." I told him, "It's only the Cubs and Braves playing." So he said: "Oh, then I don't care." He's only three; he's already decided not to care about the Cubs.

When the Cubs were down 3-0 in Game 7 of the 2003 NLCS, I put on my rally cap and Kerry Wood immediately hit a home run. For the rest of the night I didn't move a muscle. So, I guess you could say I was a little superstitious. When the Cubs lost, I got phone calls from everyone. It was very sweet; it was an outpouring. My life, though, went on immediately after it happened. Being a Cubs fan, I had already been through 1984. In a game in June, Ryno hit two home runs and a little nobody by the last name of Owen gets a base hit to win the game, and that was the year I fell in love with the Cubs. They go up 2-0 on San Diego, and I was bragging to everyone, "Oh the Cubs are going to the World Series." I remember bragging one night, and my father walked into the room, looked at me, smiled, and then left the room—it was very poignant. He didn't say anything. He knew. And then they went on to lose three games. So I'm immune now. But I didn't watch a single game of the 2003 World Series.

The bleachers are insane. I will never sit in the bleachers again. There's everything but baseball going on there. The fans are aware that the game is on, and sometimes they're even cognizant that there's a score. But it doesn't matter. It's an afterthought to the fact that they're in the bleachers in Wrigley Field. There are two kinds of fans in Chicago: there's Cub fans and there's Wrigley Field fans. The latter are there to enjoy Wrigley Field, and the game really doesn't matter. I'm a prude, I guess—I wasn't offended, but I was more eyes/face-forward, focus on the game, so that I didn't have to testify later on. Heavy petting, there were some illegal substances. People were throwing up. Thirty guys waiting with baseballs so that they can throw theirs out and keep the good one. Kind of a **Grateful Dead** atmosphere.

> Do you know what Jerry Garcia said to Elvis when he first saw him in heaven?
> "Hey King! Guess who your daughter married."

Rick Wilkins and Luis Salazar were two guys who could hit the high fastball. I don't mean the high fastball that's up near the shoulders; I mean the fastball that's over your head. I remember the year Wilkins hit 30 home runs; it must have been the last year he hit double digit home runs. There was a game, when it was the seventh or eighth inning and they're going to walk Wilkins, but they aren't going to walk him intentionally. They're hoping they can just throw around him and see if he'll get himself out. The pitcher throws one in the dirt. Wilkins, of course, swings. Throws one outside, Wilkins swings. So, he decides he's going to go up the ladder, the catcher is literally standing up, it's a rising fastball.... Wilkins hits it on the rise up into the right field bleachers. Cubs win. I thought Wilkins was going to be an All-Star catcher for a lot of years.

I lived in an apartment where there was no access to a radio that would get reception. The only Cubs station in St. Louis is 880 WCV/Highland, the all-Catholic religion station. It's run by Larry Rice, who bought the station for the sole purpose of getting his message across to Cubs fans during the commercial break. But I couldn't get reception in my place, so I'm out in my dad's Mercury every single night, no air conditioning, listening to Pat Hughes and Ron Santo.

During the 2003 playoffs, I had to change my schedule. Every year, me and my parents and my fiancée and her son go out to dinner for my birthday at Chevy's Mexican restaurant. For whatever reason— this was for the fourth game at Wrigley Field, Cubs-Atlanta Playoffs—I thought the game was going to be in the daytime. So I had to call and cancel dinner, not wanting to tell them that I'm skipping to watch the Cubs game. So we schedule the birthday party for that night. Then, I find out that the game is at night. I can't tell my father that I'm going to miss my birthday for the Cubs game. I'm trying to figure out how to duck out of dinner.

We get out there, and my fiancée's kid finds a carousel to ride around on for like ten dollars, and there's the excuse I'm looking for. I walk out of the restaurant and start watching the game in the basement of Sears. But there's no way to avoid dinner. My brother knows what's going on. Soon enough my father figures out what's going on, too, and the only ones who haven't figured it out are my fiancée and my mother. Dad had a pager that gives you updates of the scores. So he starts knocking on the table to let me know what the score is. First knock, Atlanta Braves. Second knock, Chicago Cubs score. The Cubs were down 6-2 and then Eric Karros hit a home run, so my brother's knocking on the table, my father's knocking on the table, and I go to the bathroom and stop at the bar to watch the game. Eventually, I'm going to the bathroom every four minutes and my mother and girl-friend are expressing concerns about my well-being and health.

Then, the Cubs mount a rally in the ninth inning, so there is *no* way I can go back to the table. Now, my father in the past two or three years has—not become a Cub fan—but he wants them to win for me. So he wants to root for the Cubs, too. So we *both* go the bathroom. We're standing there. There's this other guy who is having a romantic dinner with his wife, and he gets up from the table and starts standing next to us. We're all talking, watching the game. Sosa comes up to the plate, Smoltz gets him. So we come back to the table, and it's not pleasant to be at the table anymore, because we left them there for ten or fifteen minutes. It doesn't matter that it's *my* birthday: I'm not get-ting talked to. Because I'm not enjoying my birthday with *them*.

It will all be worth it when it really *is* next year.

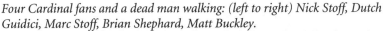

Four Cardinal fans and a dead man walking: (left to right) Nick Stoff, Dutch Guidici, Marc Stoff, Brian Shephard, Matt Buckley.

BASEBALL MAKES
STRANGE BEDFELLOWS

Bob Shapiro

Bob Shapiro might live in Arlington, Virginia but he is still a Cubs Season Ticketholder. He attends about 15 games annually at Wrigley. His Cubs memorabilia collection is considered one of the finest in the country.

Bob Shapiro (left) with his father.

My father grew up in Chicago. He was a Cubs fan since he was a boy. My best recollection is that I was probably four or five years old when he took me to my first Cubs game. I remember coming in and there seemed to be something magical about it. It was big, which you would think would be intimidating for a small child, but there was something that really captivated me about sitting there and watching these men play a game, which I gradually grew to learn and love. I had a very fortunate and very pleasant childhood, and a big part of that was rooting for the Cubs and going to Wrigley Field. It was a good chance to bond with my father. We don't have a single conversation, regardless of the time of year, where the Cubs aren't mentioned.

My dad always talks about **Augie Galan**, who played in the 1930s. The other player he always talks about is Lou Novikoff, who was called the Mad Russian. He was in the Cubs minor league system in the 1940s, and was one of these can't-miss stars. He came up to the

> After grounding into a double play in his last at-bat to end the Tigers' pennant run in 1967, Dick McAuliffe went the entire 1968 season without hitting into a double play. Only two others in the history of baseball, with 500+ at-bats, have ever accomplished that feat: Augie Galan (1935) and Craig Biggio (1997).

Cubs and just totally bombed. Apparently he had a number of neuroses, among which was a great fear of the Wrigley Field vines. I've read somewhere that he feared there were spiders in the vines. My dad's dad, when he heard that there was somebody called the Mad Russian, insisted that my dad take him to a Cubs game.

I've really gotten to know a number of the 1969 Cubs. I was able, on one occasion after one of the Emil Verban luncheons, to have Ernie Banks to my house. We were finished with the luncheon early and I drew the role of being his chauffeur for the day. I live very near the airport, and we stopped by the house. We chatted for a while. I have a full-size arcade Cubs pinball machine in my house, which was made in the mid-1980s. The scoreboard is the Wrigley Field marquee. I had seen it advertised new in a catalog, and a few years later, I got in touch with a pinball and video games dealer and told him, "Whenever you see a good used one, give me a call." No more than a month later, there it was. Ernie loved it. I had to tell him: "Ernie, we've got to get you to the airport." I had him autograph the machine. His famous saying is, "Let's play two." He signed it, "I've played two."

I was chair of the Verban Society the year that Hillary Clinton came. Of course, this is before she became a Yankees fan. She made a wonderful presentation about growing up as a Cubs fan, and somewhere there exists a copy of what she said. It was obviously the kind of speech that she had a heavy hand in writing. I remember introducing her. At that point I had worked for the government for nearly twenty years, and I had been saying to my parents the night before, "I've been working in the government for twenty years, I work a relatively senior position. How do I meet a former first lady? Through the Cubs." When she said goodbye, because I had related a story about my parents, she said, "Well, give my best to your parents." When I talked to them, I said, "Hillary Clinton sends her best." And of course they were like, "*Come on.*"

When the book *Wrigleyville* first came out, the author Peter Golenbock was doing a book promotion on Opening Day. My dad and I have gone out to Opening Day for easily the last twenty years. I wasn't able to get to the book signing. I called the bookstore to see whether I could get an autographed copy, and they asked me if I wanted to have it personalized. I said no, just a regular autograph. Apparently, the communication went slyly awry, and when they gave Peter the book, it must have indicated to be personalized. He saw the name Robert Shapiro—keep in mind the book came out during the O.J. trial—my inscription says, "Best wishes to Bob Shapiro. And let's win one for The Juice." I've always treasured that copy of the book for the inscription.

A Cubs fan is extremely loyal, eternally hopeful, and able to deal with regular adversity. The experience of being a Cubs fan—where we were in our lives during certain Cubs games—is a big part of the Verban Society.

In August of 2003, there was a baseball card show in Chicago, followed by a charity dinner for the 1969 Cubs. I took my dad there, and I think he knew that I knew Ernie Banks, but didn't know the extent of our relationship until he actually saw us interact at the dinner. I remember thinking it was kind of like a MasterCard commercial: "Dinner with the '69 Cubs. 100 dollars. Having your dad see you interact with Ernie Banks. Priceless." Banks even invited me to his latest wedding. He's probably been married three times. I didn't go; it was in Barbados.

I just acquired a Cubs-Red Sox World Series pin for 2003. This one escaped destruction.

During the Seattle Mariners first year in 1977, they measured their distance to the fences in fathoms. A fathom is 6 feet. For instance, where a park may have a sign that denotes 360 feet, the Kingdome would have the number 60.

THESE TEN THINGS ARE SEVEN REASONS HE LOVES THE CUBS

Joe Hutchinson

Joe Hutchinson may qualify as the biggest Cub fan in Arizona. Joe, 50, moved to Glendale in 1967.

Joe Hutchinson (left) and Ron Santo

Remember that net the Cubs had for foul balls by home plate. Long gone. I'll never forget how the ball would go up and every kid in the stands would "whoop…" People don't realize, until you bring it up to them, that was part of going to Wrigley Field. Watching that ball go up the net and every kid in the house making that "whoop." They just changed it. It was the best. And then how it was so spontaneous. "We want a hit." It was silly, but it was really terrific. It was really fun. And the Andy Frain ushers. The Andy Frain ushers would be up there and when the kids would start the chaos they would wave their hands just like a conductor and really get you going-walking up and down there. "We want a hit, we want an out." And, I remember too our little, "SANTO…Santo, Santo, Go, Go, Go." Andy Frain ushers were classic. The white gloves, the white hat, the navy blue outfit. Classic. And Ladies Day was on Tuesday, where all ladies got in free, that was a day. The thing that is really important to remember is that a lot of moms were home moms and didn't work.

My Aunt Mary who had eight kids would pack up the station wagon and drop us off at the game. We'd go in, she'd watch the game at home, and tell us, "Start walking home, and I'll pick you up. Start walking home and I'll pick you up on Irving Park past the cemetery there." So, those are things you just don't do today, having all these kids dropped off at the game, you could get in for practically nothing.

It was like a daycare. It gave moms a chance to do whatever they wanted to do at home; iron, whatever, and she knew her kids were safe at the Cubs game. Can you beat that? The other things that changed too is that all grandstands and upper grandstands were open seating. There was not assigned seating. First come, first served. So, if you got to the game early, you could get that first seat by the rail, the dividing line with the box seats. That was primo if you could do that. And then as the game progressed, you could move into the box seats.

Now, with all the security, you can't do anything. So, kids today might not ever have the opportunity to get close to the dugout or the field. Very rarely, you can do it, just maybe, prior to the actual game start, but they shoo you away right away. You have to have your ticket. It's a 9-11 issue and it's a bunch of bull. It's an excuse. Just like here in Arizona, they won't let you bring stuff into Bank One Ballpark anymore unless you have a clear bag and they look at everything. All the little Cub duffel bags that I still have, I can't bring them in. They need to start concentrating on real terrorists and leave the regular folks alone. My oldest daughter came to visit last May. She lives in Portland, Maine now. In fact, she's Miss Maine, USA—she's finishing up her reign. They confiscated a one-half inch nail clipper from her kit on a plane. What is that girl going to do? Is she going to take down the whole plane like, "Nobody move or I'm going to cut everybody's nails?" It sounds facetious, but that's what it is. It's an outrage.

My wife went to San Jose and found the article, "Pipe down, Dusty fans; Alou is masterful," by Skip Bayless in the October 8th edition of the *San Jose Mercury News*. "The Dusty lovers have come out of hiding. Giants lose, Cubs win. Out pops the glee club. See, they say, the Giants miss dear old Dusty! Told you so! No, let me tell them something: The National League Manager of the Year should not be the Chicago Cubs' Dusty Baker. It should be the man who replaced him and overcame obstacles that would have turned Baker into an excuse-making wreck. It should be the man who pushed more magical buttons in one season and postseason than Baker did in 10 years with the Giants. It should be Felipe Alou. The Giants were much better off without dear old Dusty. In the 2002 post season, the Giants often won despite Baker's moves and ultimately couldn't overcome them in the World Series games 6 and 7. This time, the Giants lost a division series to the Marlins in spite of Alou's masterful managing. Give Baker this season's Giants, and they wind up in a dogfight with Dodgers and Diamondbacks for the N. L. West. But Alou's Giants won 100 games, buried two rivals whose payrolls were up to $25 million higher and easily led the majors with a 28-12 record in one-run games." Then there's another excerpt in here, "Alou got over being a player and wearing wristbands a long time ago. Alou keeps an arm's length away and manages ruthlessly. He's more of a distant father figure, a distinguished general, a baseball version of Tom Landry, operating from above with cold-blooded wisdom."

The Chicago media has not taken Dusty to task for games six and seven. Do you mean you don't go out after the fan interfered to calm the team down and rally the troops? What the hell's wrong with you? You sitting there on the bench twiddling your thumbs. You have to have the leadership.

You noticed how they wear these trendy, contrasting uniforms that come dark blue or black. I am a traditionalist. Look at the Cardinals. Look at the **Red Sox**. Look at the Yankees. Look at the Braves. Now the Cubs are wearing these stupid blue batting practice jerseys. They look like softball players. Not one other game for the division championship did they wear their road gray with Chicago on the front of their chests proudly displayed. That just irritated the hell out of me. That's got to be changed.

Things have changed so much because guys want to be individuals. Look at Barry Bonds, he wears uniforms like pajamas. They go down to the dirt. That to me is a disgrace of wearing the uniform of a major leaguer. Can't his dad, his dad's dead now, but Willie Mays tell him, "Hey guy, you have to dress for success." That's one thing I'm really big on is wearing the pride of a major league uniform of the city you represent.

> The Sam Malone character in Cheers was patterned after former Red Sox pitcher, Bill Lee. Bill Lee once demanded number 337 from the Boston Red Sox because 337, upside down, spells Lee's last name.

What does Wrigley Field mean to me? Daytime baseball, Bleacher Bums, Fun. When that one playoff game in Oakland started at 10:00 Eastern time on a weekday and finished, because it was extra innings, near 3:00 in the morning. The advertisers want people who have money. The people who have money have good jobs, they have vacation time, they have flexible time and if it's their team, they are going to take off and they are going to watch the game.

I wasn't shocked and I wasn't for it when Wrigley put in lights, but to this day, I won't go to a night game. I just won't do it. I do appreciate the fact they made them blend in to make it look old fashioned instead of just putting up steel columns. They did a nice job with it. But I won't go to a night game even if it's a World Series. The houses in the background, the "L" are all part of it. That's why it's better than Fenway. At Fenway you're closed in. It's relaxing to see the trees and the lake from Wrigley.

Two Americans were caught in Mexico attempting to smuggle drugs, one was a Cub fan and the other a Cardinal fan. They were brought before the captain of the firing squad who informed them that he would grant each one a last wish providing that it was reasonable. The ugly Cardinal fan said he could die in peace if he could hear the late Cardinal announcer Jack Buck say "That's a winner" one more time. The captain said, "This is your lucky day. We have cable in the palace, our head of security is a moron and a Cardinals fan, and he tapes every game." The captain turns to the Cub fan and asks if he has a reasonable last wish. The big, good-lookin' Cub fan replies, "I sure do, *senor*!" The captain says, "Well, what is it?" And the Cub fan says, "Shoot me first."

SHORT STORIES FROM LONG MEMORIES

Ditka was going to sing in the bottom of the seventh, but he ran a little late because he was playing golf and traffic was backed up. So we go to the bottom of the seventh, and Steve Stone takes the microphone and says, "The coach hasn't arrived. I guess I have to do it." Then, all of a sudden, here Ditka comes. He bolts in like a bat out of hell; he grabs the microphone, and in his Knute Rockne style of "Take Me Out to the Ball Game," he starts. I'm five booths down from where he is, and I'm just holding on to the key like I do with everybody. Then he starts—it looks like a polka tempo so I'm going to have to pick it up. About a quarter of the way or halfway through, I caught up with him. He went on and I just kept up with him.

The amazing part is that we scored seven runs in the bottom of the inning. We scored a touchdown—he was rallying the troops! Usually the performers come into the booth before they sing, and we go over it. I'll ask, "How are you going to sing—like a one, a two, a three? Let me hear you." He came late so he just came right to the booth, and I picked up his tempo. He was ahead of me, but I said, *No, no, I'm going to catch up with him*. People didn't know what was going on. I say it was like a 33 rpm record going at 78 rpm.

I don't know who's been the best. Vin Scully was excellent; he did it like an Irish tenor. He appreciates the song and what it means to baseball. We had Kenny Rogers, the singer, not the pitcher. He did an excellent job. He came into the booth afterward and said, "I want to thank you. It's an honor." We've had Walter Payton, Ernie Banks, and Muhammad Ali. Ali couldn't sing, but he was there. You get to play with all these people in different fields—Hall of Famers, singers, actors, announcers—it's great.

Ditka wasn't even the worst singer to do it. Harry was no Frank Sinatra, so if someone sang it off key, so be it. it turned out great when Ditka did it the first time, because it put "Take Me Out to the Ball Game" on the map. After that, everybody was saying. "Now who's going to sing?"

Mike Ditka epitomizes Chicago. He was a hardworking, put-it-on-the-line type of player, and they loved that. I still see tapes of him in that game against Pittsburgh, the day after Kennedy got shot, when he ran through the whole team. And if you win, that's the icing on the cake. Since he left, the Bears have never been the same. That one season, 1985…I can't remember a more dominant football team, and the fans loved it. He would tell the media off in no uncertain terms. He didn't care. He told the Vikings he had roller skates on in Minnesota. They loved that. That's what Chicago is.

——GARY PRESSY, Wrigley organist, Ditka accompanist

I haven't really seen any big fights here…out by Sox park, but not here. Where you see the fights is actually down by Murphy's. You'll see the squad cars down there all the time and generally someone's fallen off a roof somewhere. That's the big thing. That's when St. Louis comes to town; that's when you know you're going to have problems because that's a big rivalry….huge.

I've known Ronnie Woo-Woo since I've been here…over 24 years and after a Cubs game, a lot of times these doors are open all night, we'd have this grumpy old engineer, Bob Bachman, this big German guy. At two or three o'clock in the morning, he's tired and upstairs sleeping. I'd have Ronnie come in here and start screaming, "Bachman, Woo! Bachman, Woo!" just to get him all ….ed off. Ronnie would do it and he'd go racing out of here because Bachman would be right after him. The only guy hanging around

Ronnie Woo-Woo

Wrigley all year is Ronnie; he's there every day. Ivy Man and Neon Man showed up recently, though. There's also a Shrimp walking around somewhere for a restaurant. There's also been a pimp and a Santa. Ronnie had a gorilla outfit on one time with a gorilla on his back or in front in a box, riding around on his big wheel bike. Sharon Stone paid for his teeth, from what I understand. The Smashing Pumpkins produced the Ronnie Woo-Woo CD.

——JOHN SAMPSON, 47, Fireman, across the street from Wrigley

I was sitting in the left field bleachers—right field sucks. It goes without saying that if you're sitting in the bleachers, you have to be wearing clothes that don't need to be dry-cleaned. When the gates open, people rush to get into the front row. So you have people who have been standing out there since ten in the morning for a 1:20 game. Someone who comes in after the game starts and comes down to the front and asks if there's any room—that's just ridiculous. In '99, there was a night game so the gates opened at five. I'm there around 4:30. Along comes this preppy-looking guy, he's with this girl, and out of the goodness of my heart, something I usually don't do, I let them in. So, the guy and the girl sit down, they're yakkin for a while, and I'm eavesdropping. Finally, this knucklehead says to me, "Hey, why don't I buy you a beer." I'm like, *I can't believe that he didn't offer this right away.* I can't remember what struck me, but I asked the guy, "Do you work for a major league team?" And he said, "Yeah. I work for the Florida Marlins...director of marketing." I tell the guy, "I'll buy *you* a beer, if you send me something." Then I'm starting to think, *What the hell am I doing? I'm buying this guy that I let sit down next to me a beer, and I'm giving him my business card.* He gave me his business card. It's a Florida Marlins business card, so I know it's real, but it doesn't have a phone number on it. This guy promises to send me something. Four weeks go by, and one day at work, I get a box. It's from Miami, open it up and it was Craig Counsell's batting practice jersey. Counsell had just been traded to the Los Angeles Dodgers. On Marlins 1997 World Series stationery, the note says, "We traded Craig Counsell, the Game 7 World Series hero, and now you get his BP jersey."

——JIM BRADLEY aka "BOO", 35, Wrigleyville, Software QA Engineer

Chapter 2

Growin' Up a Cubbie

Let it be a Closer…

Experience Is What You Get When You Don't Get What You Want

IT WAS IN *TIME* MAGAZINE... SO, HELL, FOR ALL I KNOW, IT COULD BE TRUE

Jonathan Alter

Jonathan Alter, 46, a native Chicagoan who grew up six blocks from Wrigley Field, now roots for the Cubs from New Jersey, where he resides with his wife and children. He is a senior editor and columnist with Newsweek *and a contributing correspondent with NBC News.*

I lived six blocks from the stadium, and Cub games were daytime games until the late eighties because of the Wrigley family. The neighbors didn't like night baseball. All during the summer, starting when I was nine years old, I could go with a friend to Wrigley Field with no parental supervision. Mother would give me a dollar for doing some chores around the house, which happened to be what entrance to the bleachers cost. She would pack a brown sack lunch. Sometimes if I was well behaved, she would give me another twenty-five cents for a Frosty Malt.

A friend and I would go there about ten-thirty in the morning, and we would watch batting practice. We would sit in the bleachers and would stay until about four o'clock in the afternoon. I would spend significant chunks of my summer doing that. Of course, in April, on Opening Day, a lot of kids from my school would always play hooky. We would always go to Wrigley Field for Opening Day! My parents were okay with that. I would say that from the time I was about nine until age fifteen, I would go to the ballpark and would be sitting in the bleachers with these Bleacher Bums, many of whom worked at night, or they were unemployed, and had time to go and lounge in the bleachers on a Tuesday afternoon. They drank a lot of beer and they swore a lot and they gave me a great taste of working class life in Chicago.

Things have changed so much. The ticket that used to cost me a dollar went for as much as fifteen hundred dollars for the recent playoffs. So, the nature of the clientele has changed. It's a little more corporate, upscale, suburban. At the time I started going, it was unemployed construction workers, people who worked night shifts and as bartenders, and a surprising number of tart-tongued, hard-drinking, hard-cursing women.

They were a particular breed of baseball fan who would show up in the bleachers and be part of our group of bleacher bums. I was a "Little League" bleacher bum because I was at least a decade younger than most. There would actually be three groups of people—the weather-beaten sixty-year-olds, who gave the impression of having a lifetime of trouble etched on their faces and had gone through the Depression. They would be sitting out there. Then you'd have the hard-drinking people in their twenties and thirties who were often between jobs. Then you'd have the kids. We'd all be there in the bleachers together. There was great rivalry between the left field and right field bleachers. We would always be taunting each other.

It was one of those idyllic childhood memories of the Cubs—except for the fact that the Cubs didn't win. It was a little bit like being an old Brooklyn Dodgers fan which you hear about from the thirties or forties. But, except for 1969, which was heartbreaking, it was a pretty rough ride.

Sometimes our family went to the Indiana Dunes—large sand dunes about sixty miles from Chicago. We didn't have a television set in that house, and my parents allowed me to go down to the car and sit for hours listening to the Cubs on the radio. The Cubs had some great announcers. The one we all loved the best, and who I got to see just a couple of weeks before he died, was Jack Brickhouse. Harry Caray was a great announcer in the 1980s. When he first came here in the mid-seventies, he had basically been a St. Louis Cardinal announcer. As the Cubs became really "trendy," Harry Caray was a great character and became a signature voice for the Cubs. But the real Cub announcer for true, long-time Cub fans was Jack Brickhouse. One thing that made him so great was that if there was a rain delay, you wanted to keep listening because he would be telling you these great old baseball stories that would go back to Babe Ruth. He could talk very knowledgeably forever, sometimes with a guy named Lloyd

Pettit, another announcer, about the old days of baseball. If you had an interest in the traditions of the game, particularly the National League, although he also did White Sox games, you could learn a tremendous amount just by listening to him.

When the Cubs would hit a homer, Jack Brickhouse would say, "Hey. Hey." He'd say, "Going. Going. Gone."

When I was a kid, I would get real upset if I realized that I had gotten to the ballpark without my first baseman's glove. I had a better chance of catching a home run if I brought my glove. My great memory is of the "game I won for the Cubs!" I've never been able to get this picture—it's somewhere in the files of the *Chicago Sun-Times*—but, in 1968, a friend and I were sitting in the first row of the right field bleachers. The Cubs were playing the **Mets**. Adolfo Phillips, who had come to the Cubs in a trade with Ferguson Jenkins, in the eighth inning, hit this towering drive which landed on top of the wall. Now, they have put a basket right out over the edge of the bleacher wall to keep people like me from interfering with the play. In those days, there were no baskets there so if a fan touched the ball, it was ruled a ground-rule double. I was ten years old, and as I did every day, I brought my glove with me to the game just for the possibility I might get a ball. I tried to make the catch and I missed. The ball glanced off my glove and off the wall back onto the field. Adolfo Phillips rounded second and went into third with a triple. The Mets started complaining vociferously about fan interference, that it should be a ground-rule double. Ernie Banks hit a sacrifice fly. Phillips scored. That was the winning run. The next day in the paper there was a picture of me with my mouth agape trying to go for the ball. I've been trying to get that picture for thirty-five years.

The peak of my obsession with the Cubs was 1969—until now! The Cubs had an eight and a half game lead over the Mets. We had a terrific team. I would go to the games there at Wrigley, and then they went into their swoon. I would come home from the game after they had lost again, and open the door and walk in a sullen, wordless way,

After the Mets had played their first nine games in their inaugural 1962 season, they were 9½ games out of first place.

more like an adolescent than an eleven-year-old, into my room. I would stay there sulking for most of the rest of the evening until the next morning when I would happily head up to the ballpark again thinking *this will be the day we turn it around*. Then that afternoon I was walking back home from the ballpark, perhaps buying a snow cone to assuage my wounds, before repeating the rituals of the previous day—returning wordlessly to my room to sulk.

We had great, colorful players in that era. There was a relief pitcher we all loved named Chuck Hartenstein, whose nickname was Twiggy, because of the British model by that name. He was a very slight player, only a little bit bigger than we were as kids, but he was extremely good. Ernie Banks would say, "Let's play two today." He was always so upbeat and so positive. He had a different slogan every year to make us feel better—like, "The Cubs will be in Heaven in '67," "The Cubs will be great in '68," and "The Cubs will shine in '69." We'd all go, "Yeah. Okay. Ernie said it's going to happen and Ernie won the MVP back in the fifties, so...." I saw his 498th, 499th and 501st home runs. He hit his 500th at home against the Braves, but I was in school that day.

Banks was on the downward slope of his career then, but the two greatest players of my youth, the '69 period, were Billy Williams and Ferguson Jenkins. I had all their cards. I never had any paper at the games so sometimes I would take the brown sack paper, from the lunch bag I had brought to the game, and drop it down to the players in the outfield. They would sign this brown bag. I've still got some of their autographs some place. There's a whole lot tied up into character building with all the losing and the yearning and realizing that life is all about waiting until next year and trying to be positive in the face of setbacks. Even when I got married in 1986, one of my friends who I had gone to all these Cubs games with, gave me a complete set of '69 Cubs baseball cards. By the end of the evening, I don't know whether a waiter lifted it or what happened, but they disappeared. That's just the way it is with Cubs fans

We had our martyr, too, a second-baseman named Kenny Hubbs, who had been killed in an airplane crash. Hubbs had just recently been named Rookie of the Year. When Hubbs was a kid in Colton,

California, his Little League team went to the Little League World Series. The pitching duties were shared by Hubbs and a kid named Jay Dahl. On the last game of the 1962 inaugural season of the Houston Colt .45s—now the Houston Astros, they started nine rookies. Jay Dahl was the starting pitcher, thus becoming the first person born after World War II to make the major leagues. The P.A. announcer that day was Dan Rather, now the CBS anchor. The next year, Jay Dahl was killed in an auto crash while playing in the Carolina League. What are the odds of that? Everybody always has to have a Roy Campanella story—or somebody who has met a bad end in some way.

The Cubs fans don't whine the way the Red Sox fans do. There's something very restful about Wrigley Field. I heard a guy on Imus attacking Cubs fans. I wanted to punch him. What happened was that they would draw respectable attendance even in years they did terribly so there was no great incentive to invest in a lot of great players because they were making money either way. Why was that? Well, because when you walk into Wrigley Field, it is like going into a park, in the larger sense of the word. Why were parks created? Why did the old British notion of an enclosed garden develop through the centuries? Why did cities when they were designed include parks? The answer is that people went there, and they felt a sense of peace. They felt better after they were there. There's something about Wrigley Field that's hard to describe to people who haven't been there. The combination of the ivy that Bill Veeck, Sr. arranged to have planted there and the lack of any advertising signs in the park and the dimensions of the field and the fact that you can see out across the horizon almost all the way to Lake Michigan and the coziness of the field—the sightlines. Then, for many years, there were no lights, so it had its own special daytime flavor. It gave you a good feeling even when the Cubs lost.

We all love Sosa here, and I'm a big fan, but I did write one article for *Newsweek* after the "bat incident." It was called "Good People Behaving Badly." I didn't buy his line on the bat. My son bought it entirely. He thinks Sosa was entirely innocent and just picked up the wrong bat.

The Yankees are just scum. They are run by scum. They have horrible values. Chicago is a tough place, but all of the values you would not want your children to grow up with are espoused by the Yankees. You do want your children to be successful, but the way to get success, by being George Steinbrenner, all those things—you don't want your children to do. The values of loyalty, optimism, future orientation, belief in finding solace and rest in a peaceful park, getting outside in the daytime, which becomes a problem for kids. I'd like to beat the Yankees, but losing to them would be okay, just as long as we get to the World Series someday.

Two boys are playing hockey on a inlet on the shore of the Mississippi in St. Louis when one is attacked by a rabid Rottweiler. Thinking quickly, the other boy takes his stick and wedges it down the dog's collar and twists, breaking the dog's neck. A reporter who is strolling by sees the incident and rushes over to interview the boy. "Young Rams Fan Saves Friend from Vicious Animal," he starts writing in his notebook.

"But I'm not a Rams fan," the little hero replied.

"Sorry, since we are in St. Louis, I just assumed you were," said the reporter, and he began writing again. "Cardinal Fan Rescues Friend from Horrific Attack," he continued writing in his notebook.

"I'm not a Cardinal fan either," the boy said.

"I assumed everyone in St. Louis was either for the Rams or the Cardinals. What team do you root for?" the reporter asked.

"I'm a Chicago Cubs fan," the child said.

The reporter started a new sheet in his notebook and wrote, "Little B——d from Chicago Kills Beloved Family Pet."

JIMMY RITTENBERG IS A JEANIUS

Jim Rittenberg

Besides being a nice, fun and exciting guy, Jimmy Rittenberg is a legend in the Chicago restaurant and entertainment industry. Born in the Garfield Park area on the West Side of Chicago, he has owned or managed 28 different restaurants around the country, including Faces, Parkwest, 59 West, Ditka's City Lights and Mother Hubbard's. He was a school teacher for six years after graduating from DePaul.

In 1948, when I was five years old, my mom took me to Wrigley Field for the first time. My dad worked nights so my mom was my baseball fan. I remember there were old wooden chairs. It was half empty so a kid could sit down and take hold of the seat next to him and bang it up and down for a rally. That was our way of saying, "Go Cubs." Phil Cavarretta was the manager. He played first base and managed. I remember a right-hander, Johnny Klippstein. Andy Pafko was a Cub in '49-'50, and he was my favorite player for a while. We used to be able to sit in center field. There were seats out there before they turned that all green. We'd sit there and wave to Andy and he would wave back to us. He was replaced as my favorite player by Frankie Baumholtz, a center fielder and a right fielder in the fifties. His claim to fame was he finished second to Stan Musial one year in batting. On the last game of that season, the Cubs were playing the Cardinals. Musial pitched to Baumholtz and Baumholtz pitched to Musial. The left-fielder was Hank Sauer. He was the MVP in '52, and he was one of my favorites. Then we got hold of Ralph Kiner toward the end of his career. He played left field and Hank moved over to right. The Statue of Liberty was a half-step faster than those two guys…pity the center fielder.

Banks and Baker came up around the same time, and they were both shortstops. They moved Gene Baker to second base and put Banks in at short. Both were very good. I do remember the right-field grandstands because when the Dodgers and Giants played, that's where all the black people sat. The Giants had Hank Thompson and Monte Irvin. The Dodgers had Robinson, Junior Gilliam, Roy Campanella. They got all the black fans.

My mom was not a huge Cubs fan, but because I was, she sucked it up and took me all the time. We had to take two buses to get there. They didn't have the "L" running out west then—it came there in the mid-fifties. It would take an hour to an hour and a half to get there, and coming home was difficult because of the crowds of people who rode the bus at that time of day. We used to pack our lunch and go. By the time I was eleven and twelve, I could go to the games by myself, both to see the Cubs and the Sox. Then you didn't worry about letting a kid do that, but nowadays you couldn't send a kid on a bus by themselves.

I've had sports bars, Mother Hubbard's and Gamekeepers, and Ditka's basically was a sports bar, and saw tons of the North Side—South Side thing. A Cubs fan doesn't necessarily hate the Sox. The Sox fans hate the Cubs. Cub fans are a little newer at this thing. The Cubs, all the way through the fifties and sixties had very little attendance, and always had bad teams. The Sox were always a contender and were at the top of the heap. They were always in second place, third place. The Cubs were always seventh or eighth place. The White Sox fans have always thought they are the baseball fans, and the Cub fans are the nouveau riche. The Cubs neighborhood had gotten real nice in the eighties. I had season tickets there in the seventies and there was nobody around me—we could stretch out. I bought season tickets to the Cubs in '75 and had eighth row, Section 38. Then they moved me up, and for the last twenty-something years, I've been right behind the visitors' dugout.

I was always a big fan of Harry Caray from when he was with the White Sox. Harry did a good job wherever he was. He was a huge White Sox fan and was good friends with Bill Veeck. Most of today's Cubs fans don't remember Harry in his White Sox days. He came over to the Cubs in the winter of '80. All the fans came in about '83. They don't have much history. Figure it out, a thirty-year-old fan, twenty-three years ago, was only seven years old.

Listening to the Cubs on the radio, there was Jack Brickhouse, Harry Creighton, Vince Lloyd—Jack Brickhouse was my idol for years. He turned out to be one of my best friends. Jack was my announcer all my life—he was the announcer for football, the announcer for baseball, wrestling. Then when Harry came in, he was the announcer for the Sox, and then Harry took Jack's place and became a symbol of the Cubs in the eighties. Brickhouse was like a god to anybody who's in their fifties and sixties in Chicago. He had such enthusiasm and he did the "Hey. Hey."

Harry and Jack were cheerleaders. They knew their baseball, but they were "us" up in the booth. I'm not crazy about having athletes in the booth, except as color commentators. I want one of us up there. Harry was us, and so was Jack.

The Cubs had a policy where they would let kids in for free after the sixth inning. We would get out of school, take the bus in May and would stand outside till after the sixth inning, catch three innings and then go home. Then during the summer, we would pick up seat cushions. The box seats weren't drilled into the ground like they are now—they were just folding chairs. They used to sell cushions to people to put on the chairs. At the end of the game, somebody had to pick up the cushions. They had certain kids, and I was one of them, who would stick around and pick up the cushions. When we turned in the cushions, we'd be handed a pass to come in free for the next game. Remember, they never, ever had a sellout.

When the George Brett "Pine Tar" game was concluded, Ron Guidry was the center fielder and Don Mattingly was the second baseman.

TEXTBOOKS? WE DON'T NEED NO STINKIN' TEXTBOOKS; WE'RE SITTIN' NEXT TO A SMART LEFT-HANDED KID

Bob Beck

Bob Beck, who grew up on Chicago's North Side, owns a chain of college bookstores. He's 82 and lives in his homes near Wrigley Field in Chicago and Hohokam Park in Mesa, Arizona.

I saw my first Cubs game in 1929. The outfield was composed of Hack Wilson, Riggs Stephenson and Kiki Cuyler. Our combined batting average in 1929 was .303. They had a great team and they won then. I was eight years old at that time, and I used to go to the ball games. We were penniless, but it was easy to sneak into the ball games. I was thin enough to get between the crossbars at Wrigley. After the game, we'd go through the seats and pick up all the trash. When we got through, they'd give you a ticket for the next game. I'd sell that ticket, and then I'd sneak in again. That was my start in the world of crime.

The games used to start at three o'clock all the time. The only time they started earlier was if it was a doubleheader, and then they would start at noon. One day I was sneaking in, and I got up on top of the wall in left field. I started to go toward the bleachers. All of a sudden, there were security guards there, so I turned around and started coming back to the stands. The announcer was describing this curly-headed, pug-nosed kid running back and forth with security after him. My mother was a big baseball fan so, when I got home, she said, "How was school today?" I said, "Okay." She said, "Well, they described you on the radio running back and forth on the wall." The Cubs used to have a Ladies' Day every Friday, and mom would go to it. She was like all the ladies that when anybody hit a foul ball, they'd scream and yell and get excited. It was a good pastime for her.

We went on a Cubs cruise to Hawaii after the '84 season. They had bingo every day, and the pot was up to around twenty-eight hundred dollars. That was one of those days when you had to cover all the numbers on the board. All the wives decided that all the husbands should go play bingo, too, so we could win it. Harry Caray and Pete Vonachen, who did the eulogy at Harry's funeral, and a couple of other buddies were there. We sat there while they were calling all these numbers out. Finally, Harry yells out, "Bingo." I thought, "Oh, God, he's screwed up somewhere." It was one of these deals where they had to check all the numbers. So he was walking up to the caller, and he was shaking and things were jumping around. I said, "Don't anybody disturb your cards because this guy may be off." But he had them all. He won about twenty five hundred dollars. He bought everybody there a drink, which didn't cost much, because you get most of your drinks for nothing. Whatever was left he told them to put in the tip jar for the crew. He was that kind of guy.

Normally, we go to Bernie's, a tavern right across from the ballpark, and we go there all the time before the game. We sit around and talk about the game, but it's gotten so popular that there are people standing around outside waiting to get in. When the game starts, people with tickets go in the ballpark. The people on the outside go in the taverns and they're still packed. I have macular degeneration and can only see about three feet in front of me. I have a head set and listen to the ball games, and I also have a pair of binoculars and I always sit within the first nine rows of wherever I go so I can watch the game that way. In this tavern, the owner, Linda Dillman, and her two boys, Jeff and Tim, were nice enough to put a special TV in the corner and that's where I sit and can watch the game regardless of how crowded it is. I can walk in and I have my little throne there to sit on.

I'm waiting to go on a bender. I'm going to have a few extra pops if we ever win this thing. After the past losses, we were very depressed. I was more depressed in '84 than '69 because we had a better team. We certainly had the best team in the National League, and we could have beaten Detroit, I'm sure…2003 though was a killer.

THE CUBS FILL THE POTHOLES IN HIS SOUL... MAYBE THE CUBS *ARE* THE POTHOLES IN HIS SOUL.

Jack Wiers

As a youngster growing up in a suburb south of Chicago, Lansing, IL, Jack Wiers, 52, pretended he was a Chicago Cubs broadcaster. Jack fulfilled his ambitions when he became the Baltimore Orioles TV broadcaster in the late 1980s. Jack now lives in Honolulu, Hawaii, where he still does TV broadcasting in addition to directing public relations for the U.S. Army in Hawaii.

Being a Chicago fan is like a penance. What did I do in a previous life to deserve this? I went to a psychic, and he told me to take penance, but it had nothing to do with the Cubs. I had to go to an ancient Hawaiian hei'eeau and put a lei down for past sins in previous lives.

I grew up in a small, blue-collar town right on the Indiana-Illinois border that got swallowed up by Chicago suburbia. When I was a kid, there were about three or four thousand people in it, and by the time I was in high school, the town was about 22,000 people. It was a classic 1950s American suburb. When I was growing up, a lot people were fans of both the Cubs and the White Sox. And I have to admit, I'm one of them. I'm desperate for a winner! Somebody has to go out and win something. I'm not a fair-weather fan—I'm a baseball fan. I would have watched whatever was available to me.

Growing up, there was peer pressure that you had to be one or the other. We grew up in a neighborhood where houses were being built every week in a classic setting—it was baby-boomer heaven. There were dozens of young boys my age, and what we did, every day after school, was go out and play baseball, football, and basketball. But we played mostly baseball. When you played baseball, you were always

Ron Santo, or you wanted to be Nellie Fox. I played third base, so I, personally, was more of a Santo-type, although I really loved Kenny Hubbs. Back in those days, if you didn't have enough players, right field was out. You never had any second baseman, so I moved over to third base. Santo was just hard-nosed, very emotional, and seemed like he would dive for everything. The front of his uniform would always be filthy, and there was a certain grit to Ron Santo that you just loved.

Boy, '69 was a great year because that was the year I graduated from high school at Thornton Fractional South. It was Thornton Township, the township had a high school called Thornton High School that split in the 1920s. The poor second school became known as Thornton Fractional. What a lousy name. And then in 1959, it split again. And then Thornton Fractional became North and South. We were Thornton Fractional South. We were the Rebels.

We were still in school when the Cubs became good in '67, and the excitement was building in '68. They were developing these players like Glenn Beckert and Don Kessinger, who was just this nothing .220-hitting shortstop who suddenly became this All-Star who could hit .270 and became a Gold Glover at short. And there were other guys like Adolfo Phillips and Randy Hundley at catcher. And in 1969, they got off to that fabulous start, and we were seniors in high school getting ready to venture out into whatever. It was a strange time in America, when we were all registering for the draft or getting our college deferments, like many of my friends. This was the last summer of our youth. That summer, I was painting houses and the Cubs were playing day games. It was a wonderful time to be outside, painting a house, listening to the Cubs game, and doing whatever you could to find a ticket. Then you would hop on the South Shore Line, the Vomit Comet, an old rickety train that you would catch in Hammond, or Gary, Indiana, and then you would take that to downtown and then catch the "L" from there and take it to Wrigley Field. It was such a heady time that a Tuesday afternoon game could be a complete sellout. I remember it being standing room only for a Thursday afternoon doubleheader against the Cardinals. There was such a euphoria that went with the team. After a victory, Ron Santo had a routine in 1969 where he would run around, jump and click his heels in the air.

Nobody in my family was a baseball fan except for me. We grew up together with about a dozen guys. My next door neighbor was a year younger than me, and we used to have games of pitch and catch behind my garage. The Wentworth Avenue overpass was about 150 feet behind us. We had a strike zone box on the wall of our garage. When we couldn't get enough guys, we would have a one-on-one game. I loved being like Lindy McDaniel, who had a fabulous forkball.

He was a Cubs reliever in the mid '60s. He was the first guy I remember who threw a forkball. I remember how that ball came swooping down. My next door neighbor, Mike Sember, could not hit that pitch if his *life* depended on it. Over the years, I became more appreciative of being able to dominate Mike Sember because he went on to become a number-one draft pick of the Cubs in 1975. He was an All-American shortstop at the University of Tulsa and actually made it to the big leagues. He was a power hitting shortstop with speed. Unfortunately, he was a byproduct of what was wrong with the Cubs, because that was an era where they didn't develop any of their players. You know what? He never got any better. It's so important for young players to be developed by good organizations. When Mike got to the big leagues, he still couldn't hit a big league curveball. He deserved a better fate, because he was a tremendous athlete. The *Chicago Tribune*, a few years ago, did their all-time prep All-Star team. Mike was the shortstop. He was considered the best prep shortstop in Chicagoland. His dad used to take us to the games. That was the type of neighborhood we had. I didn't realize it at the time.

I was fifteen when I first went to Wrigley. A friend of mine and I got a couple of tickets and went on the three-hour South Shore Line odyssey to the ballpark. The train was rickety. You always wondered if it was going to fall off the track as it would wobble its way to downtown Chicago. The train was hot and crowded and sweaty. It was really a lousy way to get into the city. There was no upside to taking the South Side. After that, you had to walk about ten blocks to catch the elevated train. That was great. The beautiful thing about that elevated is that you practically bump your nose on the Wrigley outfield wall when you step off the escalator at the L station. You're stepping into another world. The ivy is dark green in contrast to the shimmering emerald green of the grass. You would completely abandon all inhibitions. You were just having fun as a Cubs fan, without any expectations, and you were part of this community that was gathering to do exactly the same thing. There was a camaraderie at Wrigley with its cigar smoke and smell of beer that you couldn't duplicate at Comiskey. Wrigley Field was Chicago family. I sat on the left field side of the bleachers, the Waveland side, where Billy Williams was. There were scantily-clad girls there that barely wore tops in the hot summer months. Maybe that was just their way of saying "hello."

My best friend was choking back tears while I was talking to him after Game 7 of the 2003 NLCS. He believed that we were going to win that Game 7 of the series with the Marlins, and I never thought for a minute that we were going to win it. He was so distraught he couldn't squeak out a full sentence. But the next day, the day after, both he and I just felt wrung out. You felt beaten up. But you still think, "You know, that was a pretty good season."

Distance makes the heart grow fonder. I really pine for that trip back, where I can go and see as many games as I can. I plan my vacations around being able to go back and see ball games at Wrigley in the summer. When McGwire and Sosa were staging their epic home run battle in 1998, I plotted my vacation for early September. I had tickets to Wrigley Field and saw Sammy tie Hack Wilson's all-time Cub record with his 56th home run. The next week, the Cubs played the Cardinals at Busch Stadium, and I was there to see McGwire hit his 62nd home run to break Maris' record. I was blessed that weekend. Here's the irony—that's my biggest Cub thrill—Mark McGwire breaking Maris' record against the Cubs. I've got a version of the extra edition of the St. Louis newspaper on my wall at home.

I despise what happened with the Mets in 1969 because it just seems so unfair. The Mets won ten games in a row, and the Cubs lost eight in a row. I believe in my heart that the Cubs were the better team in 1969 and that somehow fate transpired against the Cubs, and that maybe for the Mets, there was a destiny that was programmed for the Mets that year at the expense of Cubs. The Mets had this completely rotten team, and all of a sudden after what—seven years—they get to win everything and be the darlings of America. And America gets to revel in the glory of loving the Mets. They get to be this magical team in this magical year, but if you were a Cub fan and you listened to the first half of the year, you thought that was *your* magical year. You knew 1969 was your magical year. Like maybe the whole '69 thing has just reaffirmed your Midwestern-ness. Like somebody's saying, "Hey guy, you're not supposed to dance, you're not supposed to revel, you're not supposed to jump up and down and get flat-out goofy, excited and get silly." You've got to get rid of that Midwestern angst somehow. A couple of beers helps you do it!

In my professional career, I met Ernie Banks, Fergie Jenkins, Randy Hundley, Billy Williams. And it seemed like these were the loveliest people you would ever meet. Maybe they were too nice! But with somebody like Joe Pepitone, it was like we borrowed some New York attitude. Nobody ever looked at Joe Pepitone, with that mullet hairdo that he wore when he was with the Cubs, and thought *this guy* was part of our culture. Ernie Banks was always this genial ambassador who always projected this happy exterior, and you knew in your heart of hearts that there was some real pain underneath there. The guy had the greatest Hall of Fame career, all to never play in a postseason game. You knew when you met Ernie Banks that you didn't want to go there, because you're sure a million other people probably did. With those Cubs teams, the defining moments *never* happened. It was *supposed* to happen. They were supposed to win that National League Championship, go the World Series and play the Orioles. It wouldn't have mattered if they had lost to the Orioles.

But it reminds me of 2003. There was going to be a celebration in Chicago. They city was ready to celebrate. The country was ready to celebrate, and then Game 6. I was off work for a couple of days after the NLCS. I was very wrung out, just kind emotionally drained, like blood had been drained out of me. I watched the World Series very halfheartedly. Watched Game 1, got no pleasure out of it at all. Missed Game 2—it didn't bother me at all when I missed Game 2. I didn't show up for any of the other games. The Florida Marlins— 2003 World Champions…unreal.

All I have to say is that when that moment finally comes, it will be the most glorious moment the baseball community at large has ever experienced. The pure joy that will come out of that will be so great. It will be the most wonderful party, and it will last—forever. Will it happen in my lifetime? I'm not sure. I would love to be there when the party starts …'cause I'm stayin' til the end.

INDEPENDENT NEWSPAPER FOR CHICAGO CUB FANS
[Dedicated to Harry, Wilma, Jack, Carmella & Arne]
P.O. Box 64-2401, Chicago, IL 60664-2401
(773) 975-2251
bleacherbanter@yahoo.com

Published Six Times Per Year
(Feb., Apr., June, Aug., Oct. & Dec.)
©2003 by Stephanie Leathers

| Vol. 13, No. 1 | February 10, 2003 | $4.50 per issue (still less than a beer) |

"The Cubs Will Be In 2003."

Prentiss Marshall

HOLY COW!!!

This has not been an ordinary off-season, so please indulge us while we reminisce.

GOODBYE, DEAR FRIEND...

It seems like we have lost at least one notable Cubs personality for several years in a row, some being more difficult to endure than others. Unfortunately, this off-season hit the Cub fans harder than ever with the loss of 100-year-old **Carmella Hartigan**. Perhaps you were one of the more fortunate to have met and had your picture taken with Carmella on your travels to Wrigley Field, but if you were not, certainly you knew her from her multiple appearances on TV during the Cub games. Carmella's beautiful serene face and the fluorescent pink hat that topped her veil of white hair were mainstays for the WGN-TV cameras as Carmella sang and smiled regardless of the outcome of the Cub games.

Those who knew her personally regarded her as a role model and vowed if they lived to be a hundred, they wanted to be "just like Carmella." If you asked her how she felt, she would always say, "I'm fine, and even if I wasn't, what good would it do to complain?" Photos were taken with her by people from around the world, from babies to grandmas, and cherished by all.

Yes, we lost one of our favorite fans. It won't be the same without seeing Carmella walk the ramp to her top row seat in the centerfield bleachers near the cameras, but we will continue to talk about her and reminisce about the time spent with her in Wrigley Field and on the numerous trips she took with us. Strange. We thought she would live forever...

THERE'S MORE ...

Jim & Mary Ellen Reinhold sustained the loss of Jim's beautiful mother, **Miriam**. She was blessed with loving family members and many true friends who have been a great comfort to the Reinhold family ...

The family and friends of **Jesse Lindsey** (one of our favorite visitors from Des Moines, Iowa) are grieving with his sudden passing. Jesse is survived by his wife, **Sharon**, his children, and best friends, **"Cub Charlie" Nichols** and Charlie's fiancé, **Mary Malloy**. R.I.P, Cowboy ...

Eddie Gold was the Sun-times trivia expert whose annual Christmas sports poem was an delight ...

Many of the bums consoled **Ray Meyer, Jr.** on the death of his mother **Marge**. The late **Ray Sr.** was the original owner of Ray's [now Murphy's] Bleachers across from the Wrigley Field bleachers. Mary Ellen Reinhold, among others, referred to Marge as "my bleacher mom of my youth ...

Ironically, within a day or two of Marge's passing, **Jim Murphy**, the former Chicago police officer who -purchased Ray's Bleachers in 1980, also passed away.

Thanks for listening. We hope that's the end of our grieving for a long while.

IF YOUTH KNEW
IF AGE COULD DO

Mitchell Snay

Mitchell Snay is the Chair of the History Department at Dennison University in Ohio. Snay, 49, was raised in Rogers Park, near Evanston.

I grew up in a house and a neighborhood that was heavily Cub fans. On the North Side where Wrigley was, most people were Cubs fans. But, on the South Side, it was like another city. It was really far away to drive. We very rarely went to Comiskey. I remember sitting there, staring at the scoreboard, to see what the Cubs score was. I got very nervous when the opposing team was up to bat for a long time, and they didn't post the score.

My dad, of course, was the one who introduced me to the Cubs, and he used to take me to Opening Day, from the time I was about seven or eight years old. I don't know how he got tickets, but he did. My mother used to write a note to the teacher to excuse me after lunch. In her note she'd say, "He's gonna have a stomach ache." Now, I think it's very odd—how did she know, three hours in the future that I was going to have a stomach ache? Of course, it was just an excuse so I could get out and go to the game. I'm sure the teacher must have known. It also became a part of our family lore. There were truant officers who used to go to the games to catch kids. But, if you were with your father or mother, you were pretty safe. When I went to Wrigley, it was like going to turn-of-the-century urban America, which was very much my roots. The park was built around that time—my grandfather would have been here, and it was a few years before my dad was born. Now, it's like a second home. I still remember the smells of Wrigley Field—with mostly cigars, and the smell of beer.

My father taught me how to keep the scorecard, and he played catch with me. We would talk about it a lot. The games in April were freezing. If you sat in the upper deck, there was a very cold breeze. My other memory is that the beginning of baseball season often corresponded to Passover. We kept Passover at the house so I was starving when we went to the games. I couldn't have a hotdog because we couldn't eat bread.

My dad took my mother, my sister and I to the 1961 All-Star game. Then they had two All-Star games, and the one in July of that year was at Wrigley Field. It was so crowded that the only seats we could get were two and two so my dad and I sat together and my mother and sister sat together. In looking back at sports books and almanacs, I realize that I have seen some of the great players.

My father died in 2001. My sister and I were talking about how excited our dad would have been that the Cubs had gotten so far in 2003. One of the things that happens to Cub fans is that the notion of the Cubs being in the World Series was so jarring because it was so inconceivable. There were so many years that passed, that unlike Red Sox fans who expected it, we never did expect it. In one sense, it was wonderful, but, "How could this be? How could it be happening?" He was very fond of the Cubs. He watched the games on WGN every day. He had a great retirement—he would sleep late, get up, shower, eat and by the time he was done, it was time for the Cubs game.

In 1967, I turned thirteen. The Cubs had the horrible fall in '69 when they lost the Division to the Mets. After that, and I think it was the combination of being so heartbroken, but also kind of in a sense, growing into adolescence that there was a series of years when I was kind of mad at the Cubs. I went, but my feelings were nothing like they had been in my youth...We didn't have a lot of the accouterments the kids have today. I remember having a Cubs hat all the time, but I don't remember having the wristbands, the small toys. Ernie Banks would always have sayings for every season—like, "The Cubs will be heavenly in sixty-sevenly." "The Cubs will be great in sixty-eight." "The Cubs will shine in sixty-nine."

I'm sure those collapses do something to you, but I'm not exactly sure what. You feel so close to something and then...That's, in a way, the wonderful thing about baseball. It's a game, and both the goods and the bads happen. In a way, anything is possible. I do remember, as a kid, poring over the newspapers. I was lucky because when my dad went to work, he worked the late shift at the drug store, so I was the first person to see the paper. I went right to the box scores, and I pretty much knew the lineup by heart so I checked everybody's batting averages.

My friends and I played games outside, and I would always pretend I was one of the Cubs and I always wanted to be a third baseman, my favorite position, so Ron Santo was my hero. When I went to a game, I was always so excited to come home and play. I notice that now with my son, who is ten. When we go to a sporting event, the first thing he wants to do right away is come back and play the sport. So there's something there. When you're a kid, you can dream that can be you some day, just possibly.

Later in life, I really began to get an appreciation for the history of the game, which is now one of my favorite things. Beginning last year, I started collecting baseball memorabilia. It started when I got an autographed cap from Sandy Koufax. I've been buying Cubs cards from the sixties. If my own son and I are at a card shop or find a mall with a card shop, we always stop in and look through their selections. I have stayed away from eBay because I feel I would go on there and never be able to get off. I know one guy is trying to collect ticket stubs for every one of the one hundred and two games Koufax won, and he's well on his way. If someone has a huge box of cards they are selling, I just go through and look for the Cubs. There is a very strong pull with Cub history, and I don't know if it's because I'm getting older or if it's because I'm an historian. I do nineteenth century U.S. and study the Jacksonian era—the coming of the Civil War is my specialty.

I always found the line between baseball and immigrant communities is very strong. There was a wonderful documentary on *The Life and Times of Hank Greenberg*. It talks about Jews all over the country and in Detroit where he played, and how much he meant to them. When I was a kid, Koufax did that to me. One of the stories was that Koufax wouldn't pitch on Yom Kippur, and that was a big deal. I don't remember the Cubs having had any Jewish players other than Kenny Holtzman.

SO SAY YOU ONE
SO SAY YOU ALL

Moose Moryn had about as much speed as your average bulldozer, but he did make the dramatic two-out catch May 15, 1960 that preserved Don Cardwell's no-hitter in Cardwell's debut with the Cubs. Joe Cunningham was the batter. Moose made this incredible catch to preserve the no-hitter. I had this huge baseball card collection, and I had every Cub except Moose Moryn. This friend of mine down the street that I used to trade baseball cards with all the time somehow got a Moose Moryn card. This came at a time when you could get a pack of baseball cards and bubblegum for five cents. Maybe it had gone to a dime, but I think it was still five cents. He got a Moose Moryn, and I wanted that card so badly that I bought it from him for $3, at that time an outrageous price. That's how badly I wanted a Moose Moryn card.

——CHET COPPOCK, Sporting News Radio personality

I was twelve years old and we had just moved into Chicago from Iowa. I was living on Addison Avenue, not very far from the Cubs. This was during the Depression and none of us had any money. Everybody knew that if the bleachers weren't full, the 'bulls' wouldn't go after the kids who climbed over the wall. The bulls were the security guards who were supposed to keep the kids from doing that, but they always looked the other way if there were a lot of empty seats up there. So the only time I ever went to any ball game was when I climbed over the wall, which was about fifteen feet tall. I watched, with great interest, with two or three of my buddies there. The Cubs lost, and I was mad that they lost, so I never went back. I follow the Cubs all the time, but I haven't been back to a game in almost 70 years.

——JOHN KEARNEY, 79, artist and sculptor of goats

We had a broken-down, cracked radio. I was the sports fanatic as a kid. I played every sport—basketball and football and baseball. When you're raised that raggedy-ass poor, sports validate you. My ex-wife used to say about our high school that there were three classes there—the cashmeres, the fur-blends, and the orlons. If I played sports, I somehow felt validated.

As a kid, I would bring any money I earned home to help feed my brothers and sisters. My mother would keep the money, but she'd put a nickel away in a little cracked cup in the cupboard. When we got enough, my mother and I were allowed to take the IC, the Illinois Central, downtown, and then catch the elevated, the "L," over to Wrigley Field. I would sit in the bleachers and fantasize about what it would be like to be a bat boy for the Cubs. Everybody who ever went there came back to the neighborhood talking about it. It was a shrine.

——**TOM DREESEN**, Comedian, on growing up in Harvey, Illinois

I went to Catholic grade school until fifth grade. The nun saw me chewing something, and she said, "Mr. Beck, where did you get that gum?" I told her I got it at the corner store. She suspended me. If I would have bought it in the cafeteria, it would have been all right, but I didn't buy it in the school. We had a few nuns who were baseball fans, but not many.

In the bleacher days, we would get four or five of us, and we'd sneak into the bleachers. We'd get there for batting practice, and then we would take turns. We'd jump on the field and run out and if there were a couple of baseballs there, we'd pick them up and throw them back to the fans in the stands. Whoever ran on the field and got caught by security, got taken in to Bill Veeck, Sr., and he would read the riot act to you, telling you where you were heading in the life of crime, but the good news was we had a baseball to play with.

——**BOB BECK**, Owner, Beck's Bookstores

Chicago was a deeply divided city, so not all of my friends were Cubs fans. That was part of it—you were a Cubs fan, and you hated the Sox! I did get into a lot of verbal squabbles over the Cubs-White Sox thing but never actual fist fights. There's a stereotype that exists out there—and in my area here, the same type thing exists between the Raiders and the 49ers—that the White Sox are a working-class team, and the Cubs are more middle class—a wine and brie, kind of team. To a small degree, that's somewhat true, probably due to the locations of the stadiums. Comiskey Park is just now undergoing some urban renewal around the area. Wrigley underwent that awhile ago.

Wrigley appealed to the North Side and the northern suburbs, which are wealthier than the South Side.

——DR. ROBERT WACHS, Palo Alto, California

When we had our second child, born in October, I told my wife, "If you plan any more of these for October, and they happen to conflict with the seventh game for the pennant or the seventh game of the World Series, honey, you're on your own." She knew I was serious—she got mad at me about it! I wanted to name him Sammy, and she would not let me.

My son, Tom, who just turned four this October always wanted to stay up late with me and watch the Cubs game, but he also wants a bedtime story. I asked him if he wanted a story or wanted to watch a little more of the Cubs game. He said, "I'll watch a little more of the Cubs' game." We were sitting there, and I turned and looked up at the screen—the game was tied 3-3 at the time. Moises Alou came to the plate, and I go, "Hey, Tom, here's your story. '**Moises Alou** hits a two-run home run out onto Waveland Avenue, and the Cubs take a 5-3 lead.' Ready?" Next pitch, Alou hit a two-run home run out onto Waveland Avenue. My son went to bed really happy, thinking the Cubs had won. The next morning, he wakes up, came into our room and crawled into our bed. I said, "Morning, Tom." He said, "Hi Daddy, what's wrong?" I said, "I've got some bad news. The Cubs lost last night." He looked at me and said, "They lost?" I said, "Yeah, they lost, Pal, the season's over." He got a little weepy. He loves the Cubs. All he wants to do is play baseball every day, and he's always on the Cubs. He was very sad when they lost. He said, "It'll be all right—definitely next year, right, Dad?" I said, "Oh God, you're a little early to be starting with that. But, yeah, Tom, definitely next year." He said, "Okay."

——JIM DEMARET, Chicago Stock Exchange

I had an aunt who lived in an apartment that was an annex to our house, and I went over to her house, where she had a color TV. Every day of the summer, from the time I was eight until I was about thirteen, I watched every game that came on WGN.

With the Expos in 1993, Moises Alou hit six consecutive home runs over a span of four games.

I remember my amazement at walking into my first major league game at Wrigley Field and smelling the grass and smelling the cigarette smoke and the beer and just being totally awed by the experience. I went with my dad, and we drove down to the city. It took us about an hour to get to the stadium, so we couldn't go to games that often. I remember listening to the Cubs going on their West Coast road trips when the games were almost never on television but always on the radio. I didn't have a radio in my room, but my parents had a clock-radio in their room, and they would let me go in their room and lie on their bed and listen to the Cubs.

——JIM FILL, 48, on growin' up in Glen Ellyn, Illinois

I have very vivid memories of when I was ten or eleven years old, coming home from school in April and May and turning on the Cubs game. They weren't very good then. There was a player, a catcher, named Sammy Taylor. It was the bottom of the ninth and the Cubs were down by one, and they needed two runs to win. I was raised as a Catholic, so I was going to parochial schools. I remember praying, "Please let Sammy Taylor hit a home run." He did. I was jumping up and down and screaming.

Most of my friends were Sox fans. We didn't get into physical confrontations, but there was a lot of verbal jibes going back and forth. In those years, the White Sox were *the* team of the late fifties and sixties, so I didn't have much ammo. I'm kinda stubborn, and my dad vaguely pushed me in that direction. The fact that I could watch the Cubs on TV in the afternoons, when I got home from school, was a major reason why I became a Cubs fan. I just loved watching baseball, and I liked to collect the cards and had shoeboxes and shoeboxes full. I wish I still had them, but my mom threw them out.

——TOM ROBISON, 52, TV news producer, WLS-TV, Chicago

I had my heart broken in '69 when I was nine. And, it was so sad in 2003 to see them look like they had been hit in the head with a 2x4—just like it was in '69. I had gotten tickets from a lottery in '84. At the time, I was working, making $152 per week as a reporter, and I was offered $600 for the two tickets, and I turned it down. That was the game that was never played. So in '89, I was cheering like an ex-wife. It took me almost twenty years to fall in love with the Cubs again. I can't believe I've dragged my kids into this. They love Wrigley Field, first, and then the Cubs. They're six and seven, and they've made a ton of money selling lemonade. In fact, during the crosstown series, a Cubs fan gave them $5 to not sell lemonade to White Sox fans. Then the White Sox fans offered them $10 to sell them lemonade. They held to the $5 deal.

———KAREN KENNEDY, 43, Chicago

Leo Durocher's girlfriend was Lynn Walker Goldblatt, who he later married. She lived in a building called 777 North Michigan Avenue right over a Walgreens. It was a posh Michigan Avenue high-rise then. At night they would often have dinner there. He liked to smoke a cigar but, when he did, she would send him downstairs 'cause she didn't want cigar smoke saturating her furniture. He would stand outside of 777 North Michigan Avenue and he would talk to anybody. I was a kid then, and my mother would let me walk down to the Tribune Building and get what we called the "Bullfrog," the first edition of the morning paper. I would, not infrequently, encounter Leo Durocher just standing there talking to anybody. He would have a crowd of twenty-thirty people around there listening to him tell his stories.

To be a Cub fan is to think of the old Frosty Malts they used to sell at the ballpark, the Ron Santo Pizzas—they were not great pizzas. They were small and could actually become quite dangerous because people preferred to use them as Frisbees. They were sold in the stands. The most unfortunate nickname for him, of course, was Pizza Belly, as he began to put on weight.

———SCOTT SIMON, Award-winning Journalist, Washington, D.C.

I had all the Cubs pictures, which Jewel Food Stores used to hand out. I'd have my mother take us to the food store, and every week, they'd have a different set of pictures out for the players. We had to go first thing Saturday morning to get that week's pictures before they sold out. They were 8 x 10 pictures. I still have them and many are signed. A lot of the players lived around our neighborhood and they were much more approachable then so they would sign the pictures.

———MICHAEL GORDON, 42, Investment Banker, Chicago

Chapter 3

Sweet Home Chicago

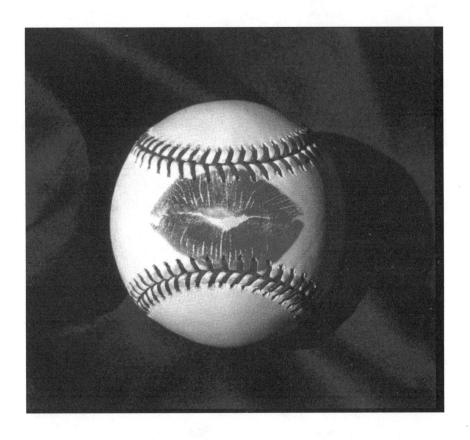

Wrigley Field—The Land of Ahs

THE CUBS PROVE THAT TRULY GREAT COMEDY IS NOT FUNNY

Tom Dreesen

A stand-up comedian, Tom "Shoot the Deuce" Dreesen, 59, who grew up in a poor suburb on the south side of Chicago, has seen all his dreams come true, except for one.

They talk about the rivalry of the Yankees and the Red Sox, and I'm not saying that the rivalry doesn't exist, but there's no greater rivalry in baseball than Cub fans and Chicago White Sox fans. There were bars you didn't go into if you were a White Sox fan or if you were a Cub fan. The rivalry between those two fandoms is just amazing. I wore my Cub hat anywhere and challenged them after a while. I just don't quit. I'm not going to let them beat me.

I boxed, as well as playing the other sports, and I wasn't a big kid, but I had the desire. If I got into a fight, I did not quit. But we're hardy people from Chicago. We come from a hardy city where the weather beats the s— out of you, where the humidity beats the s— out of you, where the Cubs beat the s— out of you, but we just keep coming back because we're hardy people.

When I was an adult bat boy for the Cubs, I wanted to show these guys how hip I was 'cause I play in a fast-pitch softball league. The first time I was a bat boy, they were playing the Giants. Their leadoff guy, J.T. Snow, got a base hit. Here I was wanting to show them how hip I was. I wanted the next guy to hit into a double play, so I said, "Come on guys, shoot the deuce,"—'cause that's what we say in soft-ball. The whole dugout looks down at me. What they say is, "Ground ball, double play. Pop his butt up." So after that they all started calling me "Shoot the Deuce." It was, "Hey, Shoot the Deuce. You'd better go out there and get those bats."

Rick Sutcliffe is a practical joker. I had to wear a hard hat when I ran out onto the field. A lot of adult guys who are honorary bat boys just stay in the dugout. But, I ran out and grabbed the bats—I did the job. David Letterman used to rag me, "I don't believe you. You don't go out there and grab those bats. Tell me you don't do that." I liked to run out and grab the bats and high-five them when they would hit a home run and all that stuff.

Sutcliffe blew a big bubblegum bubble and stuck it on top of my hat while I'm sitting there in dugout. I ran out on the field when it was time to go get a bat, and the whole crowd starts laughing and pointing at me. I'm thinking they're laughing because I'm a comedian they recognize. I'm waving back at them—looking like a big dork! He also had the WGN camera guy cued that he was going to do that.

Another time, he has a huge glass of Kool-Aid. He puts a hole in the cup, and he covers it with his finger. He told the camera guy, "I'm gonna hand Tom this drink, and it's gonna squirt Kool-Aid all over him." What he did was—the next time a ball was hit out to the out-field he started looking at it and saying, "Oh no, Tommy, hold this for me." Naturally, like an idiot I grabbed the cup to hold it, and the stream shoots out all over my uniform—this on national television.

Another time, he tells me, "When you go out to pick up the last bat, tell Frank Pulli, the umpire, that I think he's the best home-plate umpire in the National League." I went out, and he was sweeping off the plate. I picked up the bat and said, "Hey, Mr. Pulli. Rick Sutcliffe said…" He said, "I don't give a d— what Rick Sutcliffe said, and I don't care what you have to say. You know what I'm saying? You're a bat boy. Pick up the bats and go back to the g—d— dugout. Don't bother me." I didn't realize it, but Sutcliffe had told Pulli he was going to do that so it was all planned. I went back to the dugout and Sutcliffe asked what he had said. I said, "He said he thinks you're the best pitcher in both leagues."

Sometimes, during my comedy shows, I would say, "In the year 1908, the Chicago Cubs won the World Series. At that time, there were forty-five states in the Union. Teddy Roosevelt was president of the United States. The world's oldest living president, Ronald Reagan, wasn't even born yet. Two years later, Halley's Comet came through Chicago. Halley's Comet has been back and the Cubs still have not won a World Series. But a fan is not someone who goes to the ballpark when the team is in first place. A fan is someone who goes to Wrigley Field the last game in September. The Cubs are a hundred and two games out—and you think they still have a chance. I've been there—forty-five people in the whole ballpark. The crowd was so intimate, instead of the National Anthem, we sang, 'Feelings.' One vendor—I said, 'Could I have a hot dog?' He said, 'I've only got one, just take a bite.' In the fourth inning, you hear the announcer say things like, 'Will the lady with the lost nine children please claim them. They're beating the Cubs eleven to nothing.'" I won the "Quote of the Year" once, getting five-hundred dollars donated to my favorite charity. It was: "When I was a little boy growing up, I used to pray that the Cubs and the White Sox would merge so Chicago would only have one bad team."

When I came out of the service, there were buses for rent and about fifty of us guys would get on a bus and go down to Wrigley Field to see the game. One particular day at Wrigley Field, fifty of us go down there, and we all go in and sit in the grandstands. In front of us, in the stands, there were fifty empty seats right on the rail. We just assumed another block of people just like us had that section. It was time to start and here they came as the game was just beginning. It's fifty of the strangest looking people I've ever seen. They were dressed odd and they looked at all of us and said, "Hi." And they wanted to shake hands and introduce themselves to us. They said, "We're from Manteno."

Manteno is a mental institution so we knew then that they were patients. So we all shook hands with them and said, "Nice to see you." They finally sit down and they start saying, "Where's Charlie? Charlie hasn't been out of the institution for over ten years." We see this goofy looking guy coming down—purple hat on sideways, orange sweater, green slacks—the goofiest looking shoes I've ever seen in my life. It's Charlie. Then we all shake hands with him.

Finally, we asked him if he could sit down. He did. Then someone asked if he was going to have a beer. A woman says, "Charlie hasn't had a beer in ten years." The beer man comes and Charlie gives the guy a dollar and gets a cup of beer. Charlie walks over to the railing, and he dumps it down on somebody's head. We're all going, "Did you see what he did? He dumped the beer over the railing."

Well, this guy from down below comes up to where they were and he points out Charlie to the usher. The usher took Charlie out, and everybody's asking where he is. Then about the fifth inning, Charlie comes back. They were all excited to have Charlie back. He calls the beer man over, gives the guy another dollar, gets his cup of beer, again walks over to the rail and dumps that beer. We were all laughing and saying, "I can't believe it. He dumped that beer over again." Meanwhile Charlie sits down, and the guy down below is screaming up at him. The guy comes up this time with a security guy. He points out Charlie and they take him out again.

The ninth inning, here comes Charlie wandering back to almost a standing ovation. Everybody in the bleachers is shouting, "Char—lie. Char—lie. Char—lie." Now guys are getting in fights about who is going to buy Charlie another beer. Sure enough—they get him a third beer, and, again, Charlie dumps the beer over the railing. This time, two cops and another guy from down below come up. They carried Charlie out like he's a wishbone to people chanting and cheering and applauding. Now the Cubs lost thirteen to nothing that day—but, it was another wonderful day at Wrigley Field!

When the Cubs win, all the years of abuse I took as a Cub fan, good-natured ribbing from friends, it will be unbelievable. I'm not Jewish but they have a great word—kvell. I'd kvell.

BEAR DOWN CHICAGO CUBS

Photo courtesy of the Chicago Cubs

Mary Therese Kraft

Mary Therese Kraft is a fine young Notre Dame graduate who booked Mike Ditka to sing "Take Me Out to the Ball Game" in 1998. Ditka's quickie rendition is now part of Cubs lore. Here is her behind the scenes story of that day.

We invited Mike Ditka to sing "Take Me Out to the Ball Game." When he accepted we were ecstatic. The plan was for him to arrive at the ballpark directly after his golf game. The game started, and we were all running around in a panic trying to find out where he was. We called the restaurant and they said he was on the golf course. The golf course called and said, "Oh, he just left." This all happened in about the fifth inning.

We had a security person posted in the parking lot and one with me up in the booth. We just waited for him to come. As it turned out, we had to decide whether we were going to go with him or not. He arrived with two outs in the top of the seventh inning. My intern at the time, Doug Thompson, was with the security guard and they ran him up there. They radioed up to us and said Ditka had arrived. So we told our P.A. announcer and our message board operator, "He's here, he's in the building—we're going to go with Ditka." Then all of a sudden the third out was made. Poor Steve Stone did such a great job of holding the crowd. He said, "We have an announcement: Ditka's in the building but he's not here yet, so I may have to sing by myself." The crowd started booing, not because they didn't want to hear Steve but, because everyone was anticipating Mike Ditka.

In the meantime, Ditka was running—this poor guy has had two hip surgeries and a heart attack—up our back stairway, which has about three flights of stairs and four ramps. We got him up to the top of the stairway, and Steve Stone said, "The coach has arrived." Everybody in the crowd just went crazy. We told Ditka we were going to prep him on the way up and that we'd be waiting for him. We meant that we were not going to sing without him. But he thought we meant that we weren't going to start the bottom of the seventh until he sang. So he just belted it out like no other. Oh, it was so funny, and his expression after was just the most comical thing we saw all year.

Everyone's faces were in a state of confusion. The crowd started to sing with him, but just couldn't keep up. Everyone started with "Take me out to the ball game..." but they just lost him after that. This had never happened; the seventh inning stretch was not sung. Everyone was just in awe. Our organist kept right up with him. He followed him to a "T", which is amazing. It was unreal. As soon as he finished, everyone was like, "What just happened?" The bleacher section did a chorus of their own and sang the whole song over again because it was just too fast.

It didn't hit anybody until that night when it was aired across the country on ESPN and CNN. Diana, his wife called and asked for a copy of it, because she hadn't seen it. People were just calling like crazy. They were laughing and saying it was the best rendition. When you look at it, you know Harry has to be laughing hysterically in Heaven because it was so Harry-esque and so Ditka-esque.

He could not have been nicer. He stayed on the air with Chip and Steve; they couldn't even cut to a commercial because it was so late. He was wonderful. He said, "I'm so sorry; I didn't realize it would take so long to get here from the golf course. I got stuck on Addison." We ask everyone who sings to autograph the scorecard and some baseballs to auction off at the end of the season. He said, "Oh, I'll sign anything you want. I feel terrible." I asked if he would mind going on WGN radio, and he said, "Oh, I'll do anything, I feel so bad." He was funny.

I had never met him before in person, and he was great. He took pictures with everybody, signed anything anybody wanted him to sign, and did a great interview with the media. He was wonderful, and he really loved it. He won an award for us, which really put this entire "seventh inning stretch" song on the map. From that point on, we had people calling us up to offer to sing because of the exposure he was able to get for us.

Ditka sang on Opening Day 1999, and I have to say that he still can't carry a tune. Our theme that year was: "This time he's on time." In '99 he sang much slower. it was important to him to come back and do it again and do it right. He's not a strong singer, but he's a phenomenal guy all around. When we approached him, we told him about the award that MLB had presented to us because of his performance. He was in awe. Major League Baseball gave us the award for "Blooper of the Year." It probably isn't something to be proud of, but it was pretty funny.

Ditka is such an amazing icon, it's really impressive. You see that stern face, that rugged blue-collar persona on TV, the Ditka that broke his arm in the locker room when he was so mad—this rough, tough guy. The first time I met him, I was almost taken aback. His face is such a caricature. He is Chicago. My generation, especially, admires him. He's got that Midwest mentality that everybody appreciates and associates with. It's that rugged image of someone who worked hard all his life, has definite morals and ethics, or at least is someone you can respect. Who doesn't really appreciate and support that?

A Chicago Cubs fan was enjoying himself at a game in the mid-'70s when television cameras focused on him and a lady friend. The only problem was that the lady friend was not his wife. The wife found out, and the fan did not receive a warm welcome upon his return from the stadium. The fan sued the Cubs and their television carrier for invasion of privacy. Because of that fan, most sporting tickets today carry fine print on the back that reads, "…This holder grants permission to the Participating Clubs and agents to utilize the holder's image or likeness in any live or recorded video display or other transmission or reproduction in whole or in part of the event to which this admits him…"

A ROSE BY ANY OTHER NAME IS A ROSE, A DYNEK BY ANY OTHER NAME IS A STREET.

Ralph Dynek

Ralph Dynek, 45, is a futures trader and owner of a carpet store with his wife, Julie. They did not buy a book on baby names for their children. They just named them after streets surrounding Wrigley.

As we got older and got into high school, we became bleacher fans. I never ditched school to go to a ball game though. What we would do is we would caddy in the morning. If that ended early, we'd jump on our bikes and head out. I lived about five minutes from one of the elevated tracks called the "Skokie Swift" which fed into the "L" downtown so we'd go with three bucks…$1.25 to get into the bleachers, 75 cents on a pop and $1 on a Polish, and we'd be in. As we got even older, we started driving. Just north of the ballpark about two streets is a street called Grace. My first daughter is named Grace after Grace Street. There is a huge Catholic property, a convent, there. The nuns, wearing Cubs caps, would actually sit out and allow people to park for a donation. It was about $5. The *Tribune* manages parking there now, but pre-*Tribune*, I'd say 1986 or so, it was the nuns who ran the show.

When our oldest son was born, we named him Addison Clark after the streets around Wrigley Field. The original idea behind naming our first-born was because Clark and Addison just rolls off the tongue, like "cookies and milk." When Addison was born, he was going to be Clark Addison or Addison Clark. Then he was born on Julie's father's birthday…the exact same date…and we fine-tuned the name to Addison Buck after Julie's father. The baby was two weeks early. Since it was her dad's birthday, we were supposed to meet him at a restaurant. We called to tell him, "Sorry we're not coming to dinner, we had the baby" and he didn't believe us. He said, "No you didn't, it's two weeks early...you're at the Cubs game." He realized he was wrong and then the second boy came along. We had picked out other names like Blaise, Mason, and a few others and we weren't quite sure what we were going to name the child. About a day after the baby was born, Julie's mother and my mother came to the hospital and said, "That's it. This child's name is Clark." The grandmas muscled up and guided us into naming him Clark. They gave us the final push. We didn't put up a big fight and the little boy's name was Clark.

When the third boy came along we had no idea what to name him. The only streets left were Waveland and Sheffield and we could not name a boy Waveland so his name is Sheffield and everyone calls him "Sheffy." Then, a few years later, our daughter Grace was born. We just could not name her Waveland. I could just see her getting her diploma and looking out at me, staring as she graduated from high school wanting to kill me, so we went with Grace...the street where the convent was. Her middle name is Waveland, though, so she's Grace Waveland Dynek.

A couple years later we had another girl and we were out of streets. There is a fifth street—Seminary—that runs right along the side there in left field; it butts up against the ballpark. We couldn't name the baby Seminary, so instead we named her Ivy from the ivy on the walls. Her name is Ivy Marie Wrigley Dynek. We didn't want her to feel left out. All the kids are named after the streets, not the ball players. The ball players come and go, but the most endearing thing to us is the ballpark; the red brick, the smells, the sounds, going there with your dad, having popcorn, playing catch with your dad, playing Little League, going out and playing all-star games, tournaments, playing softball, American Legion ball; a lot of baseball being played over the years and every now and then a trip down to the ballpark to rekindle your love for the beloved Cubs.

RUNS 'N HOSES

John Sampson

John Sampson, 47, a member of the Chicago Fire Department is Assistant Cook at Firehouse #78—directly across the street from Wrigley.

Everyone always asks if we ever get balls into the firehouse. Back in '84 Ron Cey hit one into the kitchen. It was a foul ball because we're on the other side of the foul pole, on the foul side. We were watching the game on TV, you could see it was coming foul and it went over the fence. It must have ricocheted into the front door and rolled right into the kitchen. I just leaned over and picked the ball up and put it into a locker. About 17 years later, this fireman from another area brings his kid to Wrigley. I'm in the kitchen cooking. The kid—at the end of the game—comes walking in, he must have been 10 years old. He sits on our bench in the kitchen, and he looks all dejected. I asked what was wrong with him. His dad says he came very close to catching a foul ball. Some guy reached out and grabbed it from him. I told him to hold on a second. I reached into the cabinet and said, "You know what, this ball was hit by Ron Cey back in '84...it's yours. Take it" It looked like it made this kid's day. He had this huge smile on his face. He never said, "thank you" because he was just in awe by this ball so his dad walked across the street and got him one of those little ball holders and they put the ball in there.

There was an Old-Timers game with Ernie Banks. Ernie came in and was looking for a belt for his uniform. We've got black uniform belts. He grabbed one. Well, he stole that one, I never saw that one again, so Ernie Banks has my belt. Billy Williams comes in with his grandkids sometimes and they hang on the rails.

One afternoon after the game, the Cubs are going to Cincinnati. They're fifty feet from us, getting ready to get on the bus to go to the airport. You can see all the players getting on. The bus pulls away and there's Rick Wrona sitting on his suitcase as the bus pulls away. Well, he just got sent down to triple-A. This was '89. I said, "Hey, Rick, come on over here. We're having dinner"...he stayed for pizza. He said, "I have to call my wife." I asked why and he said, "She's waiting at the airport and she's going to be in tears because we're going back to Iowa." When she pulled up she was crying because she'd just gotten used to living in Lake Point Tower.

Every now and then we have to go across the street and unlock the players' cars...they aren't the brightest people. They make a ton of money but all they do is play baseball. Bob Dernier to name one locked his keys in his car. His alarm kept going off at the ballpark. Fergie Jenkins did it a couple times when he was coaching. The two nicest guys that ever played for them since I've been here were Shawon Dunston and Turk Wendell. Wendell would come over with venison stew. One day my son, Ryan, and I walked across the street to Wrigley and there's Fergie Jenkins and Turk Wendell in the bleachers shooting bows and arrows at a target on the field. Here I am the big fireman and Turk says, "John, you want to try it?" I said, "Ok, whatever." They had this little target sitting there at second base. It was a big foam deer. Nobody is on the field, so I just grab this big bow and pull it back. You have to be stronger than hell to pull those bows back. Here's my kid watching me with Fergie Jenkins and Turk. All of a sudden, once I got it past my shoulders, it was really easy. I bring it back and I didn't even come close to the stupid deer. You kind of get to be a little bit of family. I talked to Shawon Dunston all the time before he left. He talked about his kids and he'd ask about my kids. He said, "Yeah, by the end of the season you're going to see me stealing bases." I asked why and he said, "Well, my contract is up and I have to have incentives here." I told him not to get picked off and the same day when he told me that, he got picked off twice. I told him, "Shawon, you're leaning!" He said, "Yeah, I have to steal some bases though, for the contract."

A lot of players come in our firehouse. I invited Tom Trebelhorn in here once. He had his little impromptu press conference out in front. He was the coach and the Cubs had this long losing streak so he stood on the bench in front of the firehouse and all the reporters were standing around. He's fielding questions and going on and on. I said, "Hey, coach...I have a question!" Now all the cameras are on me.

This is right in the middle of the whole Whitewater thing with Clinton and Hillary. I said, "What's your take on this whole Whitewater thing?" All the reporters got this puzzled look on their faces. All of a sudden they put the cameras back on him as if he has an answer for it. I was cracking up. He's shaking his head. I said, "Ok, never mind, I have another question." The cameras are on me again, waiting for me to ask. I said, "Are you hungry?" He said "yes." I asked if he wanted to come in for dinner and he said, "Ok, great." He hopped off the bench, came in and shut the door. We have reporters pounding on the back door of the firehouse trying to get him to answer more questions. I had to ask him one question. I said, "Tom, you have to do me a favor. It will probably never happen, but you have to do me a favor. My son loves Ryne Sandberg, he's his idol. Give him the bunt sign, just to move a runner across to second base. I've never seen him bunt, he's a prolific hitter." He looks at me and nods. I think it was the next week when Ryne Sandberg retired. I swear to God, I was watching the game, Sandberg stepped back, he got the sign. Sandberg retired the next day. I never did ask him about that…if he really gave him the bunt sign.

Zimmer was a happy-go-lucky guy that would come over. Billy Conners….I was good friends with him. Remember when Pete Rose tied Ty Cobb's record at Wrigley Field back in '86 or '87? I got the Wheaties box top and I had the ticket because that was my son's first baseball game-he was there to witness Pete Rose tying Ty Cobb. I had Billy Conners bring the Wheaties cover over there for Pete Rose to sign and I got the ticket stub in an envelope. You just get to meet the players, and they're like everyone else so it's kind of funny to see everyone hooting and hollering, especially when they drive by in their Escalades.

Our firehouse gets called into Wrigley all the time. Generally, when we go in there, it's not a pretty sight because there's something going on. Usually heart attacks. There's been heart attacks where we're working and people are stepping over us trying to get by. We were there for Hee Seop Choi when he bounced his head on the third base side against the Yankees. We pulled the engine and the ambulance on the field and picked him up. We generally go to the first aid station on Addison for heart attack victims, breathing, broken arms and legs… stuff like that. We had people fall off the grandstands into the box seats before. We go in for little rubbish fires and difficulty breathing. We were put here in 1915 in this spot because the ball park was put up in 1914. That's why the house is here…for the ballpark. In 23 years we've been stuck in traffic once. Everyone thinks it's a problem, but it's not a problem at all. We have the big cowcatcher in front of that rig and people just move out of the way.

We had an ambulance run there at Waveland and Kenmore during that whole McGwire/Sosa thing. St. Louis is out there and taking batting practice. McGwire is up. We were getting pelted with balls on the corner while trying to work on a patient on the ground. We had to have somebody stand over us with a baseball glove because the balls are hitting the fire truck and raining on us.

In '84, the problem was "how bad are the Cubs going to beat you?" They were that good. They had the pitching, they had the relieving; they had everything. The feeling was that they were going all the way and you wondered how bad were they going to kick your butt. In 2003 you wondered if they could hold on and win. That's why their pitchers had to pitch so many innings. They had to go eight and nine innings because they had no middle relief and it showed at the end. The whole problem was coaching. Where was Clement? You put your starters in. I'm at home watching this wondering what this guy was doing. That was the problem in '84. I think they pitched the one pitcher instead of Rick Sutcliffe because the coach wanted to save Sutcliffe for the first game of the World Series. You have to get there first. I couldn't believe it.

I'm a Yankees fan too because I can't stand the Sox. I actually hate the Sox. If they were in the World Series and there was a good movie, I'd go rent a DVD or something. I could care less about the Sox. But I like that one guy that's a die-hard Sox fan on the South Side. He says, "For every home run hit against the Cubs, it's free beer."

I've always told all my significant others that when I go, I have to be cremated. I want them to dribble the stuff on the ivy in the outfield during a Cubs game. I'll be there somewhere. Then I want them to throw a little on Waveland so I'm always around.

WRIGLEY FIELD

MORE FROM THE FIELD OF SCREAMS

We went to the workout game and the home run hitting contest at the 1990 All-Star game. After all that, my cousin and I are in my Toyota in the traffic, and Bill Murray knocks on my window and said, "Can I have a ride?" So I gave Bill Murray a ride. It was right outside Wrigley Field. He was walking by, and we were in the right spot at the right time. He and his brother got in the car with us. He said hello to us and told me just to drop him off in a couple of blocks. I said, "No, no, I've got this opportunity. Where do you want to go?" He said, "Well, actually I'm going to the Lake. I have a friend who has a boat." So we took them on a five or ten-minute ride, and he signed an autograph for my cousin. He was as nice as can be. We talked about the Cubs a little bit and he wanted to know what I did, and he talked to my younger cousin a lot. He was great.

——**DAN SCULLY**, Cub Fan

Wrigley Field is a special place. It's the best ballpark in the world to watch a game. When I, at age 57, walk into Wrigley Field, it reminds me of my childhood because it hasn't changed, besides the fact that they put lights on the roof. When I walk into the concession area, it hasn't changed one bit. It reminds me of a lot of good times I had with my dad and with my family. There was a guy who used to sell hot dogs outside of the ballpark. I really liked the smoky links. They're kind of a smoked hot dog. I don't think they sell them anymore.

——**BOB OLSON**, Barrington, Illinois

One hot summer day, one of those 95-degrees-in-the-sun days, my family and I had gone to a Cubs game. I was ten years old at the time, and the Cubs were facing the Reds. When we'd entered the stadium I had bought a hot dog and gone to sit down. Our seats were about twelve rows up from first base, so you can imagine the great view of the field we had. Soon, the sun caused my hot dog to start to wrinkle up like a raisin, it was so hot. "Mom," I panted, "can I go up to the balcony in the shade?" After begging and pleading with them, my parents finally gave in and I ran up the stairs.

As I entered the cool, refreshing shade, I sighed in relief. Then everyone around me stood up. I didn't know what to do. I looked straight up and saw a baseball flying towards me. After what seemed like an hour, the ball came down and hit off one man's hand and bounced to the floor. "*Wow! I have a chance to get this ball,*" I thought. But it was if I was cursed, the ball started rolling away from me. "Oh, no," I said aloud. Then it was as if everyone started coming at me. They were trying to get me out of their way. I dove under all these men throwing their bodies at me. As my stomach hits the floor, I look straight ahead and see this white object with red laces. I reached for it and my hand finally found it. I stood up and threw my fist up in the air and a rush of applause greeted my ears.

——DAN COSTIGAN, 13, Mokena, Illinois, aspiring writer

Everybody who comes to Chicago wants to go to a Cubs game, even when the Cubs suck. So these four girls were sitting down in front of us. They had stuffed their pants and coats with beer and they were getting a little loopy so, just out of the blue, they turned around and stood up on their chairs and just flashed their chests at the crowd. The crowd got a bonus that day.

When you go to a Cubs game, most people go there just to people-watch. The Cubs have been so stinky for so many years—but they always fill up the stadium. The young women come out in droves. They wear as little as they possibly can. They drink as much as they possibly can, and they just walk the park. That's what you do at a Cub game. It's pretty unbelievable. You get people there who, when asked who won, say: "I don't know." Asked, "Do you have any idea what the score was," they reply, "Noooo."

——PETE ALDWORTH, Hinsdale, Illinois

To me, the smell at Wrigley was what was special. Think about this—you're driving through a neighborhood and you come to a stop sign. Lo and behold, there's a ballpark in the middle of this neighborhood, not just a ballpark—Wrigley Field! That's the same ballpark that Babe Ruth pointed in—the famous point. Now you go inside that ballpark, and you think about this—you're going to sit in the seat that your great, great grandfather sat in, that your great grandfather sat in, that your grandfather sat in, that your father sat in, that you're sitting in, that your son will sit in and that your son's son will sit in. You're going to sit there and watch a game that all your ancestors watched—the same game in the same seat and for a moment, only for a moment, time stands still. In this hectic, crazy world, time stands still.

But as a little boy, it was the smells. I can't tell you how poor we were—I'm not trying to give you a Charles Dickens story, but the smells of food and the hot dogs and everything there. The excitement and the people and cheers—it was like being in this holy place, this shrine.

By the way, I still feel this way when I go to the there now—I still get the same excitement in my stomach when I'm walking up those stairs up into Wrigley Field. You walk out and you go, "Wow, look at this."

——TOM DREESEN, Los Angeles, California

Back in 1998, my sister arranged with her company for us to go out and play on the field at Wrigley. My son, who was then about nine, and I went out and pitched in the bullpen. We ran the bases. We went up to the ivy and played catch in center field. Ernie Banks and Jack Brickhouse were sitting in the dugout signing autographs, and we got those. Just very shortly thereafter, Jack Brickhouse died. During the 1996 Democratic convention, all these political reporters got to go and take a swing at home plate batting practice. We got three pitches each, and I missed all three of them—but it was great to come up to the plate at Wrigley Field.

——JONATHAN ALTER, writer, New Jersey

The Lakeview Baseball Club on Sheffield had a sign that used to say AC 14 58 95. The AC is "Annos Cubbies," year of the Cubs. The 14 was how many years it had been since the Cubs won the division, the 58 was the number of years since the last time they won the pennant, the 95 was for the years since the last time they won the World Series. My son and I went to the doubleheader  near the end of the 2003 season. That was one of the most amazing days I can ever recall at Wrigley Field. When the Cubs won the second game, they took down that 14 and only had one zero to put up. They put up that zero, and the few thousand fans that had some clue what those numbers meant went absolutely ballistic. It said AC 0 58 95.

——STEPHEN GIVOT, 53, Chicago

Wrigley Field is great for girl watching. You see all these beautiful women. I was with a co-worker at Wrigley Field, and we got there early and saw Harry Caray on the golf cart they used to take him upstairs to the booth. He was very impressed with this girl who was with me. Harry was very impressed by any girl!

I had a co-worker and somebody in his family died. They cremated him and wanted to spread the ashes at Wrigley Field, like from the bleachers or something. The Cubs management said, "No." So they took the urn anyway and did it themselves before one of the games.

——**DANIEL SCULLY**, postal store manager

When I was seven years old, in 1977, my father took me to my first Cubs game. It is a spectacular event for a youngster to experience, and not just because of the game. There is an entire world bustling within Wrigley Field. It's a foreign fun world of sights, sounds and smells. I was wide-eyed. Dad even gave me money to buy my own food…and none of it healthy. I ran down to the concession areas and saw something I had never had before…NACHOS. I quickly secured a little origami cardboard box filled with the sharply aromatic and yellow glowing snack. I took one huge scoop with an unknown green vegetable wagon wheel on it and chomped. Now, mind you, prior to this I didn't even like black pepper on food because it was too spicy for me. So, needless to say, my entire skull was blazing from the spicy cheese and the jalapeno slice. Teary-eyed and snot-ridden, I spat out the remaining hell-fire, and tossed the nachos in the trash. For the rest of the game I was miserable and I didn't eat spicy food again until I was well into college. Now, when I eat anything spicy, especially nachos, I immediately return to that day and think—GO CUBS!

——**TOM ZAHORIK**, 33, Senior Producer—Atari, Baltimore, MD

John O'Malley and I were so excited to be at Wrigley Field that day. The Cubs were playing the Dodgers in a doubleheader, and we were there. Two games in one day; we were in heaven. John came from a big Catholic family, and I was the tag-along friend that day. Mrs. O'Malley dragged all seven of us on the L-Train from Wilmette to Wrigleyville. She didn't take any guff from anyone. The first game was a good one. It even went into extra innings. Our day couldn't have gotten any better. The game went 15 innings and I don't remember who won. All I remember is Mrs. O'Malley standing up after the first game was over, and telling all of us we were going home. We shouted, "What? There's another game!" She replied, "You have already seen two games. We are leaving." John's sisters didn't care; they were happy to leave. We were shocked! We made the long, sad walk to the L-platform, complaining under our breath. There wasn't much we could do. It was common knowledge that you didn't mess with Mrs. O'Malley.

——TODD MIZENER, Photojournalist, Quad Cities

My friend, who shall remain nameless, told me one of the funniest Cubs stories I can remember. As you may know, at Wrigley, the men's bathrooms have big troughs to pee in. And the sinks to wash your hands are round and big with water flowing. My friend's uncle goes in and starts peeing into the sink, thinking it was the place to go. Luckily, no one was currently washing their hands, and everyone there seemed to just let him finish and let him leave. Afterwards, there was much laughing ... but no one was going close to that sink.

——SCOTT GRISSOM, 34, Nashville, TN

In the summer of 1996, some friends and I had bleacher seat tickets for a game against the Atlanta Braves. The four of us walked around to the rear entrance of Wrigley to stand in the ticket holder's line. While in line, I noticed that the two men in front of me were acting a little nervous, a lot of whispering and looking over their shoulders. Within a couple of minutes, I realized that one of the men was trying to hide a gallon jug under his shirt. I thought that it might have been filled with margaritas or at least something alcoholic.

Being a stand-up kinda guy, I offered my help. The men were up for any suggestions at this point. So I placed the jug in my rather large camera bag, which I am rarely without, and proceeded to stand in line. The two's tension seemed to ease as they tiptoed through the ticket turnstile.

Now, here I am, ticket in hand and an over-weighted camera bag, entering behind them. Before I cross into the promised land, I'm approached by security. "What's in the bag?" he asked. Okay, so now I am the one who is nervous and looking over shoulders. The problem in front of me was that I had no idea what the penalty, if any, was for BYOB-ing at a public place. Digging deep into my intellect and wit I managed to scrape up enough words for my brilliant response, "What bag?"

He promptly mocked me with his minimum-wage smirk and just as quickly, opened my camera bag. And there it was. Busted. My first concern was if I had enough change in my pocket to make my one phone call, which consequently was long-distance. The gallon was snatched up, top popped, and placed under the nose of the Wrigley Rent-A-Cop. After a long and deep breath, he put the lid back on, returned the jug back to my bag, and told me to proceed.

When I asked why it was alright to pass, he replied, "If you think that you can get drunk on what little amount of alcohol that may or not be in there, good luck. You getting up every two outs to take a leak is punishment enough."

Long story short, I spent the better part of ten minutes freaking out because a couple of idiots wanted to smuggle in a gallon of lemonade to a baseball game.

——SCOTT EVANS, 34, Photographer, Nashville, TN

Danny Schuman with his grandfather, Sid Rosset

When my grandpa first started going to game, he found a parking lot on Grace Street, a convent of some sort, which still exists today, but today it's run by the Cubs for parking revenue. Back then, it was run by the nuns. I remember my grandpa pulling into this lot. The nuns were in their full black habits, and they all had blue, plastic Cubs helmets on their heads. They would say, "Hello. How are you doing? Would you like to make a donation to the convent for parking today?" My grandpa would say, "How much do you recommend?" They'd say, "Two dollars." He'd give them two bucks, and we'd pull right in.

I remember my grandpa would cut out the standings and send them to me in '71 when the Cubs were doing well. All those players were All-Stars, and he'd cut out their stats and send them to me in the mail. We both lived in Chicago, but he was just so into it that he wanted to cut them out and send them to me with a note attached, like, "Hey, D.J., check out how everybody's doing." When I would go away to Camp Ojibwa, a sleep-away sports camp, he would send me clippings of the standings and the stats and articles to read. Probably my earliest memory of really knowing the team, being into the team is '71. I would have been eight then.

When I was in my late teens, early twenties, I would go to the games early to sit in the bleachers and watch batting practice. We'd do a lot of heckling of the players. Darryl Strawberry was always a huge guy to heckle. We would say, "Fe Fi Fo Fum, Darryl is a ——— bum!"

There was this woman, about fifty years old, who sat in the bleachers, and we called her the "Chicken Lady." She would wear a long-sleeved sky-blue spandex top and she had blond hair, and she made chicken sounds. Then there was the "Bleacher Creature," Jerry Pritikin. I think he's been in the bleachers for every game for decades. He used to wear a hat that said, "Bleacher Creature" on it. And there was Ronnie Woo-Woo.

The great thing about Chicago is that you can leave your office at one, go to the game for six innings, and be back by three-thirty or so. I was shown on TV in Game 1 of the Cubs-Marlins series, and I got close to seventy-five calls and e-mails.

——**DANNY SCHUMAN**, 40, grew up in Highland Park

I went to school at DePaul University, which is a mile and a half from Wrigley Field and I bartended down in that neighborhood at the Blue Parrot from '92 till about '96. I was bartending and going to school. Usually I'd get up around ten o'clock, then I'd get on my bike and ride up and down the lakefront. Then 1:15 would roll around, and I'd find myself somewhere up near Wrigley Field magically every day. I'd lock my bike to the stairs leading up to the WGN truck, Then I'd go scalp a ticket for three bucks about midway through the second inning and just go in and watch the ball game. Those years the park wasn't all that packed, so it was usually easy to get a ticket. You'd go in and find some Cub fans and hang out and find out how bad the Cubs were doing. You'd have the wonder and the joy of them having a win that day or, you'd put on your Mark Grace jersey and go find a couple of girls that were sitting there with Mark Grace jerseys on.

In all of that general area, there are die-hard Cub fans all over the place. They don't just hang out at Wrigley Field. There's a lot of walking in that area, and there's a bar every fifty feet. A lot of times people would go to the Cub game and bar-crawl their way back. So, ten or twelve Cub fans would walk into the Blue Parrot with their Cub hats and their Cub jerseys on, stumbling and mumbling and cheering, 'cause at that point, they had no idea whether or not they'd won or lost the game. And it didn't really matter 'cause they'd hit fifteen bars on the way back to the neighborhood. People loved the 2:20 games on Fridays. They'd go to the games and the game would be over about five or five thirty, and by the time they'd pub-crawl back to me at the Blue Parrot, it would be eight o'clock,. My shift would be ending and I'd think, *Thank God I don't have to deal with these idiots walking through the door right now.*

You could see them coming a mile away. Here come twelve guys with Cub hats. Get out of the way. It's eight-thirty. They're walking back from Wrigley.

————**JIM DEMARET**, Chicago Stock Exchange

One name that has gone largely unmentioned in Cubs history is John McDonough. John McDonough has been the head of the promotions of the Cubs for probably the last twenty years. He has been the one who has guided the Cubs—with crappy teams—through the '80s and the '90s and filled that stadium. He is the one who recognized the marketing possibilities of the neighborhood. He befriended all the bars and, unlike the White Sox who didn't want any bars around the new ballpark because it would cut into their beer sales, McDonough takes the opposite slant with the Cubs, saying, "It's great to be part of the neighborhood." He has the guys advertising in his programs; he sends them parties; he works the neighborhood like a pro.

————**JIM RITTENBERG**, Mother Hubbard's, Chicago

My dad was a huge baseball fan. He was a Chicago policeman, and he played for the Police League. He had aspirations of being a ballplayer, but they didn't pan out. He always liked the Cubs. He was from the West Side originally, and you picked your team because you weren't tied to either the Sox or the Cubs.

Ferguson Jenkins was one of my favorites. He gave me a baseball bat during a White Sox–Cubs exhibition game at Comiskey Park. I don't remember how old I was at the time, probably 12. He broke a bat and was walking back toward the dugout and tossed me the bat that he had just broken. I walked out of the ballpark with that bat with Fergie's name on it, and I felt like it was the Holy Grail. I've had a bunch of great memories at Wrigley. One of my favorite moments was when I went on Mother's Day one year on tickets that Second City arranged for me. I was there with my mother—kind of a selfish gift to give my mother on Mothers' Day—but she was indulging me. Jody Davis hit a home run, and I remember calling it, saying, "Mom. Jody's going to hit this ball to you." And then he actually did it! She thought about that as "her home run."

There was a guy named Chester out in the bleachers I used to sit with, who claimed not to have missed a home game in thirty or forty years. His seat was reserved. He just sat there and philosophized the entire time. He'd talk about guys you hadn't heard about so much—like Andy Pafko. There's this play called "Bleacher Bums" that was written years ago in '78. Joe Mantegna and Dennis Franz were maybe in the original cast. The history of the bleachers is the best part of the Cubs. The right field bleachers—the ones right behind Sammy Sosa now—are a little bit more rowdy than the left field bleachers. There used to be seats in center field, but the Cubs fans would put on white T-shirts so that the hitter couldn't see the ball coming. That's why they closed the seats.

—————**MIKE HAGERTY**, 49, Los Angeles, California

I grew up on the East Coast and I never had season tickets. Going to Opening Day at Wrigley Field is one of the coolest things in the world. I actually flew out from Europe in 2003 to go to Opening Day. Then it got snowed out, and I couldn't take the next day off, and I was really bummed. I remember thinking, *this is what's being a Cubs fan is all about, a baseball glove on one hand and a mitten on the other.*

Wrigley Field is a cathedral. To see the ivy being rust colored in October was such a gift. Chicago showcased so well. When I moved to Chicago fourteen years ago, I told the agent that I only wanted an apartment with a view of Wrigley. Now I overlook the lake, and I never wanted to move downtown, but I love the fact that I can be in Wrigley in seven minutes.

—————**MARGIE MCCARTNEY**, Global Event Partners, Chicago

Wrigley Field is sacred ground. There's religious connotations. It used to be a cemetery and I think a monastery was here, but to me…It's absolutely sacred ground. It's the Taj Mahal of ballparks. One of my favorite times is being there for batting practice. It's just a slice of Americana. I don't care if I ever get back. You've got the ivy, the scoreboard, the surrounding neighborhood. And living in Wrigleyville is great. The one thing we don't have is tailgating, but you don't need it. There are so many establishments to go to, Murphy's, Sports Corner, Bernie's, you know, Cubby Bears. It just goes on and on and on. There's a party atmosphere that goes on before, during, and after the games. In 2003 it just got ratcheted up and there was magic in the air. The only thing that has changed is that there are more yuppies around. Some of the older buildings got torn down to build the yuppie palaces.

——JIM BRADLEY aka "BOO", 35, Wrigleyville, Software QA Engineer

In 1977, Alan Hartwick, a TV cameraman from Grand Rapids, Mich., wrote to every Major League team—except for the Chicago Cubs—to announce he was becoming the first free-agent fan. He wrote, "I have been a Chicago Cubs fan for 20 years. Whether the score has been Pittsburgh 22, Chicago 0, or Pittsburgh 22, Chicago 1, I have stuck with the Cubs to the end. But I don't have a contract with the Cubs' organization. All the Cubs have given me over the years have been a couple of season schedules and games postponed because of darkness. At this moment, I am a fan without a team. I will sign a contract with the ball club that makes the best offer for my services." Hartwick got calls from 10 teams. He accepted the offer from the New Orleans Pelicans, even though it came from a minor league team. The Pelicans flew Hartwick and his wife to New Orleans to throw out the first ball on Opening Day.

Chapter 4

I Saw It On the Radio

I Never Met Harry Caray
But I Knew Him All My Life

SIMON SAYS

Scott Simon

Author and host of "Weekend" on National Public Radio, Scott Simon, 51, lives in New York but is "always a Chicagoan." Simon once had a goldfish "Ernie," a turtle "Sweet-Swingin' Billy" and another turtle "Fergie."

I wrote a book called *Home and Away* which came out in 2000 and details, among other things, my love of the Cubs. It's a personal memoir of being a sports fan.

I was about four years old the first time I went to Wrigley Field. My father took me, and my godfather was Jack Brickhouse, the old Cub announcer. I'll never forget being brought onto the field. In those days, they didn't have the little cubby bear on the sleeve. They had a different Cub emblem. I remember seeing that emblem and the greenness of the field, which was larger by far than any other park I'd been in at that point. I remember the sun shining on the field. They were going through batting practice. The players were just so friendly, and their smiles were so nice. They were spitting onto the ground, and I'd never seen a man spit like that before. I thought that was hilarious. In any event, I'll never forget Uncle Jack introducing me to Stan Musial. Stan the Man was in the batting cage waiting to take his swings. He had three **bats** in his arms. I'll never forget that he had the nicest smile on his face and he said, "Hey, Scotty, how you doing?" He seemed to be a genuinely nice man.

My father and Uncle Jack had a radio show together on WGN called Brickhouse and Simon. My father had grown up on the East Coast and became a Cubs fan. His favorite player was Ernie Banks because

> Orlando Cepeda used more bats than any player in history. He believed each bat had exactly one hit in it. When Cepeda had a hit, he would discard the bat. He had 2,364 hits in his career.

Ernie was his first name, too. I actually, to this day, probably don't have to tell you Ernie Banks would say, "It's a beautiful day for a ball game. Let's play two today." Every time before I do a live broadcast, I say, "It's a beautiful day for a radio show. Let's do two today." I always do that, and a couple of times over the years that I have either forgotten to say it or we've been too busy with late-breaking news or something, it seems to us, superstitiously, perhaps, that there's always been some kind of series of technical problems. So, superstitiously, we would not think of not doing it.

I remember the night of September 11, I was anchoring our coverage, and I said to cohort Sarah Barotelli, "I don't have the nerve to make that page over the paging system." It just seemed so insensitive to say that it was a beautiful day. Sarah said, "Well, do it very quietly, because we really need for things to go well." So I did.

Probably all of my time as a kid I understood there was something special about the Cubs, not that they were the greatest team in the world—far from it—but that they were the team that most needed people to believe in them. That was just in the culture then and was what everybody imparted to me. The great Ernie Banks was always the best player never to be in a World Series. They didn't have play-offs in those days. You would hear phrases like, "Well, you can never tell about the Cubs, with the exception of Ernie Banks, there's not much talent there."

I was explaining to someone last night that I have voted for Republicans and Democrats. I have voted for Socialist Worker Party candidates and for Libertarians. I have lived all over the world. Really the one constant in my life, all of my life, has been my love of the Cubs.

We have never before been this far, only to see it yanked away from us. Bob Costas, very memorably and happily, once remarked that the Red Sox are grand opera, but the Cubs are farce. It is not unusual for the Red Sox to play in the post-season and then lose. It is unusual for the Cubs to play in the post-season. This is uncharted territory. They've never before gotten beyond the first round of a playoff. To be within five outs of getting to the World Series and then lose the game with the train of events that began with this totally bizarre and unseen circumstance of the poor fan nabbing the ball out of Moises Alou's mitt....

We are in the process of adopting a daughter and since we live in New York she will probably be a Yankee fan, but she will know that her father is a Cubs fan. When it comes time to make the choice that really lasts a lifetime, I hope I will have introduced her to the joys of being a Cub fan. But, it'll still be up to her. Now that does not dissuade me from getting her little Cub outfits to wear. I have two nephews in France, and I send them Sammy Sosa gifts all the time.

Uncle Jack, for many years, had this home run call, "That's it. Back. Back. Hey-hey!" And I was told by a woman I was seeing a number of years ago that men of my vintage from Chicago, when they achieve that moment of fruition in the act of love, completion, if you please, will frequently shout, "Hey-hey." I shared this with Uncle Jack, and he was delighted, exultant that his phrase would be enshrined in generations to come. The last words he said to me every time we would take leave of each other—I would kiss him, and he would say, "Hey, you keep saying 'hey-hey' now, Kid. You keep saying hey-hey."

I never had a relationship break up because of the Cubs. Over the years when I was single, I would be involved with people who would just not understand my devotion to the Cubs. I remember the first baseball game my wife and I went to was a game between the Los Angeles Dodgers and the Mets. That was before she knew much about baseball, but she just loved the Yankees and the emblem they were for the city of New York.

Any fair man could have projected that Greg Maddux was going to be a very good pitcher. They perhaps did not know that he was going to be one of the greatest pitchers of all time, but still.... I still put the Broglio trade above that. I honestly can't tell you that Greg Maddux being on the team subsequent to 1993 would have made a significant difference. But I really think that had Lou Brock been on those teams in the 1960s, the Cubs could have won a pennant.

Mark Grace used to complain. He'd say, "This isn't a team. This is a theme park." The point of that being he felt as a player that the Cubs fans are, to a degree, reconciled in a way Yankees fans and Red Sox fans are not. That's one of the reasons we've had this consistently enormous attendance from year to year to year that has little to do with their performance on the field.

Uncle Jack had a dream, which he told me on Thanksgiving of 1969. He told me there's a dream he's harbored for several years that there will be a seventh game of the World Series between the Cubs and the White Sox, and this was before they installed lights in Wrigley Field. It will be getting dark. His dream was that Ernie Banks would be coming up in the ninth inning, no matter how many years it was, even if they had to call him up from out of retirement. Billy Pierce would be called out of retirement to pitch for the White Sox. For this last play, Banks will foul off balls and Billy Pierce will keep putting them in the strike zone until finally the count is 3-2. At that point, it's getting dark, and they're worried if anyone can see. Bill Veeck will shake hands with the Cubs owner, then P. K. Wrigley, and the two of them will agree to call it a draw.

I go to games at Comiskey Park to see the White Sox. It can be almost frightening to be there on a Sunday afternoon in the summer when it becomes a young suburban teenager drunk fest. There is less of a sense at Comiskey Park that "We come to enjoy the sunshine and the family atmosphere." And, in fact, the crowd can get a little angry when the White Sox lose. I go there, and it doesn't bother me, but it's not the baseball atmosphere I would use to interest my wife in baseball, for example, when we first started going to games; whereas, she loves Wrigley Field.

I've had an awful lot of fun as a Cub fan over the years. The thought occurred to me yesterday that this is something I've wanted to happen all of my life. This is something that my father wanted to happen all of his life—and it never did. This is something my grandfather wanted all of his life but never really saw, since he was born in 1908, the last time they won a World Series. You have to go back to before my grandfather to have been alive to see them win a World Series. That's amazing—one of the founding franchises of Major League Baseball.

I do think there are some Cub fans who have gotten, over the years, perversely proud of our losing record, "Our grief is worse than yours." I don't feel that way, and I don't like to feel that way. There's a lot to be said for the Yankees and the pride in that franchise. They establish a gold standard really that other people have to meet from year to year to year. But the Cubs, to me, for all of their imperfections, and the fact they're owned by a major American corporation, and they pay out millions of dollars, but for many of us, our love of the Cubs begins with the fact that you look at this team and you usually think that this is still a franchise and a team and a ballpark and a neighborhood that makes this game worth thinking of as a national pastime. This is what the game is supposed to be. It's supposed to be a neighborhood game. You're supposed to have at least a few players on the team who the fans just love and have this high-profile personality trait. These are not faceless people.

What I remember about Ferguson Jenkins when he pitched was that he not only was a great pitcher, but he was a determined hitter. He was a much better hitter than pitchers usually are. He worked at it. He said, "It only helps me." And he would get up there and take his swings. When he won a game he would often have a hit or two in addition to whatever his pitching stats were.

John Elway, Deion Sanders and Billy Cannon, Jr. were signed by George Steinbrenner for the Yankees and given $100,000+ bonuses. All three quit baseball for the NFL. In the 1979 Major League Baseball draft, the Kansas City Royals drafted Dan Marino in the 4the round and John Elway in the 18th round....Also, in the same year, the Royals hired a Missourian for their Group Sales Department. He left five years later for a job in the radio business. Say hello to Rush Limbaugh.

THE BEST IN THE BUSINESS

Chet Coppock

Sporting News Radio's Chet Coppock, 55, is credited with bringing the sports magazine format to radio. Well, that and his snazzy suspenders. Chet will tell you that Jack Brickhouse was the most special broadcaster and most special man he ever met in his life. And Coppock attributes at least 110% of his ad-lib ability to the study of the brilliance of Jack Brickhouse.

I took my boy to see Game 6 of the League Championship Series with Florida, when Prior was on the mound and saw the occurrence with Moises Alou and the young kid from Northbrook, Steve Bartman. And to hell and be damned with all those people, in my opinion, who tried to lay the blame for this most recent Cub failure on the kid, who did what, basically, any fan in the world is going to do—that is to instinctively reach out for a foul ball. And it wasn't just the kid for heaven's sake. It was a living, breathing British soccer scrum with all these people who were reaching for this foul ball.

I'm in Las Vegas, I had to leave on Wednesday morning, so I saw Wednesday night's seventh game from a hotel along The Strip. And when it was done, there wasn't any feeling of desolation or desperation. There was no feeling of "where's the arsenic," let's rewrite "Leaving Las Vegas." It was just a feeling of something that had been said to me when I was about ten years old. That was, "Kid, remember, the Cubs are on earth to break your heart." And to revise that to be more metaphorical in terms of where I was on that given night, I think that slot machines, the Chicago Cubs and the Boston Red Sox all have been placed on God's earth for one express reason, and that is to break our hearts. But, in my case I was very, very fortunate.

Early in life, my father was very close to Jack Brickhouse, who, of course, for many years, was not only the voice of the Chicago White

Sox, the Chicago Cubs and the Chicago Bears, but was the single, most powerful individual in Chicago during the so-called Eisenhower years, next to Mayor Daley. And, I'm going to throw you one that probably nobody else will give you. Jack Brickhouse did more for race relations in the city of Chicago than either Martin Luther King, Jesse Jackson or any politician of any color or any extraction that you can name. And the reason why is very simply because, when I think about Ernie Banks playing for the Cubs back in the mid-1950s at a time where we're still looking at *Brown vs. Board of Education*, we had yet to get to Meredith in Mississippi, we had yet to have Wallace standing with defiance outside of the University of Alabama, when Gene Baker was playing for the Cubs and to flip a coin when Chico Carrasquel and Luis Aparicio were playing for the White Sox, Jack Brickhouse made it known in very vivid and very colorful terms over black and white television mind you, on WGN, that blacks were to be accepted, that Latinos were to be accepted in our living rooms in Chicago with the same sense of grace and the same sense of warmth that we would offer our next door neighbors, as Caucasian as they may be. So, this sounds crazy, but for a young Chet Coppock, the Chicago Cubs became a life- growing situation for me in that my first sports hero was Harlon Hill, who played wide receiver for the Chicago Bears and is arguably one of those so-called "greatest football players never to have earned a ticket to Canton and the Pro Football Hall of Fame."

I just fell in love, like any other kid did, with Ernie Banks, and it became almost a religion. I went to Sunset Ridge Grammar School out in Northfield, Illinois, which is just west of Winnetka, which, of course, is the Big Wind from Winnetka. This ultra rich, very tony suburb is the home of New Trier High School, which I attended. I would run home every day, and I ran home really with two express purposes. One was because you were dying to see Ernie Banks swing the bat hoping that he was going to hit a walk-off home run. And, number two, to hear the incredible passion and the remarkably friendly, strikingly Midwestern delivery of Jack Brickhouse. And I don't think there is a broadcaster in Chicago, who is over the age of 40, for example, maybe even over the age of 35, who wouldn't tell you very honestly and openly that, at least, part of his or her style is the direct influence of Jack Brickhouse. And over the years, my gosh, from the time I was born in '48, this ball club's in a window where it doesn't even get a look at the first division until 1968, but there was always an attachment about the Cubs that was, at least for me, stronger than the White Sox.

Because there was Ernie Banks and then, around '60 or '61, the arrival of this pugnacious bulldog of a third basemen named Ron Santo, who at once was like Jake LaMotta in baseball spikes, tough and tenacious. I remember him running out of the dugout at Cubs Park to get into a fight with Gene Mauch. Not too many people know about this, but there was a terrible feud between Durocher and Jack Brickhouse. Durocher could not stand the popularity of either Banks or Brickhouse, Leo being a very markedly selfish individual. And to the everlasting credit of both "Brick" and Ernie, they really took the high road with Leo Durocher at a time when Leo was making their lives absolutely "H-e-l-l, with a capital H."

In 1969, opening day, cold as hell, I'm in Cubs Park, I'm a young punk, I'm only 20 years old, I'm working for WFLD as a sports writer and sports reporter. I'm in the house when Willie Smith hits this dramatic, Sistine Chapel, Caesars Palace, Rembrandt of a home run to beat Philadelphia, and this cascade, this wave of jubilation, began in the City of Chicago, and, of course, it wound up being, in typical Cub fashion, massive, massive disappointment. But it's really ironic to me because I've never seen this with any other club in my life. Thirty-four years after the fact, here is a ball club that finished second, won 92 games and finished eight games back, behind Seaver, Koosman, Gentry, and **Gil Hodges**, who is a brilliant manager, terribly underrated for the New York Mets. Thirty-four years after the fact, this town still has a love affair that is as rich, as textured with that ball club as it was in 1969.

I mean, that was the ball club that never had to say, "We're sorry." A couple of years later, "Love Story" was released with Ali MacGraw and Ryan O'Neal, and the classic line was, Ali saying to Ryan, as she

> The title character in the current sports comic strip *Gil Thorp* (no "e") is named for Gil Hodges and Jim Thorpe.

was dying of cancer, "Being in love means never having to say you're sorry." And the same thing can be applied to the Cubs in '69, the Cubs in '84 with San Diego, or the Cubs in '03, being ahead and then losing to the eventual World Series champion Marlins in the NLCS. Basically, the application is being in love, as this city is with this ball club, means never having to say you're sorry. Now I'm telling you if the Cubs are taking it on the chin in New York the way they got bopped, the way they just caved in, in '69 or the way they caved in against San Diego in '84 when Durham had the wickets and let that ground ball slip through his legs, or here in 2003 where Baker clearly made blatant managerial errors in Game 6 and Game 7 with his bullpen and with Kerry Wood, if he's in New York with the tabloids, if he's on his own in Philadelphia, good God, they're going to drop kick him in—choose one—the Hudson River or the Atlantic Ocean. Or worse than that, leave him in some strip joint in Atlantic City. But, here in Chicago, it's like, well, "They sure gave us a great run."

One thing that I found to be strikingly atypical of Cub fans was, and I really blame this on my people in the media and Steve Stone, the Cub color announcer, who is one of the big perpetrators of this, the Bartman kid who reached out for that foul ball. It was the most harmless, most innocent act in the world. You are at a ballpark, you buy a ticket, it's a playoff environment, he's not conscious of what he's doing for God's sakes. He's no more conscious of Moises Alou than a guy running the Boston marathon is of the people who are lining the hill when you get to the twenty-three mile mark. All he knows is that this is his chance at a foul ball. And again, there was this collision of human flesh trying to get the sucker. You can't blame him because Alex Gonzalez blows the lock on a double play ball a couple of moments later, but Stoney goes on the air and, in this very whiney voice, says, "I just can't believe any Cub fan who would want us to win would do something like this." I heard it by replay and I wanted to say, "Stoney, for gosh sakes, will you wake up and realize not everybody played the game. The problem with you is that you're so high and mighty, having been a Cy Young winner and then occupying this seat in the broadcast booth, you can't see reality. He did what any fan would do for gosh sakes."

But here again, it's so far in the deep dark past because eternally, eternally with every Cub fan it's interesting. In my office at Sporting News Radio, as I began to piece together my show, guys were not talking about, "Gosh, we could have gone to the World Series, son of a gun, the New York Yankees and Joe Torre could have been here— Jeter and Giambi and Posada and Mariano—the Cubs could have been in the World Series for the first time in 58 years." Instead, all the people are talking to me about what the Cubs should do in 2004.

And that's the very essence of why next year, they'll draw 2.9 million and, even though they have the worst parking facilities in North America, they will always draw; and, why despite the irrevocable charm of the outdoorsy, almost-Disneyland atmosphere that exists at Wrigley Field, it's also a place of just terrible facilities, the longest concession lines in North America. It's hard to explain, but ultimately, ultimately with the Cubs again, being in love means never having to say you're sorry.

To carry it one step further, being in love means, not only is next year this year, the next one hundred years are going to be this year. Brickhouse had a great line with it. I was with him in '81 when he did his last home game for WGN television. He was kind enough to invite me up to the booth with my TV crew for Channel 5 and it was a stirringly emotional moment. The Cubs were playing a meaningless doubleheader against Philadelphia. After the ball game, Jack and I were walking down and, I remember Lou Boudreau and Vince Lloyd hopped up before we did, they gave Jack his space because they sensed that there would be some type of response for "Brick." When they got down to what was known as the "catwalk" right by the Pink Poodle, which used be the old press room in Cubs Park, all of a sudden, there must have been about 2000 fans that began chanting, "Jack, Jack, Jack," and it went on for about fifteen minutes. Two ironies emerged within me. One was the incredible display of passion for this man, who probably broadcasted more losing ball games than any man in baseball history. Number two was, being as close to Jack as I was—Jack was the godfather of my daughter, Lyndsey—I was crying harder than Jack was.

To me it captured the kind of, gosh, how would you define it really? It's like a core that exists between the Cubs and their fan base. And, no matter how bad things are, I mean Baker should be getting torched in this town right now. If this was San Francisco for heaven's sakes, if this was Los Angeles, I'm convinced that Dusty right now would be absolutely woodshed bound, he'd be tied at the wrist and people would be clobbering him. But, even our media in town, when it comes to the Cubs, is remarkably passive because we all fall into this, this little niche of realizing that the Cubs are Maui in their own way. The Cubs are the south of France. The Cubs are the eloquence and the old-fashioned European feeling of being Montreal. But yet, the Cubs are also Des Moines, Iowa. And they're Rockford. And they're a hick town down in central Indiana and they're these nomads who come in every year from Fort Wayne or come in from **Benton Harbor, Michigan,** who are lured to the ballpark.

So, ultimately to be a Cub fan, to me, is the most enjoyable experience in the world because there's no pressure. It's not like being a Yankee fan. I mean, heaven forbid, now that the Yankees lost to Florida in Game 6 in the World Series, all of Staten Island will triple their dosage of Prozac. But in Chicago with the Cubs, we still have the coolest marquee in the world on the corner of Clark and Addison. We still have the Cubbie Bear, we still have Sluggers and Hi-Tops, we still have the Harry Caray monument, we still have "Hey, Hey" flags on the foul poles, we still have Ron Santo's uniform and Billy's and Ernie's retired, we still have this charcoal-broiled oven with twenty-four ounce strip steaks just simmering to the point where you can just smell how good they really are. We have that flavor. It's a flavor that does not exist at Fenway Park, no matter what they say, doesn't exist with college football at Legion Field in **Birmingham** or down at Tiger Stadium in Baton Rouge or beneath the Golden Dome at South Bend. It only exists in Cubs' Park. And forevermore it means being in love means never having to say you're sorry.

> The state of Michigan has more golf courses than any other state in the Union.

> The New England Patriots once played a regular-season home game in Birmingham, Alabama, in September, 1968.

HELLO AGAIN, EVERYBODY

Bea Higgins

It was a wild ride for Bea Higgins during the 26 years she served as Harry Caray's personal secretary...initially at an ad agency, later full-time in St. Louis.

When we got the Griesedieck account, the boss I worked for, Oscar Zahner, believed that beer and baseball went together. And he was instrumental in getting Harry here. He came in 1944, doing hockey and a few things. Then the baseball broadcasts started in 1945. He had been working in Kalamazoo, Michigan. Paul Harvey, who would later become famous, was the news director there and had hired Harry to do sports.

When Harry started, Gabby Street was with him and none of the articles I've read mention Gabby Street. He really was a father image to Harry, a wonderful man. Gabby was in his eighties when he was broadcasting with him. They just enjoyed each other's company so much. Gabby died in 1951. Then Gus Mancuso came on. He used to be a catcher with the Cardinals. Then, later, Stretch Miller was on. And then Jack Buck. Oooh, Jack was so wonderful, too!

When Harry first started, he talked a little fast. And I remember the people at the brewery calling my boss and saying, "I don't think he's going to work. He talks a little bit fast." My boss said, "No. He's good. He's got something. Just hang in there." And, of course, my boss turned out to be right.

Harry also broadcast Cardinals and St. Louis Browns road games via Western Union ticker. That was set up in the Paul Brown Building. I'd go over with the engineer and get everything set up, watch him broadcast. The ticker tape is just saying, "ball one, ball two," and he's leaning back, saying, "It might be. It could be. It is." You know, practically falling on the floor.

One interesting thing: after he broadcast the games for a while, he had never had these kinds of paychecks before. He said there were two things he always wanted to get if he ever had any money: One was a new suit at this exclusive men's shop in St. Louis, the other was a convertible. And he got both of them.

I can't remember what the suit looked like, but I remember he called and I met him downstairs on Eighth and Olive, where our building was, and rode around the block with him in the convertible. He was so thrilled with these two things that he always wanted and now he was able to buy.

After I got married and started raising my children, I quit the advertising agency. I kept handling all of Harry's mail out of my home until he left St. Louis. He was a fan's person. I know with the mail, he read every letter and signed every letter. And he'd get upset if a fan didn't like him, because he wanted to be liked.

To me, the mail went either way. They loved him or they hated him. There wasn't any in-between. They loved him, adored him. Or, they didn't like him at all. When I was answering his mail or doing something for him out of my home, I would always have the broadcast on. But I wasn't really listening to who got a strike or a ball. I was listening to what he was saying. And, by the end of the evening, I'd say, "Uh-oh, I'd better write that down. I'm going to get a letter. Or he's going to get a call from the brewery. Or from a player."

Somebody would make him mad and he'd want to answer them. And I'd say, "You can't say that." He'd say, "Well, what do you mean?" I'd say, "Because you just don't say those things." And he'd say, "Well, that's what I want to say." I remember one day, I said, "I'm not going to answer that. Answer it yourself." And the next day he called and said, "Are you off your muscle?" And then he'd say, "Well, answer the damn letter the way you think we should answer it."

One other thing I want to mention about his mail. We got letters—obviously, people wrote for them—from blind people very often saying, "We can almost see what you are saying." And, you know, that's quite a feat. His mail was absolutely amazing. I know when he had his accident in 1968, I went to the hospital and I'd say there were fifty big brown bags full of mail—easy. I've got a picture of me standing there with all this mail in the room. I never thought he'd walk again—or at least for years. And he said, "I'm going to walk before spring training." And he did. It was sheer determination. But he had that determination.

After Harry's departure from St. Louis in 1969, I didn't talk to him all that often.

The last time I saw him, I had been in communication. He wrote me a nice letter when my husband died, and he sent his book when that came out. We really hadn't kept in touch like I wanted to. It just gets away from you. But I did see him in 1993 while I was working at another job in Clayton (Missouri) and he was staying at the Ritz, which was only two blocks away.

We were talking on the phone, and he said, "I'm going to walk up and see you." He came up, and we had a nice visit for a couple of hours and that's the first time I'd seen him since he left St. Louis twenty-four years before. He seemed to be very, very happy when I saw him the last time and I was so happy about that.

They loved him here in St. Louis. People came in droves whether the Cardinals were winning or losing. That's the kind of pull that he had. The main comment about his broadcasting was, "He makes you feel like you are sitting right in the ballpark."

HEAR ME NOW, LISTEN TO ME LATER

I knew Harry because he lived just a couple of blocks from where our restaurant is. I started working here in '68 and, of course, he was coming in here then. When the Cardinals were in town, he'd come in sometimes twice a day. He'd come in before the game and have lunch and whatever. And then end up here at some point at night after the game, if not immediately after. He used to make the rounds pretty good.

I happened to be at work the day Harry was fired by the Cardinals in 1969. Harry walked in and nobody at that point had heard he got fired. He asked if he could use our private dining room to have a press conference, and I said sure.

There wasn't a large entourage at that point. He said, "Have somebody get me a Schlitz." And I said, "Harry, you know we don't have any Schlitz." At that point, all we carried was Anheuser-Busch products. He goes, "Well, I want a Schlitz. Send somebody over to the store to get me a Schlitz." And I said, "Harry, you don't want to do that." He said, "No, damn it, send somebody to get me a Schlitz." Again, I repeated, "Harry, you don't want to do that." He said, "Damn it, Carl." And I said, "Okay, you got it. Who am I to argue?" So I sent a guy across the street and he came back with a Schlitz, and Harry, during his interview, made sure it was visible.

Harry regretted that move all the rest of his days, because he was an Anheuser-Busch guy and truly loved Gussie."

—————CARL COWLES, Owner, Busch's Grove Restaurant, St. Louis

I knew Harry Caray when he was in high school. He went to Webster Groves High School here in St. Louis. I had a cousin who went to Webster Groves. Harry and my cousin were a couple of years older than I was and, through my cousin, I met him. As a matter of fact, at one time he was a wannabe basketball player. This was before the days of the **NBA**. It was AAU ball, good basketball. He was on a club

> In March 1954, the Lakers and the Hawks played a regulation, regular season NBA game using baskets that were 12' high rather than the usual 10'...the next night they played each other in a doubleheader. True facts, believe it or not!

with my cousin and several other athletes from Webster Groves High School. Through my cousin, I ended up on the team, too. Harry and I sat on the bench together.

——**BING DEVINE**, Former Cardinal General Manager

My dad bought me an old Volkswagen Bug. I drove up and down the hills of Black Earth trying to get a station from Peoria, Illinois to hear the last game on Sunday of the '64 season. You couldn't get KMOX during the day.

On an old reel-to-reel tape from 1969, I have this tape of what was rumored to maybe be Harry Caray's last game, the game against the Mets when he, at the end, was somber about everything. He said he didn't know what his future would hold, and if he'd be back with the Cardinals or not, but he thanked all the Cardinals fans and management for all the years in St. Louis. Then **Charlie Finley** hired him in Oakland. A year later, he went to the White Sox, and the rest is history.

——**STEVE SCHMITT**, 56, Black Earth, Wisconsin

When Harry Caray first started announcing the Cardinal games on the radio in 1945, he'd describe every fly ball to right as "all the way out to the Griesedieck beer sign on the right field wall." Once TV came in, everybody could see how far out the fly balls really went. Then we knew that Harry sometimes exaggerated just for the sake of getting the sponsor's name on the air.

——**NATE WILLIAMS**, Middleton, Wisconsin

When I was sixteen, seventeen years old I went to a lot of games. After the games, I would get autographs. I'm in the Marriott one day and I see Harry Caray and a couple of other people coming down the hallway laughing and talking. People are asking him for autographs. I used to carry this book around and anytime I'd go to a game, I'd have players autograph this book for me. It had a lot of different pictures in it, and I'd get the autographs on the pictures or on the inside cover. I opened the book to one of the inside pages and said, "Mr. Caray, I'd like to shake your hand and say hello. My grandpa used to

> The Oakland A's colors are green and gold because their late owner, Charles O. Finley, grew up in LaPorte, IN and loved Notre Dame...when he bought the Kansas City A's, he changed their uniforms to those colors.

bring notes to you at the stadium." As a youngster I was very aware of the scent of Budweiser. It was almost like Harry had cologne on and it was Budweiser, kind of overwhelming. So I shake his hand, and he takes my book, and he says, "What's your name?" I say, "My name's Craig." He signed my book and hands it back to me, and he says, "Nice talking to you," and he pats me on the back, and they walk on and go out the door and head over toward the stadium. I grab my book and just waited for it to dry. I'm looking at it and it said, "Harry Cow, Holy Craig," right there in the center of my book.

———CRAIG BALL, 34, Harry Caray Fan

Harry Caray was a pretty good gin rummy player. One of the things he always said after a few hours' playing was, "The Big Possum walks late." I hated when he said that, but he ended up using that on his broadcasts quite a lot. He'd also say, "What are martinis mixed with?" He'd lay his cards out on the table and say, "Gin."

———JEROME HOLTZMAN, Retired Sportswriter

Harry Caray was my guy. I used to listen to Harry every night from 1960 until I got interested in girls in high school. Harry made things exciting. You wished you were there. He had that distinct voice and he made you want to be at the ball game. I remember in 1978, I'm in West Lafayette, Indiana at a Howard Johnson's on a recruiting trip and I flipped on the TV. I hadn't heard Harry's voice since 1969—we didn't pick up any Oakland games when he was announcing there and we didn't pick up any White Sox games on this side of the river. I'm in the bathroom, and I'm hearing Harry's voice. It was a White Sox game. He had the effect on me of thinking I was twelve years old again, listening to him. When Harry died, my cousin and I drove to Wrigley Field. The shrine they had outside of Wrigley Field was basically Budweiser bottles. We went down and contributed to the shrine.

———NORM RICHARDS, St. Charles, MO, Former Houston Astros Scout

What impressed me most about Harry Caray—above and beyond the fact that he was Peter Pan, above and beyond the fact he was in many respects a guy who because of his orphan upbringing in St. Louis always thought the other shoe was going to fall and thus he figured "I better cram twenty-eight hours into every day" was the fact that when you had the opportunity to visit with him in a casual but private

Sports Illustrated

, 1969   50 CENTS

HE RAUCOUS NEW CUBS

on Santo leads off first

THE FRANTIC NATIONAL LEAGUE

Sports Illustrated

SEPTEMBER 8, 1969 .50 CENTS

CINCINNATI'S PETE ROSE   **CHICAGO'S ERNIE BANKS**

Sports Illustrated

AUGUST 30, 1971   60 CENTS

HERE COME THE CUBS

Ferguson Jenkins wins his 20th

Sports Illustrated

SEPTEMBER 24 1984

WHO DO YOU LIKE?

Cy Young Award Candidates Rick Sutcliffe And Dwight Gooden

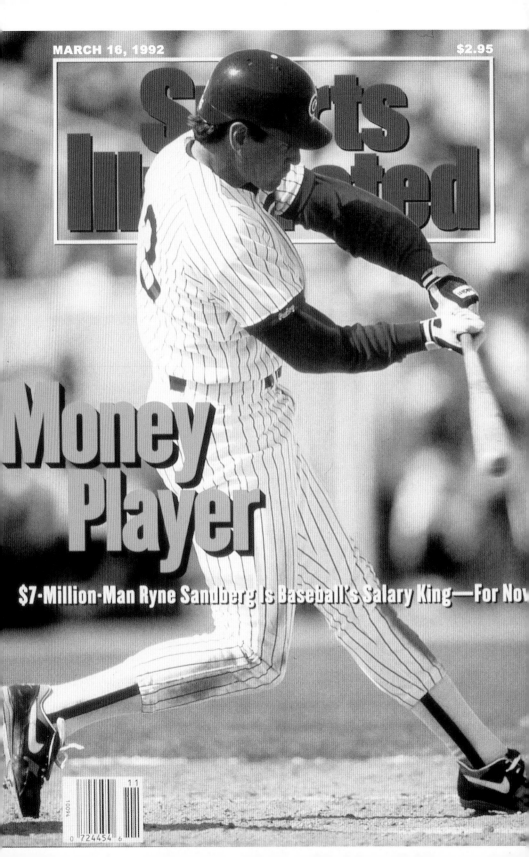

$2.95

Sports Illustrated

Money Player

$7-Million-Man Ryne Sandberg Is Baseball's Salary King—For Now

Sports Illustrated

PRESENTS

The GREAT HOME RUN RACE

MARK McGWIRE AND SAMMY SOSA

Sports Illustrated

BASEBALL PLAYOFFS

Do You Believe?

Kerry Wood Leads the Cubs Into Magical Territory

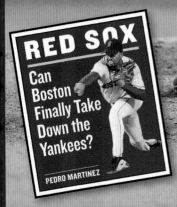

RED SOX

Can Boston Finally Take Down the Yankees?

PEDRO MARTINEZ

OCTOBER 13, 2003 www.si.c
AOL Keyword: Sports Illustr

Isle

209

🚭

**NO
SMOKING
IN
SEATING
AREA**

WE'RE ON A
MISSION
FROM GOD

Jack Buck wearing two caps
Wrigley Field, June, 2001

FOX SPORTS NET™

Cubs fans' view of a Sammy Sosa home run ball

Cardinals fans' view of a Sammy Sosa home run ball

A Great Lake
A Great Park
A Great Day

**The first of many curves
in the bleacher area**

This is not a Norman Rockwell painting. It's 30 minutes before batting practice prior to a Cubs-Cardinals game.

Happy Holidays!

atmosphere, you found another man. His voice would change. His octave level would change. He was always remarkably honest.

That was the essence of Harry. Harry loved tweaking us. Harry loved being a "Peck's Bad Boy," and this goes back to an element of his St. Louis childhood, which wasn't very comfortable. I've read innumerable stories about Harry crying during the holidays over very acute feelings of loneliness.

Harry had one quality very few of us ever achieve. Harry developed the ability to tell management and the people he worked for to go straight to hell and get away with it, because he was so damned talented. And sponsors were so in love with this guy. His relationship with Budweiser. He literally kept Falstaff Beer on the map with the White Sox back in the early 1970s. True Value was in love with him.

I remember one time being in spring training down in Florida decades ago. The late Jack Drees, who himself was a legendary broadcaster, and I were having dinner. Then we began going down Highway 41, stopping at a couple of joints. Finally, it's about one-thirty or two in the morning, and Jack said, "Do you want to have one more belt?" I said, "Sure."

We stopped off at this little honky-tonk, walk in and there are about ten hard-bodies dancing on the dance floor. I look over and there's Harry standing in the middle of this pack of girls, dancing. He yells out, "Come on in, kid. There's plenty for everybody."

———CHET COPPOCK, *The Sporting News* Radio Network

For a while I really had Harry Caray down pretty good, imitation-wise. I did him every day. We got a kick out of it. I did it in front of Harry. I did it on the Cardinal team bus. When people imitate you, you've got to be somebody. They don't imitate people who aren't anybody."

He loved baseball to the point where he thought fans sometimes might be cheated by lackadaisical play. He was not ashamed to talk about it. I remember things he said about Kenny Boyer. He loved Kenny Boyer. Harry never said anything because he disliked somebody. He said it because he thought they could do a better job. It wasn't malicious.

If he ever said anything about you, and he heard you were looking for him, he was right there for you. He'd come walking into the clubhouse. He'd stick his face right in your face. He was not embarrassed to put his face in your face and say, "You got a problem with something I said?" He did that with Tracy Stallard in 1965. It was Stallard's first season with the Cardinals. Tracy was supposed to do Harry's pre-game show. He didn't show up. Harry marched right in the clubhouse. I was there. I saw it. Harry walked up to Stallard and got right in his face. He said, "If you ever do that to me again, I'll bury you. If you don't want to be on my show, tell me. But don't ever try that again."

I don't think I saw him in anything that matched. That's why I enjoyed him so much, to see him in a pair of shorts out there. I always looked forward to seeing him in the spring. I called him "Coach." I called him that for a long, long time. Harry made a lot of people better people, by either coming out to the ballpark or listening to a broadcast. I was glad to be a friend of his. I learned a lot from him. He'll be remembered for a long, long time. Baseball has lost a lot of great people, front-office people, broadcasters. It will go on forever. But baseball will always have a place for people like Harry Caray.

———BOB UECKER, Ticket Master

The rock group, ZZ Top, was visiting Wrigley Field one day to sing the National Anthem. They were sitting on the bench. Harry came by to do his pre-game show with the manager at that time, Jim Lefebvre. Here's two guys with Blues Brothers hats, blue jeans and long beards and mustaches and sunglasses. Harry sees them and says, "Hey, who are you guys? I'm Harry Caray. Are you guys rabbis?" They said, "No. We're ZZ Top." Harry asks, "What kind of a religion is that?"

———BRUCE LEVINE, Chicago Sports Personality

We're on Rush Street. It's late, really late. I said, "Name me eleven guys who hit fifty or more home runs in a season." There were about fifteen guys in there drinking. So Harry started. He named them and named them and named them. All of a sudden, he got up to ten and couldn't remember the eleventh guy.

I knew who it was, and Harry said, "All right, damn it, I can't think of it." So I said, "Oh, I don't know. I knew there were eleven." Everybody stood around and said, "I don't know, uh…."

So Harry finally said, "That's it. This is bulls—. I've got a book back in my room." He left the bar at around four in the morning. He got in a cab and went back to the Ambassador East. He rummaged through the room, woke up Dutchie and then came back to the bar about a half-hour later. But in the meantime, I had told everybody in the bar, "Ralph Kiner."

When Harry walked back into the bar and had the book up over his head, we all shouted at the same time, "Ralph Kiner."

Well, he walked over to me and said, "Dreesen, I can forgive you for a lot of things, but I will never forgive you for cheating me out of half an hour of quality drinking time."

Years later, I saw Harry down on the field before a game. I said, "Harry, how are you doing?" He said, "Tom, I haven't had a drink in two years." I said, "Really!" He said, "Yeah." He said, "You know all that stuff how people tell you that you can have just as much fun not drinking as you can drinking?" I said, "Yeah." He said, "They're full of s—. I've never been so bored in my entire life."

——**TOM DREESEN**, Comedian, Los Angeles

When I was with Montreal, we were playing at Wrigley one day. After I finished throwing, I was in the training room getting a rub down, watching the game on TV. Harry Caray was in center field announcing the game. Tim Wallach was the hitter. Harry said, "Line drive caught by Ron Cey at third! What a catch!" Actually, Wallach had struck out and the Cubs were throwing the ball around the horn. I don't remember what announcer Harry was working with, but the other announcer said, "Harry, they struck out Wallach, and the Cubs were just throwing the ball around the horn." In typical Harry fashion, he replied, "Whoa! That would've been a great catch!"

—**BILL GULLICKSON**, 44, Chicago-area native/former major-league pitcher

How could I ever forget Jack Quinlan! He would always start the game off the same way, "The Chicago Cubs are on the air. How you doing baseball fans? This is Jack Quinlan along with Lou Boudreau." As a matter of fact, my son Jack…one of the people he is named after is Jack Quinlan. I like to thank Jack London, Jack Kerouac, Jack Quinlan and I don't want to slight Jack Brickhouse. But Quinlan I always thought was the best. And as a matter of fact, I wrote a column about him one time, about how I thought he was the best. Kids today don't have the same connections with the radio guys as we did. Like my little internal voice may go around talking to myself, and I'm often talking to Lou in Quinlan's voice. That's how deep that connection is. If somebody could hear me they would probably ask,

"What's this, your invisible friend?" and I would have to say, "No, this is Lou Boudreau," because I talk like Jack Quinlan.

I was talking to Jack Buck, who was a wonderful guy, about it. Actually, Buck and I were having lunch, and I don't mean to drop names; we weren't actually friends, but I admired him a great deal. So I mentioned something about Quinlan, and Buck said to me, "You know, I think he was the best." And of course that is the kind of guy Buck was. And I'm not so sure that Jack Buck wasn't better than Quinlan. But, since it was Quinlan I grew up with, I thought Quinlan was the best, although Buck would be a very close second. He was always so excited when he'd say, "The Chicago Cubs are on the air! How you doing baseball fans? This is Jack Quinlan and Lou Boudreau coming to you from Wrigley Field where the Cubs have been red hot and have won two out of ten..." or whatever, and he didn't mock them. I'm mocking them when I say that.

Quinlan was always so excited, and Boudreau was a perfect foil if you remember. Boudreau would always drive me nuts when he'd go, "It's going, going, caught at the wall." And my heart would be soaring one minute and then...but Quinlan was the real hero; when I loved the Cubs with a deeper passion than I have now. Do you know what I mean? I'm a big Cub fan, but there was a time when I truly loved them, and it was in those years and it was Jack Quinlan. I can remember writing poems, "The Year of the Baby Bear." I was a child who was really hooked. One hundred pounds of drugs and class action lawsuits for people like me for the time we wasted on the Cubs. And that bear logo, like the camel logo, Joe Camel, it was meant to hook youngsters, and there I was, hooked completely and totally.

———BILL McCLELLAN, 56, Chicago Native, *St. Louis Post-Dispatch*

As a young child in the early fifties listening to the games on the radio, the first announcer I remember was Bert Wilson. He was the consummate Cubs fan. One of his comments was always, even during the course of a game, "I don't care who wins, just as long as it's the Cubs." Jack Brickhouse's voice was just synonymous with my house. We always had the Cub game on, ever since I was a little kid, and he was like a friend. Harry Caray was a great personality, and he did a lot for the Cubs, but I never liked Harry Caray—because he broadcasted for ten years for the Chicago White Sox. When he was broadcasting the White Sox games, he used to talk about the North

Side fans and all the Yuppies on the North Side and said some pretty negative things about Cub fans when he was the Sox announcer. So when he came over to the Cubs, I could never forget that. Most of the Cub fans really embraced him because obviously he was a sensational personality. I guess most Cub fans have a short memory, but I don't.

——**BOB OLSON**, Barrington, Illinois

We only had one radio, and it was in the dining room where I would listen to the games. A lot of times the announcers had to be very good because they weren't at the ball games. They would get these reports on ticker tape and they would have to use their own enthusiasm. They had a little noise deal in the back of them to give crowd noise and clapping and all that stuff. It was much more difficult to announce then. Pat Flanagan was the Cub announcer and Bob Elson was the White Sox announcer. This would have been in the thirties.

——**BOB BECK**, bookstore owner

I lived on a farm near Clinton, Illinois, and we had the radio for games. I still go to bed with WGN and wake up with WGN. I've listened to Brickhouse. I've listened to them all. I remember we would take a transistor radio to school to listen to the games, and it was all right because the teacher was a fan, too.

Living out on the farm, we could only get **WGN and WLS**. If there wasn't a game on WGN, we would tune in WLS and hear John "Records" Landecker. Brickhouse was boring to listen to. I was just a kid and would be driving a tractor through the field and listening to the Cubs—they just always got beat. You just expected them to lose. It was like the crops we were growing. It's going to come up, and we're going to harvest it, and the Cubs are going to lose. That's it. My grandma, who is 86, sits down in DeWitt, Illinois with one of those huge, old satellite dishes and watches every Cubs game. She also listens to them on the radio.

——**MATT FINK**, Chicago commodities trader

WGN and the Cubs are owned by the (Chicago) Tribune Company. WGN is an acronym for "World's Greatest Newspaper"…WLS—Chicago is an acronym for "World's Largest Store"—it was started by Marshall Field.

My grandfather owned a refrigeration and air conditioning whole-sale company, but at earlier times, he was in the radio business. He was the first big radio distributor in Chicago in the '20s. The Cubs used to advertise a lot on the radio, and my grandfather would adver-tise the Majestic Radio, the brand they distributed, so he was involved with ballplayers a lot...

The Emil Verban Society was created in Washington. When I lived down there, I was a member—kind of ex-pat Cubs fans. George Will was involved in it. It's a way for the Cubs fans to stay together in Washington. It's got a fair number of prominent people in it, like David Broder. Ronald Reagan had been an announcer for the Cubs in the thirties so some people who wanted to get in good with him joined just for that reason instead of being real Cub fans. When Reagan was doing the announcing, they didn't have a signal that would reach from Chicago to Des Moines so he would see what came over the telegraph—"Hack Wilson grounds out on two-two pitch." He would then have to recreate, such as, "Fouls one off for strike one. Caught the outside corner for strike two." He'd have to make the whole thing up. That's all part of the Reagan lore and helped make him the Great Communicator.

——JONATHAN ALTER, 46, *Newsweek*

Harry Caray would be aware of my birthdays. Up in the booth, they get a list of events from the media relations people, and they read off of that. He was reading that it said, "Happy 39th" in italics, 'cause every year, he would wish me a happy 39th birthday. One year, he said, "Thirty-nine? Who's she kidding? I've known her for 39 years at these ball games." On another occasion, he said, "Thirty-nine? What does she think she's Jack Benny or something?" And he called me Mrs. Jack Benny.

——CAROL HADDON, 56, Glencoe, Illinois

In 1983, I got to spend the day in the booth with Harry Caray. It was called, "Spend a Day in the Booth with Harry," and my parents either won it or bought it at a charity auction and they gave it to me as a birthday present. Before the game, I got to go down to the production truck where Arne Harris was. He was director and producer for WGN for all the Cubs games. Arne gave me a tour about how every-thing worked down there. I was still in school at the time and was interested in broadcasting so that worked out very well. That was a really cool operation. It was also where I happened to lock my bike up for three years prior—on their steps—when I attended a game. I asked them if they ever wondered whose bike that was. They said, "You mean the Univega?" I said, "Yeah, that's mine." They said, "So you're the one who locked it up there for three years." Then they took me up into the booth right around game time. I got to meet Harry Caray and Steve Stone. I was shellshocked the first inning or two, just sitting back and listening and taking the game in—they've got quite a view from up there. I was stunned that I was up there with Harry Caray. Between innings, I would ask them questions about baseball and about broadcasting games. I figured if I directed my questions to Steve Stone, Harry would pipe in. It worked that way a lot. Sometimes, I would just ask Harry a question. I asked Harry about broadcasting for the Cardinals and then for the Cubs. At first he gave me a dirty look and was pretty defensive, "I'm a Cubs fan 'cause they're the best team, and they've got the best fans." When I phrased my question a little better, he softened up and said, "No, honestly, I am a die-hard Cubs fan now, and it has a lot to do with the fact I broadcast them currently. But, out of all my years and all my experiences with baseball, my years at Wrigley Field, which is the best ballpark on the planet, and after all the time I spent here, I've really grown to love the Cubs, and they're my team." I tried to stay out of their way 'cause I knew they had a job to do. They mentioned my name on the air, and I said one thing, but I don't recall what it was. I'm sure if it was anything good, I would have remembered it, so…. My friends had told me I had to scream something while they were on the air so they could know I was there. They said, "You've got to yell s— or something." I said, "I'm not going to swear."

——JIM DEMARET, 37, trader, Chicago Stock Exchange

I did not like Harry Caray. I thought he was a big, oogy, big mouth who wasn't always watching the same game that everybody else was. I didn't like him. I loved Jack Brickhouse—loved his enthusiasm and thought he was a better announcer than Harry Caray—I may be in the minority on that. I thought he was great. I love Steve Stone, although he doesn't have the big personality those two had. He knows more baseball than both of them put together.

——CISSY GREENSPAN, Glencoe, Illinois

We were at Wrigley for the baseball. I was a serious baseball fan. We were there with scorecards talking strategy with the people behind us. We became fans by listening to Jack Brickhouse broadcast the games. We would imitate him. I had a penchant and a talent for doing commentary and play-by-play and would entertain the other kids in the neighborhood. I watched and I said, "I can do that." By high school, another buddy of mine felt the same way, and we started taking reel-to-reel to our high school to do play-by-play. His name was Frank Mazzocco. Then we used to go downstairs in his basement and set up the reel-to-reel and then do an entire Cubs broadcast. We would turn down the sound on the television. We even had our own commercials. My friend went on to become the play-by-play broadcaster for the Minnesota NorthStars, and now the University of Minnesota Golden Gophers. Remember in the movie, "Fargo" when the father-in-law is sitting in front of the TV, and William H. Macy says, "Whatcha watchin' there, dad?" And he says, "Gophers." That's Frank announcing in the background.

I gave up my broadcasting ambitions because it seemed too far-fetched to imagine. We grew up in a blue collar neighborhood where aspirations were modest. Your world was people who worked in a steel mill, people who were truck drivers, people who were milk men, people who were policemen, or people who were teachers. It was hard for us to project because we never had access to those types of people. They were mythological. They were bigger than life. These Cubs stars were bigger than life.

When Harry Caray first decided to broadcast from the center field bleachers in Comiskey Park, I heard about it. Frank and I looked at each other and were both like, "We're there. We are *so* there." That's when I met Harry Caray. We were parked right next to Harry and Jimmy, and we had our shirts off, and we were drinking beer. They just brought out their table and set it up in the middle of the game. I remember we had a big cooler full of beer and by the fifth inning, that beer was *gone*—and Harry got them to bring us another cooler full of beer! It was a Wednesday afternoon at Comiskey Park. The world stood still—well actually, it spun faster.

——JACK WIERS, Long-Suffering Cub Fan

Chapter 5

Bleacher Creatures

Where Did The Fans in Section 151 Go? Try Section 8!

YA CAN'T GET INTO HEAVEN UNLESS YOU'RE A CUB FAN

Jerry Pritikin

Call him "Bleacher Creature" or "Bleacher Preacher," but Jerry Pritikin, 66, is a one-of-a-kind Cubs fan.

After the 2003 NLCS, I would have been heartbroken, but there was no heart left. It was my father's fault. Back in 1945 when the war had just ended, my father treated me to a two-wheeled Schwinn bike and a J.C. Higgins mitt. He gave me a crash course in Baseball 101 and Cubs history and took me to my first game. The beauty of Wrigley Field is still etched in my mind. He taught me how to keep score, and about three weeks later, the Cubs clinched the pennant. I asked him to take me to a World Series and he said I was too young. He promised to take me the next time. I thought this promise would be fulfilled. I got on the bandwagon of the Cubs in '45 when they were winners, and I just assumed the bandwagon would stop at a pennant one day. The following year in '46, I used to clean up the ballpark at Wrigley after the game, and got a free pass to the next game. I saw about 20 or 30 games that year. The pennant was flying on the pole from the 1945 team, and I kept looking at it all summer-long. I remember someone telling me that summer, right before we went back to school, "Wait till next year." That was the first time I ever heard that phrase.

My father, ironically, used to clean up what they called the old West Side Ballpark; when he was eight or nine years old, he cleaned up the West Side Ballpark in 1906 when the Cubs won 116 games, when they had guys like Tinkers and Evers and Chance. So my father was my guru; he indoctrinated me, and it got in my system at an early age.

My first opener was in 1947, and my father got us box seat tickets, and we sat next to Bing Crosby and Gene Autry. They were playing the Pirates and Bing Crosby was part owner of the Pirates. I remember asking my father what a cowboy was doing there. Less than a month later, I was back at Wrigley Field. It was packed for the first game that Jackie Robinson was going to play. One thing that was unique was that half the people brought binoculars for a look at the future Hall of Famer. I have never experienced anything like that since.

I always equated my youth with Wrigley. The majority of the houses around Wrigley stayed the same all that time. There were some character changes outside the ballpark. There used to be coal silos out along the left field line that eventually were knocked down, but everything else remained the same, year after year after year. I always felt young at Wrigley Field until the Tribune Company bought the club, and then they started making changes. There were so *few* changes. The old batting cage used to be along the right field line; now it's filled with seats.

I remember my first time at Wrigley. The stadium was so majestic. We lived in Albany Park, which is about maybe five miles from the ballpark. We had to take three old-fashioned streetcars to get there. You'd come to the front of the park—now its red—when I was a kid it was green. By the concession stands, they had bigger-than-life paintings of old-time Cub ballplayers and a couple of the then-current ballplayers. As a kid, it was like looking at the Mona Lisa. At the Riverview Amusement Park we used to buy baseball cards for a penny, 5x7, sepia-colored with signatures in white ink: I remember thinking, "How do they do that with white ink?" So when I walked into the ballpark and saw those giant pictures, I remember thinking they were just like those baseball cards. As you walked into the ballpark, it was, well, not like walking into the Grand Canyon, but something like that—this ballpark, with its double-decker stands, and the scoreboard that seemed to be miles away. It left an impression. It happened to be a fantastic sunny day, so it made it even better. A ballpark should only be illuminated by sunlight. I'm not into night games. The way I put it is this: Most people will tell you Brock for Broglio was the worst trade in baseball; Uh-uh, it was was lights for an All-Star Game.

My brother was a Cardinals fan. One night I remember he wanted to listen to the Cardinals game and, of course, he was saying that Stan Musial was better than Phil Cavarretta. Subliminally, he may have been successful in making me a Cardinal fan, but they were like a second team of choice. In the '40s, the Cardinals were also a pennant winning team. It seemed like some of their ballplayers had more colorful names than the Cubs, but I remained loyal. When the Cubs and Cards played, I was rooting for the Cubs and he was rooting for the Cardinals.

When I was a kid, a lot of the players at the ballpark seemed to have a lot of gray hair. Of course, I was young, and my father didn't have a lot of gray hair. The ballplayers looked old. I didn't realize until later that I started going to the games during a war year, so a lot of those guys were old-timers.

I was a photographer in the '70s. In '84 I brought my camera to the ballpark every once in a while to take pictures. There was one situation where I wish I would have taken a picture but didn't. I had come out of the ballpark after the Cubs had won the second game in the playoffs, and the few Padres fans there were being taunted, of course, by the Cubs fans. There was one Padre fan who took off his Padres shirt and set it on fire. Of course, the Padres went to San Diego and won three times in a row. I wonder about that fan. I often think maybe he gave up a little too early.

Sometimes, I worry that if the Cubs ever got in a World Series, World War III would break out. Then I saw a play by W.P. Kinsella called *Last Pennant Before Armageddon*, and it was a similar idea. You almost expect something would have to happen to take the joy out of it. If the Cubs had won in 2003, I really believe there would have been the biggest celebration since the end of WWII, which was the last time the Cubs won the pennant.

Recently, I've been priced out of the ballpark. The so-called cheap seats in Chicago aren't cheap anymore. The 2003 bleacher tickets had prices from $24-30, depending on their so-called "important games." They sell the tickets in February, and if you don't buy a ticket in February, the chances of finding a ticket on the day of a game at the price printed on it is like finding weapons of mass destruction in Iraq. The majority of people sitting in the bleachers are not real fans anymore. I once came out with a tee shirt that said, "Real fans are an endangered species." The little guy doesn't have a chance. My father used to say, "Hey, let's get some of your friends, we'll go out to the ballpark today." And it didn't bankrupt him. Today, you couldn't take three or four kids out to the ballpark unless you're extremely rich, and I guarantee you'd have to stop at the ATM.

Maybe it's a surprise that I wasn't a big Mark Grace fan. Mark Grace and Rick Sutcliffe both had a habit of spending time with the yuppies. They didn't come out to the bleacher area. So many of the visiting team's players, even, a first baseman like Andres Galarraga, or a manager like **Jim Leyland**, would come out and talk to the people, look up to the fans and keep a conversation with them. Mark Grace was never out there. But he was a dependable player. I just wish he would have spent more time with people in the cheap seats.

I made my first sign in 1981. It said, "We have just begun to fight," and there was Ernie Banks' signature on it. In the mid '60s, I moved to San Francisco. Whenever the Cubs came there, I was at Candlestick Park, and every year, except 1969, I always went back to Chicago to visit my parents and friends in the summer and spent at least a couple of weeks in the bleachers. You hear a lot of Cubs fans talk about the heartbreak of 1969. I didn't have a heartbreak that year because I got wrapped up in the peace marches that they were having in San Francisco. That was the only year I didn't get into Cubs baseball.

I have great memories of Harry Caray. I once was doing publicity for a pickle company called Bubby's Kosher Pickles. I sent some pickles up the booth when Harry Caray was up there, and he started eating them on camera and his assistant had to say on air, "Don't worry; there's nothing wrong in the booth. That's just Harry eating kosher pickles." I remember when I first really met Harry Caray. In 1984, the Cubs opened up in San Francisco, and I was doing the publicity for a sports store called "The Locker Room" at that time, where I

Former Colorado Rockies manager, Jim Leyland, was once a second-string catcher for Perrysburg, Ohio High School. The starting catcher was Jerry Glanville.

dedicated a Chicago window. We sold more Cubs merchandise than they did San Francisco Giants merchandise. It looked like they were going to win the pennant for a change, and Dallas Green was their manager. I created a "Dallas Green for President" campaign at that sports store, which is two blocks away from the Moscone Center, where the Democratic National Convention was going on. Well, I got 50 Democratic delegates to wear "Dallas Green for President" buttons into the convention. And Harry and Dallas came into the sports store to introduce themselves, that was my primary introduction. Halfway into the '85 season, Harry asked me to appear with him on the 10th Inning Show. He introduced me as John Q Public and, about two years later, he tabbed me the Number One Cub Fan in the country.

In 1984, whenever the Mets came to town, there was a Mets pitcher by the name of Roger McDowell, who used to throw a Frisbee to the fans. The next time the Mets came to town, I had a Frisbee with me. For about two or three years we would play Frisbee. In 1987, the Mets were coming to town. I brought my Frisbee with me, and there was rain that morning, so I knew there wouldn't be any batting practice, but I always got to the ballpark when it opened. Roger McDowell comes running out and says, "Where's your Frisbee?" I went in my bag to go get it and one of the ushers—there were only three people in the stands at the time—says "Don't throw it." I tell him to look the other way, and I threw it. And he says you're out of the ballpark. I had gone to some 67 straight games; it was in September, maybe, and I got kicked out. I called Dallas Green on the phone and told him what had happened, and he said, "Come to the office. I'll try to get you into the ballpark." But when I came to the office, the same guy who kicked me out was there, telling me to get out of there or he would call the cops. So I called the *Chicago Sun-Times*. *Sports Illustrated* picked up on it, too. It wound up being a national story. I got Roger to sign that Frisbee. The following fall I went to the winter meetings and brought a Frisbee with me and got Bart Giamatti, Harry Caray, and Jack Brickhouse to sign it.

I started getting called the "Bleacher Preacher," but when I started out, I called myself the "Bleacher Creature," back in 1984. When the Cubs were real hot, I made bumper stickers that said, "How do you spell belief? C-U-B-S," with "Bleacher Creature" underneath. Someone in the bleachers asked me if I was aware that there was a whole section in Detroit called the "Bleacher Creatures." I told him, "No." So I reworked it and would always say, "There are many bleacher creatures. But there is only one bleacher preacher." Later I did a search on "Bleacher Preacher." There was some guy with a Web site, wearing a Harry Caray tee shirt. I went on another search, and there is another guy, a real preacher who calls himself the "Bleacher Preacher," and ironically, he started out calling himself the "Bleacher Creature."

I only went to two games in 2003. I went to the opener, because my friend Carmella Hartigan passed away just a few months short of her 102nd birthday. She used to be known as the "Lady With the Pink Hat." Every once in a while, when they would pan the crowd and get a hold of her, Harry would say, "There's the lady with the pink hat." This lady used to take two buses back and forth to the ballpark, and once went for seven years without missing a game. She also once had a brain operation in February, and she was there for the opener two months later. I called up her son before the 2003 opener so that I could take her pink hat with me. She was truly a Cubs treasure. One time, they actually had her throw out the first pitch. A few days before that, I had taken her out to the park to teach her to throw underhand. A Cub fan saw her practicing with me, and came over and said, "I know Cubs pitching isn't that good this year, but is Carmela going to pitch for the Cubs?"

When Clemson University plays in a bowl game most of their fans pay their bills with $2 bills to show their economic impact...and increasing their chances of a future invitation.

THE CUBS FUTURE IS HISTORY...

Rick "Panama" Farlow

Rick lives in Osceola, Iowa and works for Data Link Communications. Some people consider him the King of Cub Fans in Iowa.

In 1990, my now-wife and I stayed at the Comfort Inn in Diversey. We sat in the left field bleachers for the first time. We scored bleacher seats for the next day's game at face value from another fan. We were set. At breakfast at the hotel the next morning, a hotel clerk announced that the hotel owner had seats for that day's game, if anyone was interested. It didn't take a rocket scientist to realize that if the hotel owner had seats they were probably good ones. We bought the seats (although they were quite pricey for us at the time, even at face value). We sold the bleachers outside of the stadium (for face) and went into the grandstand. We got to our seats. Ten rows behind the brick looking right down the third base line. Incredible seats. The Cubs won. Later that day, we met Harold Beider, the hotel owner who had the seats. He requested that his staff call him when we returned to the hotel so he could speak with us. Harold was a tremendous Cub fan and we thanked him for the seats and told him the story of my first game when I was four years old. We talked for probably an hour about the Cubs, the great seats, Wrigley, restaurants, everything. Harold realized my passion for the Cubs and offered the seats to us anytime we came out, if they were available. We graciously accepted his offer and took his personal card. When I called the next spring to check on available dates, I was shocked to learn that Harold had died sometime that winter. I gave my condolences and sat in shock. But it wasn't over. I wrote a very eloquent letter to Harold's daughter describing our day at Wrigley in Harold's seats and our great conversation we had the opportunity to have with him. His daughter wrote back to me thanking me for the letter and offering me the seats anytime they were available. We sat in row ten looking down the third base line for the next five years. Finally, Harold's son took over ticket disbursement. He did not recognize my name and opted to not allow us to use the seats. It was a great run—Sandberg, Dunston, Andre Dawson—great era at Wrigley. I proposed to my wife in those seats. The seats were gone, but the Bleacher era was about to begin. The Bleacher era—the run for a championship.

1994—another beautiful summer day at Wrigley. We have now successfully kept our vow to return to Wrigley for five years. My brother Ferg, our friends Bubba and Mookie are sitting in the left field bleachers and a dude is sitting behind us—laughing at our "clownish" behavior and eyeing the Iowa Hawks jersey Ferg was wearing. The dude is Jim "Boo" Bradley. The chance meeting now lives in infamy.

The Cubs win, Boo engages in conversation and we all hit a Wrigleyville bar after the game. Then Boo shows us his apartment, second building back from Waveland on Sheffield. He has pictures framed of Bill Veeck planting the ivy (among others). We make a pact—Opening Day every year! I now have nine opening days in a row. In 2000, we name the group: NUTCUP. Northside Urban Traveling Cubs United Posse. We are on a mission from God. A World Series Win.

In 1998, the Cubs win the wildcard. They are once again in the playoffs. I score tickets on the phone. SROs for games three and four. The Cubs have to play the Giants in a one game playoff for the wildcard. I have tickets and a plane reservation from Denver to Chicago if they win. On business, watch the game at a bar in Las Vegas, New Mexico. The Cubs win. I'm going to my first playoff games at Wrigley. I buy the entire bar two rounds. Cubs win. However, the Cubs don't win game three. No game four. We'll be back.

2003—This is our year. Opening Day was snowed out. They played on Tuesday. The Cubs won the home opener. It was thirty degrees.

It's October 2003. The Cubs win the division. Ferg attends the double header that wins it. I score playoff tickets, once again getting through on the phone. First and second row of the right field bleachers. The Cubs are up 3-1 in the series. One win in two games and the goal is achieved. We arrive in Chicago by planes, trains, and automobiles. We arrive in the bleachers and post our small 8x11 sign "We're On a Mission from God." After losing Game 6, we stay in Chicago and score tickets for Game 7. Limited view seats but good ones. We post the "Mission" sign on the pillar in front of us for all to see. We all know what happened. The quest continues. Wait till next year.

There are just so many Cubs memories…Going to the Billy Goat downtown and talking the bartender into giving us a hair from the chin of the stuffed goat head over the bar. The goat hair goes onto Wrigley from the left field bleachers on opening day…The cab rides. Wild-ass cab rides…Jake's Pub. My wife and I found the place the same year we met Harold Beider. Jake's is now our traditional bar. I am friends with the owner and his cronies and we meet and drink every year now. NUTCUP arrives at Jake's Pub the evening before Opening Day every year. Rituals are imposed. Rubbing the nose on the mounted deer head at the end of the bar. Shots of Schlitz beer. Listening to a couple of Johnny Cash songs. A vow that "This is the year…" collecting a Murphy's Bleacher beer cup on Opening Day for the collection (now standing since 1989)…I love the Cubs. We will win a World Series and I will be there…in body or in soul.

Chicago Cubs pitcher Randy Myers was attacked on the mound by a fan in Wrigley Field in 1995. After pinch-hitter James Mouton hit a home run off Myers, John Murray jumped from the stands and ran toward Myers. The hurler, trained in martial arts, dropped the fan with a forearm, and the two wrestled on the ground before other players and security personnel pulled the fan away. Murray, a 27-year-old bond trader at the Chicago Board of Trade was banned from Cubs home games for a year, given 18 months probation, a $500 fine and ordered to volunteer 200 hours of community service.

HE GOT ME IN ON A CATTLE AND OIL DEAL...AND I'M GONNA MAKE A LOT OF MONEY AS SOON AS THE CATTLE START GIVING OIL

Matt Fink

Now a commodities trader living in Naperville, Illinois, 38-year-old Matt Fink grew up in the Clinton, Illinois. Clinton is just north of Decatur and was home to Joe Axelson, publisher of Between the Vines. *Axelson, who was a honcho with the NBA's Kings, publishes from his home in Coronado Beach, California.*

The first time I remember being at a Cubs game was when I was about fifteen years old. My dad, Uncle Fred, and about ten of us drove up Route 66 in two cars and went to a Cubs game. I go out to Sox Park here in Chicago and it's a beautiful ballpark, it really is, it's a great ballpark. The young kids love it. But—there's just nothing like Wrigley. There's nothing like it since they built the new Bears' Stadium. But Wrigley is just special, every time you go. When I was single, that's where I lived. It was so much fun, even when they were losing.

There's no place like the bleachers. I always sat there when I was single. It's just a wild place sometimes. There were girls there doing things they shouldn't have been doing. At two o'clock in an afternoon game in April when it's freezing and we're all sitting around in our snowmobile suits, these girls are there in halter tops and showing their boobs and all that stuff. I'm twenty-five, twenty-six years old thinking, *That's great, but your boobs are gonna freeze off.* They were a fun bunch of gals and there were some regulars out there, but they were not for me.

I'm sure you know about Ronnie Woo-Woo. This is the funniest thing about all Cubdom. Ronnie Woo-Woo is this black street guy. I don't know if he's mentally challenged or if he just puts on. We've never been able to figure it out. He just walks around Wrigley—has been for at least thirty years. The people in Chicago have paid for new dentures for this guy. He dressed up in a pin-stripe Cubs uniform, the whole thing. And he runs around saying "Ronnie Wooooo, Ronnie Wooooo! Cubs Wooooo!" That's his big trademark. When I lived down there, you could wake up at three in the morning, after a Cub victory, and Ronnie would be standing in front of your apartment going, "Ronnie Wooooo. Wooooo. Cubs win!" He would just keep going on and on and on. His name is Ronnie Wickers. I would guess he's close to fifty years old now. People give him tickets. They let him into the game.

This buddy of mine kept bugging me to take him to a Cub game. He had great season tickets and I had these crappy tickets, so he let me sit in his good seats. His kid, who was about six or seven years old, came up and said, "Buy me an ice cream," in the middle of the last inning. I was wanting to watch so I didn't get it for him and told him we'd get something later. We walk out of the ballpark and there's Ronnie Woo-Woo dressed in a Cub uniform. That was '85-'86, Shawon Dunston's era, and Ronnie looked just like Dunston. I went, "Zack, there's Shawon Dunston." He ran up to him, and then his father came up, and I said, "Bruce, there's your son with Shawon Dunston." "Oh, you son of a b——, that's Ronnie Woo-Woo." I've got this picture of this little boy, Zack, who's now a twenty-one year old at U of I, with Ronnie Woo-Woo that looks like it's Shawon Dunston.

When the Cub fans went to Atlanta, biggest beer sales in Atlanta history—not just the stadium, Atlanta everywhere. Beer drinking is just part of baseball and the Cubs. They cut off the sales in the seventh inning so you can just see people stocking up toward the end of the sixth. But, you never see fights in Wrigley—it's a love fest.

I guess the maddest I've been with the Cubs would be '84 with Leon Durham. Everybody talks about Bill Buckner letting the ball go through his legs in the World Series. Leon Durham let an easier ball go through his legs in San Diego. I had just come out of high school, and I can remember watching that and thinking, *You've got to be kidding me.* I was playing junior college ball at the time.

QUICK HITS AND INTERESTING BITS
BLEACHER BUMS

The night after Glenallen Hill got traded, he came out to left field to the regulars—all the ballplayers know the people who are there all the time in the stands—and gave each one of them a bat. That was how much of a tie he had to those guys that were all sitting there. I would have gotten one had I made it to the game that night, but getting to night games in the city is always a challenge. All these guys are purists. I sit with them because they know the game of baseball. You can talk to them about the history of baseball, you can talk to them about Wrigley Field, and you will know about baseball by the end of that game. I know more about baseball now than most guys do. Now these guys are always in the same spot. Same position. Scorebook. Same thing every game. The first pitch, the bottom of the first inning, we'd take the last name of whoever was in left field and do the fee-fi-fo-fum chant to him. In the bleachers, you get anyone from 100 years old—a woman who died last year at 98, actually—to the really young. The tradition and purity of the American game is the best part of the Cubs because it's the best part of baseball.

———ANGELA SMITH, 39, Bleacher Creature

There are season ticket holders in the bleachers and most people aren't aware of that. Every year I get tickets to the last game of the year, thinking, if they're in the pennant race and that last game of the year means something, it's going to be so exciting. Normally that isn't the case and there are all kinds of tickets available at the end of the September. People thought it was so cold. Personally, I say it'll be cold in January; I want to see some October baseball, baby. In 1997, it was Ryne Sandberg's farewell day and Harry Caray's final, *Take Me Out To The Ball Game.*

Back in 1998, the Cubs played the San Francisco Giants in a playoff game for the wild card berth. I was sitting on my couch here, and I live on 3708 Sheffield, so I live right by the ballpark. The Cubs had lost that day, they had had their fate in their hands, and the only other way to get in was for the Colorado Rockies to beat the Houston

Astros, and sure enough Neifi Perez hits a home run and the Rockies beat the Astros. So the Cubs got a favor from the Rockies to get into the playoff against the Giants. As soon as he did that, I go bursting off the couch, run out my back door and through the alleyway you usually see when people hit home runs. I make a decision, I'm going to run down Waveland, not Sheffield… Imagine people were already in line just in the event that Colorado did win. I go running out there and get in line, and the line is probably already 700 deep and winding down Addison. I'm just thinking, "Don't sell out! Don't sell out! Finally, I get up close to the ticket windows. There are probably six or seven people lined up at each one of the ticket windows. I'm waiting in line, and there's a girl in front of me who's taking forever. I'm like, "What the hell is she doing here, she can't make up her mind." So I decide to bust over to the window next to me. I might have been second or third in line at my window and I was like fourth or fifth at the new window. As it works out, I get up to the window and the girl still hasn't made up her mind. I get tickets, last row in the lower deck, four of 'em. As I'm walking out the line, no more than fifteen seconds later, I hear him say, "GAME SOLD OUT." And I look back and the people in the other line behind the girl were still there. There is a God, and he's a Booman and a Cubs fan.

That was a great game. Michael Jordan threw out the first pitch. Bill Murray sang the seventh inning stretch, and the whole place was just electric. I still remember Mark Grace catching a pop fly in foul territory and just jumping up and down, and I'm just like…I was at that game.

——JIM BRADLEY aka "BOO", 35, Wrigleyville, Software QA Engineer

Chapter 6

Dirty Birds and Dirty Sox

Say What You Want About the Cardinals and the White Sox... Frankly, "Losers" Comes to Mind

ST. LOUIS BLUES

Bill McClellan

Chicago native, author, and journalist Bill McClellan's "On My Own" column appears in the St. Louis Post-Dispatch. *A 1965 graduate of Chicago's Fenger High School, McClellan graduated from Arizona State University and has resided in St. Louis since 1980.*

I was a Cub fan as a kid, even though I grew up on the South Side of Chicago, which was White Sox country. Back then the White Sox were usually pretty good and the Cubs were not so good, usually in eighth place. But I loved the Cubs dearly. My great friend Larry Less and I used to take the bus all the way from the South Side to watch them.

The people of my generation never give up the baseball team they grew up with. I gave up the Blackhawks and the Bulls and the Bears long, long ago. But the baseball team that you grow up listening to on the little Hitachi radio late at night when they were playing in Los Angeles, you never give up on that.

I missed the '69 collapse because I was in the service and wasn't able to follow it on a daily basis, but it still broke my heart. I came to St. Louis and there was no hiding the fact that I was a Cub fan. So I wrote columns about the Cubs, and when you're a Cub fan in St. Louis you're treated like a drunken uncle at a party. You know, with some amusement, not much anger. People are amused by you and tolerate you even though they don't want their children to grow up like you. And that's true except when the Cubs are winning. When the Cubs are winning, people become less tolerant of me because they take their Cardinals so seriously here.

It's a great rivalry. I go to the Cub—Cardinal games and I wear my Cub hat ,and people are good-natured about it, generally. I have two children, a daughter who is at the University of Illinois and a son who's in high school, and I've tried to raise them both to be Cub fans. With my daughter, I've succeeded, and she's a big Cub fan. The 2003 playoffs were very tough for her. And my son, despite my efforts, became a Cardinal fan. It's just hard to raise a little boy in St. Louis to be a Cub fan because of the peer pressure. Ozzie Smith was a big hero of his and all his friends were Cardinal fans, so he turned against me back when he was five or six. My wife was really proud of him, you know, how he was standing up on his own; and I'd say "Well, today the Cardinals, tomorrow drugs."

She's from Arizona, from Tucson. She's sympathetic. I couldn't take my kids to a Cub-Cardinal game because they were so at each other's throats all the time. It was not good-natured. So I would take one to one game and the other to the other game. You see it was no fun with them going after each other. So my wife is always, in that fight, a little sympathetic with my son Jack, because she felt that we were ganging up on him.

It's that old saying, "If they didn't break your heart, they wouldn't be the Cubs." I've had this happen before. To my daughter the 2003 playoffs were like a secret initiation into a church. You know with Cub fans it's almost like a religious thing as far as the value of or righteousness, of suffering, and so this was her first time really to see something that looks like a sure thing taken away. I remember 1984 in San Diego. I didn't go to San Diego, but the paper sent me to the two games in Chicago. The Cubs won the first two, and all they had to do was win one of three in San Diego. And, we had Sutcliffe, who was invincible, our Goliath. But I had a bad feeling about '84 that I didn't have in 2003. I really thought with Prior and Wood that things would work out. That's it, of course, Prior and Wood hadn't lost back-to-back games since the previous year. The Marlins aren't that good. It isn't like this was Atlanta or the 1927 Yankees. These were the Marlins for God's sake! Now they're World Champs twice in seven years.

Living here in St. Louis it doesn't seem any less intense, and you've got the comments that were being made around the end of the year, like when Cardinals pitcher Steve Kline said he wished that Mark Prior would take a line drive to the forehead and they wouldn't have to see him again. With stuff like that I have not seen any lessening of the intensity. The fans are usually pretty good. It's intense, but it isn't. Going to a St. Louis Cardinal game with my Cub hat on doesn't make me feel like I'm going to Oakland wearing a 49er's jacket or Yankee Stadium wearing a Red Sox cap. I don't feel that my life is in danger, but it's still very intense.

There are a lot of similarities with the South Side of Chicago. In Chicago, as you probably know, you can't like both teams. It just works out that way, that you can't be a Cub fan and also pull for the White Sox, or vice versa. Those aren't real fans. The real fans like one and hate the other. So I grew up hating the White Sox, and my best days—and they were rare—were on those days when the Cubs won and the Sox lost. Oh, how I loved that! But that didn't happen that much. Like I said, the Sox were always in second place behind the Yankees it seemed like, and the Cubs were always in eighth place. I can remember being hugely excited as a child when the Cubs were having a big three-game series in Cincinnati and fifth place was on the line. If everything broke right, we could end up the weekend in fifth. That to me sounded like unbelievably good news, the Promised Land, fifth place.

My favorite Cub over the years, no question, was Ernie Banks, number 14 on your scorecard, number one in your heart. One of the things that happened here that really broke my heart was when Ernie Banks came to town promoting some product. I forgot what in the heck it was. But he was going to be on one of the local TV stations. He was staying at the Ritz-Carlton, and apparently, somebody there said, "You ought to call this Bill McClellan. He's a big Cubs' fan and he writes columns in the local paper." And maybe they told Ernie that McClellan would probably boost whatever product he was pushing. And, of course, I would have. No question I would have. I came in, I'd been to court or something, and I was going through my voice mail and heard, "Bill McClellan, this is Ernie Banks. I'm here at the Ritz." So, of course, I immediately called over there, but he had already checked out.

Now, when I was growing up my favorite pitcher was Dick Drott. He struck out 15 Milwaukee Braves in one game. As a matter of fact, I kidded our sports writers when Kerry Wood came up a couple of years ago and was so good, I said, "You know, I don't mean to jinx the kid, but he could be the next Dick Drott." Of course the younger sports writers didn't know what the heck I was talking about. It was that "drunk uncle" again.

My dad took me to my first game at Wrigley Field. I remember thinking it was really special. But my dad didn't take us to many games, maybe one White Sox game and one Cubs game. After that I would take the bus with a friend of mine.

I don't think there's a curse. It's all fun and because it's the Billy Goat, a newspaper bar, and growing up in Chicago I had never heard of that. Maybe we were just so unhip. While we didn't think there was a curse, we were always astounded at how the Cubs did so poorly when they were so good. We knew all the players; I don't mean knew them, but you know George Altman and Moose Moryn and all those guys. We thought they were great. So we thought, *how could a losing team be this good?* We never thought of it as a curse.

I did get in fights on the South Side, but I can't remember any of them being about the Cubs. They were always about different things. We were silly kids and we'd fight. I can remember fighting kids from the Catholic school. But I don't ever remember getting into a fight because I was a Cub fan, and again a big part of that is just that the Sox always did well. If the Sox had been the eighth place team and the Cubs had been the second place team, I probably would have gotten into a lot of fights because then they would have thought, "Oh, you smart-aleck." But as it was, "Oh, you Cub fan." I was not a tough enough kid to start the fights, and there was no need to fight a Sox fan because they could just tease us.

The Cubs' pitching looks great and they finally have a third baseman. They just seem to come together and then split apart. It's almost like some kind of amoeba. You have a chance, and then the next year, who knows what happens; unforeseen things happen, you have injuries, somebody else gets a hangnail. I don't know, and I don't look to next year with unbridled optimism.

There are quite a few Cubs fans in St. Louis, and actually several in the media, but they keep quiet about it. I'm about the only one who's upfront; everybody else feels that to be popular you have to be a Cardinal fan. It's like these newscasters that you get, they came from Memphis last week, but they're already talking about "us"; all of us in "Cardinal Nation." All of us, but one, Pal!

WHITE SOX FANS ARE PROOF THAT HELL IS FULL AND THE DEAD ARE WALKING THE EARTH

Jim Demaret

Jim Demaret, 37, is a trader at the Chicago Stock Exchange. He lives in Glenview, Illinois.

I was never forced to choose sides when I was younger because people just tolerated you. I didn't know any White Sox fans so they were just really another team to me. There was not great animosity until I started working at the Chicago Board of Options Exchange, which was probably eighty percent White Sox fans. They made it impossible to tolerate the White Sox anymore. It has a lot more to do with the fans than it has to do with the team or the organization.

I remember the 1977 White Sox team, the South Side Hit Men. I won't say that I was cheering for them or rooting for them, but I thought Richie Zisk and Carlton Fisk were decent ball players. I thought they were fairly interesting and a decent ball club but they didn't go anywhere. It was never a thing about the team or the ball players; it just became a thing between the fans. You'd get phone calls at two in the morning with people laughing and saying, "Go Marlins." You answer the phone and there will be snickering and "I told you so." and "Cubs suck." That's the way it was down on the floor. It wasn't "Go White Sox" it was "We hate the Cubs." They hated the Cubs more than they rooted for their own team. I have found it impossible to deal with White Sox fans.

There were a few White Sox fans who rather enjoyed the good-natured ribbing back and forth of "We hate the Cubs," and "Go White Sox," and "We understand that you hate the White Sox and are rooting for the Cubs." There would be a lot of good naturedness there, but I would say that's the minority of the White Sox fans. The majority of them are shown in the incidences at Comiskey Park in the last few years—people running on the field and attacking the umpire. Just the way Sox fans generally behave is trashy. I don't want to call all of them trash—some of them are trash. The best way I would describe them is that they're more interested in hating the Cubs than they are in rooting for the White Sox. They're Yahoos that way.

When I was ten or eleven years old, we were taking our mitts, and we were going down early to Wrigley to catch batting practice. I caught quite a few balls. The only problem we had was that they didn't open the gates until eleven-thirty or noon in those days. The Cubs were always done with batting practice, and the opposing team would be taking batting practice. We'd sit out in the bleachers and we'd catch a few out there. If we weren't in the bleachers, I've caught my share of foul balls at other games.

Back in the eighties, it was always dangerous to go sit down the right field line, not the bleachers, but behind the bullpen and back in that corner. For a year or two, there were constant fights breaking out in that section. I don't know why, but it was weird. The girls at Wrigley are interesting, and the cameramen don't miss them. Many of the women were there to watch the game, but a lot of the female fans would come to root for their "Player of the Hour," whoever he was at the time. I remember there were quite a few times when all you had to do was put on your Mark Grace jersey, walk around and find some girls rooting for him. You would strike up a conversation about how great Mark Grace was and what a great ball player he was, buy her a few beers, and the next thing you know, you're out to dinner. After that, whatever happened, happened.

My wife is from New Jersey, and she claimed to be a Mets fan when I first met her, but I haven't seen much evidence of that of late. She's beginning to understand my commitment to the Cubs, and 2003 was helpful to her. She made a grave mistake back in 1998 and scheduled a family trip overseas to Amsterdam to see her sister while the Cubs were in their playoff pursuit. She said, "I do not see what the problem is." I said, "You do not schedule trips in late September and early

October if the Cubs are any good in June." So, she has learned that lesson since then.

My oldest daughter is six, and she likes the Cubs. For the last three years, we've been pulling our four kids' names out of the hat when the playoffs start and everybody gets one team from the American League and one team from the National League. Last year when we did it, my youngest was too little. Every year we kick two teams out, and last year the two teams we kicked out were the Cardinals, because I can't stand them,—if any one of my kids would root for them, they'd have to move out—and the Yankees, because I figured it probably wasn't fair for someone to be handed the winner right off the bat. And, I also really can't stand the Yankees, but I can't say that around my wife because my in-laws are Yankee fans.

Everybody drew a name, and my eldest drew the Anaheim Angels last year. She has become now an Angels fan because they won the World Series and she wants to go see the Angels. I'm really torn with, "Okay, maybe next year, the Angels will play the Cubs, and they'll come to Wrigley Field 'cause I really hate going down to Comiskey Park. I refuse to go there, but if her team's playing there, that might have to be a big sacrifice. Maybe I can get my wife to take her, because I really don't want to set foot in that place unless the Cubs are playing there.

We went down there two years ago for the Cubs-Sox series. The neighborhoods around Comiskey Park are not nice. You park in the lots around the field and hope they are pretty well protected. It was a Saturday afternoon, and the Cubs won 8–4. Sammy homered. The place just started going nuts. The Cub fans were cheering, and the Sox fans were yelling them down 'cause they hate Sosa. They say, "He sucked when he played for us." We said, "You guys are just p———- because we pulled off the steal of the century—trading George Bell for Sammy Sosa." They're still mad about that.

My aunt was actually dumb enough to schedule her wedding for that Saturday in 1984, which was Game 4, so we were at her wedding reception. She said there could absolutely not be a TV at her reception. She couldn't figure out why all of her nephews and her brother and her brothers-in-law and half of the other male guests who were from Chicago were not attending the wedding reception, which was held at the Westin Hotel in downtown Chicago. The groom was from Boston so there were people there from out of town. She had worked for TWA and was on international flights so she had friends from out of town.

She had given strict instructions down at the bar that if any guests came down from the wedding to not serve them and send them back upstairs. They looked at her like, "Are you insane?" She didn't want her wedding screwed up by the Cubs when they were trying to get into the World Series. What she hadn't counted on was that a whole bunch of people had rooms at the Westin that night, and we all just went up to our rooms. Finally some of the women came upstairs and knocked on the doors and told everybody to come back down to the reception. We all said, "You're insane." My aunt finally caved in and put a TV over by the bar so all the men would come down and join the wedding reception. That's where we were when Steve Garvey hit the home run off of Lee Smith. That was pretty brutal.

The next day, I was watching the game with my dad. When the ball went through Durham's legs, my dad got up, kicked the footstool over, and said, "I can't believer these f——— are going to do this to me again." I imagine he was referring back to 1969. He got up and walked out of the house. I turned around and said, "The game's not over." He said, "Yeah, it is." He walked out the door and came back a couple of hours later after he had cooled down. But he knew the game was over at that point.

The guys at work are reveling in the Cubs loss to the Marlins.. They're loving it. I had one White Sox fan actually say to me, "I bet five hundred bucks on the Marlins and five hundred bucks on the Over." He said "It was three-nothing, and I thought, 'Oh my God, the Cubs are going to the World Series, and I'm gonna lose eleven hundred bucks' and all of a sudden here comes that idiot fan touching the ball. Not only do I have a twenty-one hundred dollar swing in my favor, but there's no way the Cubs are going to the World Series. This is better than the White Sox winning the World Series." They were laughing and cheering it up and having a good old time with it.

THE WHITE SOX ARE LIKE A GOLF COURSE—ONE PRO TO THE CLUB

Robert Wachs (left) with friend.

ROBERT WACHS

A Workers' Compensation physician in Palo Alto, California, Bob Wachs, 57, grew up a Cubs fan on the northwest side of Chicago until age fourteen, not far from Humble Park.

In 1984, the Cubs looked like they were doing pretty well, the year after Elia had that tirade about the fan support, so I started pretty early to cut out articles about them. That was their first success at all since '45 so I made an album out of it. I remember a relative came to visit and looked at me in disbelief that a 38-year old man would spend his time doing something like that. It was just clearly that he was not a fan—that's all. I've only taken the album out three or four times since I made it, but not at specific times.

I'm a card-carrying member of the Die-Hard Cubs Fan Club. It was something officially offered by the Cubs fifteen or twenty years ago. They sent out this membership card to some of us. There were never any meetings, but I do remember meeting an old buddy from high school who had moved out here, too. We had known each other in the early sixties, and then twenty years later, coincidentally, I saw him at a Giants game. I don't think I even knew he lived in California, but we both pulled out our Die-Hard cards. There was nothing really active about it. You paid five bucks to them, and they sent you the card.

To me, the Cubs are a major element of the diversions of my life. I'd like to think I still have some sense of the proper values in life, and so I have a loving marriage and kids that are doing fine and everybody's healthy; and that's what's important to me in my life. But the Cubs are providing a major diversion. I follow what they do. Without the Cubs, some other diversion would have to substitute for that.

The difference between Cubs fans and Red Sox fans has to do with expectations. when something like this happens to the Cubs, it's not such a terrible thing because we didn't expect to be there in the first place. In a way, it's harder for Red Sox fans, because they have higher expectations. They expect to be there, and then find a way to screw things up. I know it's a crazy thing to say, but one of the most important things you can do to be happy is lower your expectations. It's true at work. It's true of everything. It's true. Think about it. Really, people's unhappiness is the gap between their expectations and their reality.

For many, many years, until the strike in '94, I shared season tickets at Candlestick Park. In my little group, I was the one who went to the Cubs games so I went to their games here pretty regularly. There were days in the middle eighties when the Giants had poor teams, and I honestly think there were days when there were as many Cubs fans at the park as Giants fan. The way I looked at it was there were five thousand Cubs fans in the Bay area who would go to games regularly. If the Giants were doing badly, there would be five thousand Giants fans, and about five thousand Cubs fans. If the Giants were doing well, there would be forty-five thousand Giants fans, but still the same five thousand Cubs fans.

I have a license plate that says "CUBSFAN." Having a Cubs theme was a natural possibility when I first got an e-mail address, and was picking a screen name. We looked through various ones and the first name I thought of, which would have been MRCUBS was already taken. So I settled for MRCUBZ. That was with AOL.

Recently, I stood up at the wedding rehearsal dinner of a friend of mine, who happens to be a White Sox fan, and read this poem I'd written:

The Poem for the Ages

There exists in this country a certain breed of men.
They sit in their stadiums filled with the promise of what might be
Nose bleeds they endure. The heights are such, you can barely see.
Who is that ant? Could it be Carlos Lee?

There exists in this country a certain breed of men.
At times their team is okay. At times it makes them blue.
But this we all know, although it makes them stew,
In their own home town, they're always number two.

There exists in this country a certain breed of men.
In 1919, eight of their heroes turned into big rats.
Some claim a thrown Series is merely an annoyance like gnats.
Compared to one or two expertly-corked bats.

There exists in this country a certain breed of men
Who embrace with lust their colorful cast.
For instance, the curse of the Bambino past.
Oops. Wrong Sox. Forgive me. I'm a guest.

There exists in this country a certain breed of men.
Their team often looks like it mostly fields scrubs.
Only five pennants and about a hundred flubs.
Compare that to the lovable ten-pennant Cubs

There exists in this country a certain breed of men.
Their GM is brilliant. A great trade he can smell.
Those schmoes to the north I don't wish them well.
I know let's trade them Sammy for the outstanding George Bell.

There exists in this country a certain breed of men.
By now you've a feeling for the gist of this special man
Like Bozo, you punch him, he pops back as only he can.
The indomitable, the immutable, our very own White Sox fan.

Not too much happened when I read it. It either wasn't well-received or it wasn't well-heard. The acoustics were horrible. My friend said absolutely nothing afterward.

HE DROVE BY THE CUBS MUSEUM OF PROGRESS. IT HADN'T OPENED YET!

Gene Siglock

Gene Siglock grew up in Alton, Illinois, dreaming of playing for the Cardinals. Instead, he was a Prudential Agent for 25 years and now is in the courier business.

My oldest son and I went up to a Cardinal-Cub game in 1984. In **Wrigley Field**, they had opened a little sandwich restaurant down the right field line. Up above it was a private club that cost thousands of dollars to join. All you had to have was a ticket stub for that day's game, and you could go in and get these deli sandwiches, shaved turkey and ham, an ice cream sundae. Prices were pretty reasonable compared to the rest of the park. Your deli sandwich and some ice cream weren't much more than getting a hot dog and a soda out in the park proper. It was decorated real nice. They had these big wooden tables that had memorabilia sealed in clear plastic on the top of the table. They had taken old seats out of the ballpark, three on each side, so each table held six people. Then they had a big counter and the cushions for the bar stools at the counter were made out of old bases. The waitresses all had these outfits on that looked like the ladies' outfits from "A League of Their Own." They had TV monitors on up there and if the Sox were playing, they'd show their game. If the Sox weren't playing, they'd show a tape of "This Week in Baseball" or something related to baseball. We got in there and got the second to last table, and there were only the

> More NFL games have been played at Wrigley Field than at any other stadium in the country. Mile High Stadium in Denver was in second place until demolished in 2001.

two of us sitting at this big table. I can look out the door and there are about three hundred people out there waiting to get in. I stopped the waitress and said "Tell those people we're glad to share the table with some of them as long as they don't mind sitting with a couple of Cardinal fans.

So this guy sat down, by the name of Bob Browning. I always remembered his name because the Reds had a pitcher by the name of Tom Browning at that time. He and his wife came in and sat down with us and we started talking. We found out that he was best friends with Jim Frey who had just become the Cub manager that year. They had gone all through grade school, high school and college together. Through Jim Frey, he got three seats right behind the Cub dugout in the front row, right where they go down the steps. Meanwhile, I had real good seats in St. Louis, in Section 140. Mister Busch's private box used to be right in the front row of our section. I got to meet a lot of people then because of the World Series and the playoffs, Skitch Henderson, Chub Feeney, etc. Celebrities would be walking up and down the aisle, and my seats are right on the aisle. I'd jump up and shake hands with them and sometimes get autographs from them. Browning and I talked, and we decided that we would swap some game tickets with each other. Later on Frey became the general manager, and, of course, I about cried when he got let go in the early nineties, 'cause that was the end of that. These seats were so great it would be like sitting right in front of the coaches' box in St. Louis. In Wrigley, there's no foul territory. The only bad thing about it is you really had to be alert because if a ball came up there, you didn't have much reaction time.

One of the first times we went up there, the kids were in school, and my wife and I went. I had an extra ticket, and my boss at work wanted to go so bad that he took a vacation day to go up there with us. We go in and sit down and the ushers will just drive you crazy. I finally just took my ticket stub and stuck it in the bill of my cap. About every five and ten minutes before the games start, they're coming around checking to make sure you belong down there. They don't want anybody sitting in those seats unless you have the ticket. I'm sitting in the middle, my boss is sitting toward home plate, and my wife's sitting toward the outfield. We're right behind where the players go down the steps so we're about a third of the way down the third-base line and maybe no more than fifteen feet off the foul line. You're so close, you could hear the players talking.

So I'm sitting there. The Cardinals had batted around once. It was about the top of the fourth inning, and Vince Coleman was leading off. Thank God for the gray road **uniforms**. I've got my ball glove there—I'm left-handed. My wife had gone up and gotten some pizza. She brought me a slice, and it was real hot so I took my ball glove off and laid it on my right knee. I bent over and was blowing on the pizza to cool it off. I had just sat back in my seat and Coleman got an inside fast ball. Even though he wasn't a big guy, when you get an inside fast ball, and really turn on it, you can really smoke it. I saw the ball was gonna just miss my boss's nose and was gonna hit me right over my right eyebrow. I'm thinking "neck muscles do your thing!" All I could do was just slam my face forward right into that slice of pizza. The ball was so close that it actually grazed my ear. That's how close it was. If that would have hit me, it could have killed me. I played ball until I was forty-five years old so my reaction was pretty fast, but it was hit so hard I just didn't have time to even think about the glove. I heard this loud whack and thought, "Oh, golly, somebody right behind me got hit and hurt bad." I looked around and luckily nobody was in the seats right behind me but two rows back and about four seats down, the guy just got his bare hand up in time and the ball was hit so hard that it busted that bone on the outside of his hand. It came right through the skin and just showered everybody with blood. The ball went off his hand and all the way down in the left field corner and the guy with the glove down there caught it. That's how hard it was hit.

Maybe three or four weeks after this happened, a little boy was sitting about three rows back and about two rows closer to home plate, and he got hit above the ear, and it fractured his skull. The Cubs ended up

> The Yankees were the first to put numbers on the back of uniforms...circa 1930...Lou Gehrig was the first athlete to have his number retired.

paying his family fifty or sixty thousand dollars in medical bills. they did it voluntarily because there's no liability for a batted ball. If a player throws a bat, that is a liability issue. You don't expect a bat to come flying in the stands, but a ball, you just assume the risk.

The fans in Wrigley are nice. They'll give you the business, but you never feel like you're in fear like you would at Shea. You would never go to Shea and wear any Cardinal apparel or you wouldn't get out alive. Wrigley is just good natured banter. I really enjoy going up there. We try to go up there at least one Cub-Cardinal game every summer. When we had those seats, we'd definitely go.

For years I took a megaphone to the games. I never used any profanity. In 1987, we were at Wrigley Field sitting in those good seats and the Cubs were playing Montreal. Hubie Brooks was playing shortstop for Montreal and Tim Wallach was their third baseman. It's so close there you can hear the players talking when they're having infield practice between innings. Hubie walks over to Wallach, probably about the bottom of the third inning, and he says, "The Cardinals are going against Dwight Gooden in New York today." Wallach says, "Yeah. Gooden's pretty tough on them. He'll probably shut them out." It ticked me off, but I didn't say anything. The game goes on for an inning or two. I looked up at the manual scoreboard, and the guy drops a "10" for the Cardinals in the top of the first inning. I couldn't resist that—I had the megaphone there. I had it turned all the way down to a "one." Pasqual Perez was pitching that day. He had the Cubs shut out. He's just going into his windup, I flipped the megaphone on and I just said, "Hey Wallach, Brooks, look what the Cardinals just did to Dwight Gooden in the top of the first inning," thinking they were professional enough they'd wait until after the pitch was made. The second I said that, they swiveled around to look at the scoreboard, and the Cub batter hit a hard one-hopper right between Wallach's legs. If it would have been about three inches higher, his voice would have been about ten octaves higher. So, the ushers come down and take my megaphone away, like it was my fault.

SOME PEOPLE THINK THAT FRANK THOMAS IS THE BACKBONE OF THE WHITE SOX. I WOULDN'T PUT HIM QUITE THAT HIGH.

Robert T. George

Robert T. George grew up in Hinsdale, IL, a western suburb of Chicago. A boy genius, George's first full sentence came at ten months old, on August 6, 1978, when he said, "We traded for Davey Johnson? He'll be a great manager some day if he can lay off the booze." George is currently a Journalism student at Northern Illinois University in Dekalb, IL.

In mid-season of 2001, I was at the Hunt Club, a North Side bar on Rush Street, after a Cubs game. There, at the end of the bar, sat every Cubs fan's most hated scum of a player, Frank Thomas of the White Sox. I decided, in all of my drunken wisdom, to approach this 600 lb. mass of lard and tell him what I thought of him. My brilliant plan was to go up next to him, order a drink, and casually turn to him and tell him how much he sucks. So, I went up to the bar and stood next to him, waiting for the bartender.

As I waited to order my drink, Fat Frank—A.K.A. The Big Herd—turned to ME and said— "You're in the wrong neighborhood!" Now, I must remind you that the Hunt Club is on the North Side.

Shocked at his ignorance, I turned to him and said, "Excuse me?"—I assumed I could not have heard him correctly. He pointed at my Cubs jersey and repeated "You're in the wrong neighborhood. Why don't you get the —k out of my bar!"

I informed him that it was he, not I, that was lost here, and security immediately came over and kindly asked me to leave their guest alone and order my drink from the other side of the bar. I obliged, and went about three feet away to the other corner to order my drink. After my friends asked me what happened, I loudly informed them of how Frankie the Gut had treated me like some lowly Sox fan. I also may or may not have mentioned his weight problem during this conversation.

Thomas, as I had hoped, heard me and sent a "Let's-engage-in-a-boxing-match" type of gesture in my direction. Security decided, at that point, that maybe it was time that I found another watering hole, and they escorted me out. As I walked away, I yelled profanities and fat jokes at "Tubs."

After getting out of the bar, I stood and thought about what bar I would go to next, and waited for my friends. All of a sudden, from behind me, I hear, "You're dead!" I turned around and angled my head up to see the .240 hitter himself, Frank Thomas.

With my liquid courage going strong, I stood toe to toe with him and just ripped him a new one...verbally, of course. I said things like, "Of course you could kick my a—, you outweigh me by 400 pounds! And, "Why don't you learn to field your position before you start talking s——!" I continued, "The only reason you wear a major-league uniform is because the Sox were bad enough to take you."

This went on for about two minutes and then things almost got very painful. I stood there like an idiot as this mass of Jello reared his right hand back, ready to knock me back to Wrigley. Fortunately, Thomas' own security guards, trying to save him from a lawsuit, grabbed his arms and wrestled him to the ground. A third guard suggested that I go on my merry way, and I wisely took his advice.

But, I stood face-to-face with the ugliest, most untalented and moronic athlete since **Patrick Ewing** and came out unscathed.

Patrick Ewing was the first athlete ever to be on the cover of *Business Week*.

DIRT ON THE DIRTY

The Cubs were never good enough for there to be brawls—and the White Sox were never good enough either. If we had seasons where they were both going into post-season play, tensions might really have arisen. The White Sox were good in '67, and the Cubs were terrible. The Cubs were very good in '69, and the White Sox were no good. There were not these years when it got that fierce between them. The trick is that neither team has been good enough for it to be anywhere near as bitter as between the Yankees and the Brooklyn Dodgers.

——JONATHAN ALTER, Journalist

Bob Olson (right) with son, Bruce.

I grew up on the West Side and at the school I went to, there were quite a few Sox fans. We got into it all the time, including a couple of fist fights. One time Luis Aparicio was the shortstop for the White Sox and Ernie Banks was shortstop for the Cubs, and this kid was ribbing me about the fact that Banks wasn't as good as Aparicio. We started shoving each other and got into a fight. In my mind, nobody was any better than Ernie Banks.

The worst trade ever was when Lou Brock was traded to the Cardinals for Ernie Broglio. They traded him in 1964 to the Cardinals for Ernie Broglio, who was a sore-arm pitcher. Brock always could run like a deer, but he wasn't a good fielder, and he was a pretty lousy hitter. For whatever reason, Brock wasn't successful in a Cub uniform. The thing that really irritated me was that as soon as he put on a Cardinal uniform—it wasn't a year or two years later—like the next day, he was a Cardinal superstar. For some reason, he lost a lot of confidence playing in Wrigley Field. He got booed quite a bit. He used to drop a lot of fly balls, and he'd strike out a lot. He probably just wanted new surroundings.

——BOB OLSON, 57, Barrington, Illinois

Sometimes in the bars, Cubs fans will shake up their beers and spray beer all over each other, usually when they have beaten the Sox in a game. Those things can get a little intense. Sometimes I'm ashamed to say I'm a Cubs fan because some people just act obnoxious.

I went to a game early this year and was in the bathroom. There was this one kid, eleven or twelve years old, in there, and he was a Sox fan. The Sox just killed the Cubs the first game this year. There was also this big guy who was a Cubs fan in there. The kid said, "We're winning," and the guy just took the kid's hat off and threw it in the urinal, which is basically a trough. I was really a disavowed Cub fan at that moment.

————**DREW MARZEN**, 24, Albany Park Area, Chicago

I didn't cry about the Cubs in '84, but I did cry in '59. Can you guess why I cried in '59? That was the year the White Sox won the pennant. I was no kid, thirteen years old, but I remember crying because they had won.

Back in those days, the White Sox had good teams. They were always second place to the Yankees—and the Cubs were horrible. So there were a lot more White Sox fans around. A kid will take that rivalry differently. Now, I don't think there are so many White Sox fans around. But we do still have a rivalry.

My brother and I have a good relationship on many levels, so it's not like a "Field of Dreams" where we fight all the time, and the only thing we can ever talk about is baseball. It does help that we are both fans. My brother is retired and spends a lot of serious time on the computer dealing with sports and the Cubs in particular. He has a very intellectualized approach to it, as to why things are happening. Now, a lot of our conversations about the Cubs consist of the statistics. We also agree about something and would be fascinated to get more insight into the Cardinals rivalry. Neither of us has ever felt that we were very much rivals with the Cardinals. When I grew up in the fifties, it was absolutely the Sox, even though we never played a game against them—that was the big rival. Then, after '69, it was the Mets.

My theory is that the Cardinal-Cubs rivalry, which people talk about all the time, but I never felt, might go back to the thirties, when both teams were very good. Supposedly, it's common knowledge that the Cubs greatest rival is the Cardinals. Growing up as a die-hard fan, I just never felt that rivalry, which was very quiet in the fifties, if anybody was even feeling it. I'm curious as to its origin. Also, there might be an age thing about it—people who remember the Cubs as a good team so someone over sixty might feel it more.

——DR. ROBERT WACHS, Palo Alto, California

As far as St. Louis people being belligerent or sending angry e-mails when the Cubs aren't doing well, and the Cardinals are doing fine, people are very tolerant and good humored about me being a Cub fan. In those unusual years when the Cubs are doing well and the Cardinals aren't, some Cardinal fans can lose their sense of humor and say things like "you ought to go back to Chicago." There are a lot of people over the years that have told me "if the Cardinals can't do it, I hope your Cubs do." There's a lot of that. That's why I call this an intense rivalry. It's, in essence, a friendly rivalry and, of course, if the Cub's can't win the division, then I always hope the Cardinals do. Not so much that I like the Cardinals, but it's a nice town when the Cardinals are here. Its fun, and people are nicer. So, I'm not one of those people who want to see the Cardinals in last place because I live in St. Louis. I like to see them do well. I certainly don't want to see them do better than the Cubs, but if I could have my way, the Cubs would win the division and the Cardinals would be the wild card team and make it all the way to the division championship where the Cubs would beat them.

My fondest memory of the Cubs playing the Cardinals would probably be a tie between the day in '84 when Ryne Sandberg hit two homers. For a Cub fan against the Cardinals, it doesn't get any better than that. And really, it was only approached by the 2003 season's four-out-of-five Cubs wins in a September series in Chicago, where the Cubs won four, and they were all good games. Actually, the Cubs should have won the fifth. That was the game where Moises Alou hit the ball and it hit the chalk. I don't think there's any question that the ball hit the chalk and we would have cleared the bases.

——BILL McCLELLAN, St. Louis Post-Dispatch Columnist

My oldest brother is a minister in Ft. Smith, Arkansas and a big Cub fan. My other brother is a Cardinal fan who has season tickets for their games. He quit being a Cub fan in '69, graduated from high school in '71 and started rooting for the Cardinals. So, we have a war. He has not called me or spoken to me since we beat them. He won't call me. He won't talk to me.

——MATT FINK, Chicago Board of Trade

I was one of ten kids raised on the South Side, and the only one born with a brain—I'm the Cub fan. My dad worked for a bank, and he was a die-hard White Sox fan. I became a Cubs fan in 1967, when I was sixteen years old. I got my license, got a car, drove down there. I looked like I was about twelve, but I sat in the bleachers and ordered a beer, and they served me. I've been a Cub fan ever since. It was the best venue in the world to watch a baseball game. I was sixteen and drinking beer. The girls don't wear much during the summer. It's just a great place to go. For daytime baseball, it's just fantastic. I started going to a lot of games.

Until that time, when I learned my lesson, I was a White Sox fan. My dad would never talk to me about baseball because he thought I was an idiot for being a Cub fan. Just today, my brother saw me in my Cub jacket, and told me I was an idiot. Half of my brothers and sisters would not even call me and say congratulations for the Cubs making the 2003 playoffs.... In the eighties, my daughter was born, and my wife would breast-feed right in the box seats because there was nobody around. That's how empty it was.

——STEVE ZAWASKI, 52, Real Estate Appraiser, Western Springs, IL

I once did a project for the Society of American Baseball Research (SABRE) to try to find out which team were natural rivals, which teams should be put together in divisions and things like that. I said to the Twins fans, "Which team do you consider your natural rival?" The answer was the Brewers, which would not have been my number one idea. You talk to Cubs, and you're supposed to say their big rival was the Cardinals. In football, I'm a Bear fan, and I hate the Packers. I don't have any strong, strong hatred for the Cardinals, but I have strong, strong hatred for the Mets. In trying to figure it out, my brother came up with the answer that years and years ago when the Cubs were good and the Cardinals were good, back in the thirties, those were our natural rivals so everybody said, "Aw, that's the team you should root against." But in my basic lifetime, the Cubs and the Cardinals were not good at the same time so the one time we really had a rivalry was in '69, and the Mets beat us. So, that's why I consider them our natural rivals. The New York SABRE chapter has a lot of Mets fan there, and they tolerate Cubs fans. They laugh at us, "You guys never win anything, so...." Their record may not be too good either, but they've won two, which is two more than I can remember.

——DR. JERRY WACHS, New Jersey Cub Fanatic

What I'm hearing is not so much anti-Yankee. People don't really care about anybody else right now except the Cubs. But, Cubs fans were thrilled that the White Sox didn't make it. The White Sox fans can't even stand the fact that the Cubs are having some success right now. There are always fights between the fans of the White Sox and the Cubs. When you have the crosstown series—when they play each other twice during the year, once at each park—they're all sold out and the bars are just jammed. You get White Sox fans yelling, "The Cubs suck," and Cubs fans saying, "You South Side, dumb Italians don't know s——."

——PETE ALDWORTH, Hinsdale, Illinois

I always found the Cubs-Cardinals rivalry interesting. It always perplexed me as a Cubs fan growing up. Here is this small metropolis of St. Louis that fields all of these Hall of Famers, always puts a contending team on the field…what's the deal here? We're the third largest city in America, and it appears that the Cardinals are devoting the resources to put a winner on the field, and we're not. I never hated the Cardinals. I always envied the Cardinals. I envied the Cardinals that they were always a smarter and classier organization.

What's the deal, I thought, that we can't devote those resources? The Cardinals put all these championship teams together, and they were always retooling, and always competing. As a Cubs fan, there is this feeling with the management like we're being played for chumps. If there's one thing that annoys me and will challenge my faith, it's that—like being the good son, you're always going to be overlooked. You're always going to show up, you're always going to give us your money, and all we've got to do is just tease you with the idea that we can have a competitive year here, and that's going to be good enough. I know a lot of people feel the way I do, because it's absolutely true.

But we don't write letters like the Yankees or Red Sox fans do. You keep supporting the team. I think it's a Midwest thing. You grow up in a harsh climate. My mother told me "be thankful for what you've got. And don't worry about what you don't have." You were never supposed to be envious of what somebody else had, you were supposed to be thankful for all the blessings you had. The small town, Midwest, work-ethic, farmer-mentality, where you may have the finest crop in the county, but you sure as heck don't go out and buy and parade around in a new Buick or Cadillac. Because as soon as you do that, there's going to be a hailstorm to wreck that crop. You're only a fraction of bad luck away from having your livelihood stomped on by Mother Nature. There is always a caution. We were taught to believe you never promoted yourself. You let your work speak for itself. There is a Midwest sensibility there.

——JACK WIERS, Long-suffering Cub fan

The Sox and the Cubs play every year. My girlfriend and I took my fifteen-year-old son to Comiskey Park to a Cubs-Sox game. I got five extra tickets for my son and some friends, who were sitting higher up. The guy sitting in front of me had all seven seats. Five of the seats he did not give the tickets away, so the seats were empty. I called my son up in the upper deck and told him to bring his friends down here to sit because the guy, who was a Sox fan, said it was okay. I'm sitting in the seat behind, next to a woman who's a total White Sox fan—Sox earrings, Sox hat, whatever. My son comes down with his five friends and they sit in front of us, and they're rooting for the Cubs. This woman gets up, goes to an usher, and said, "These five kids don't have tickets for these seats." They did have permission to sit in these seats. I looked at her and said, "You b——." And I don't do that—I'm usually a real gentle person, but she was starting to mess around with my kid. The usher came down and asked to see their ticket stubs. The man said he didn't have the stubs because no one was using the tickets so he didn't bring them. The woman said, "Get them out of here. I want them out of here. They don't belong here." We really almost got in a physical fight. She said, "Why don't you take your kids and your Cub hat and go to the North Side." I said, "Why don't you take your Sox earrings and shove them up your a——." I never had gotten in a fight with anybody. I said, "Lady, I've never really been an anti-Sox fan but, from now on, because of you, I am going to hope the Sox lose every game they ever play, you miserable b——." I sat and stared at her the rest of the game.

——BONNY BECKERMAN, 53, Glencoe, Music Producer

Chapter 7

The Era of the
E.R.A and the ERA

Earned Runs and Equal Rights
in a Woman's World

EQUAL RIGHTS
EQUAL RITES

Cissy Greenspan

The 48-year-old Glencoe, Illinois homemaker didn't really marry her husband because he had Cubs season tickets, but it was a plus.

My older brother, who is five years older than I am, took me to my first game when I was twelve and bought me my first hat. I remember all about that day. I remember where in the bleachers we sat. He took my best friend with us and he took his good friend so there were four of us.

When Wrigley owned the team, they had weekend and holiday packages where you could buy fifteen games that were Sundays and holidays. In '78, my brother and a girlfriend and I did that, and we had seats five rows behind home plate. What I wouldn't do to have those seats now. We went to a lot of games then.

When the Cubs lost the final game of the 2003 season, I was so sad—I wasn't prepared for how sad I was gonna be. The next morning I was standing in the shower feeling so sad, and I didn't want to do anything. I went down to my computer and wrote my sons a letter. I have three sons who are all huge Cubs fans and we went to so many games together this summer. They are eighteen, almost fifteen and twelve. When they were gone in the summer to camp, I wrote them all every day telling them what the Cubs did the night before. That's just what they expect. So I wrote a letter and made three copies of it and put it on their desks so they would get it when they went to their rooms. I told them, "We're all feeling sad. Every now and then, things happen that we can get a life lesson from. This is one of those times. Don't close your heart to the Cubs. We've had such great times." And, I reminded them about the Yankee series in June and about how we have six seats in a row, and we all sit in the sun, and we sit in the cold and how the thing that meant the most to me about the Cubs was that it was something we shared together. How many things can you really share with your teenage sons? But we all had such a good time together. We wanted to be together. They wanted to be with us. The games that we weren't at, we were watching together on TV. It really brought us together. That was why I didn't want them to feel sad. I wanted to tell them that life is long and it wasn't really about the winning, it was about how exciting the ride was. All three of them said, "Great letter, mom." That's really what it was—it was the ride.

My good friend Bonnie's only son and my oldest son are very close friends. We live around the corner from each other. Bonnie works full time, except during the summer on Fridays she can leave work early. So, when we get our season tickets, I pull all the Friday games, and we go together.

We laugh a lot when we go to the games together because we're these two middle-aged women sitting in a sea of drunken businessmen. We're so into the game. I don't like to go to the games with casual fans. I don't want to go and sit and talk about other things. I want to go and be in the game and talk about the game and talk about what's happening. Bonnie and I do that together.

One of the things Bonnie and I always talk about are these women coming to the ballpark dressed the slutty way they do. What are they thinking? Why are they doing this? I went to games when I was twenty-two years old and could have worn anything I wanted, and I didn't parade around dressed like they do. It's a joke to me. I don't think the ball players notice them, but maybe the men who are there in the crowd do. I guess it's as good a place as anywhere to get picked up.

I remember all the Opening Days I went to with my brother. I always tell my kids, "I remember the year I had to brush snow off my seat, and I was as happy to be there as if it had been eighty degrees." I didn't care. I still feel that way. I miss my brother, who moved away about a year and a half ago. I told him that so many times during the 2003 season and particularly in the last week of the season that I just wished he was here. It killed him not to be here. It was sad that he wasn't here.

I met Ryne Sandberg once in a jewelry store. He was buying something, and he was so lacking in any personality. I went up to him and said, "My sons wouldn't forgive me if I didn't ask for your autograph. Do you mind? You probably hate this." He said, "No, no, give me a pen." He wasn't unfriendly—he was nothing! Mark Prior strikes me that way, too. They're so into their craft that they never develop a personality. They start when they're twelve years old and they see how good they are and don't ever develop a personality. people tend to work on their personality—*unless they don't have to.* It's like being a beautiful girl. Sometimes they don't bother to develop a personality because they can get by without it.

I'm not a lover of Sosa. He's another one who is temperamental and will never admit to weakness. He had a couple of big flubs this summer. He never said, "I'm in a slump, and I'm gonna get out of it." He would never acknowledge he was in a slump. I felt bad about the cork thing because my kids felt bad. I'm sorry that he didn't say, "I'm sorry I did it." I felt let down by him. The kids thought he was something special and it doesn't seem like he is now.

I can't wait until next year. That is what I said in my letter to my kids, "It's only four months until spring training, and they'll be back before you know it."

There was a near brawl in St. Louis' Busch Memorial Stadium in 1986. The female fans at the Cardinals-Cubs game grew tired of standing in lines to use the restrooms. Scores of women stormed the men's rooms. Said one disgruntled male fan, "I offered to share my urinal with one of the gals, but she told me to buzz off. I was just trying to be hospitable. After all, this was a men's john…But she was a Cubs fan."

DO THEY STILL PLAY THE BLUES IN CHICAGO WHEN THE BASEBALL SEASON ROLLS AROUND?

Rainy Horvath

For 54-year-old Rainy Horvath, a college professor residing in Scarsdale, New York, being a Cubs fan is a philosophy of life that defines you.

When you're a Cubs fan, it's not just an aspect to your life that's in proportion to everything else. Being a Cubs fan is a philosophy of life. It's defines the way you live. It's like I didn't pick the Cubs, the Cubs picked me. I love the Cubs because they've been a part of my life since I was a young person. I guess I love the Cubs, too, because of what they represent.

To me, they represent all these wonderful intangible qualities like optimism. If you're a Cubs fan, you're a die-hard optimist—you have to be. They represent the feeling that there's always tomorrow. They represent hope. To me, they'll always represent Wrigley Field and day-time baseball. The Cubs have suffered a lot—for almost a hundred years.

That first major league ball game that I ever attended, I bonded with the Cubs—the young, hopeful, idealistic person in the late sixties going to the Cubs game with everything that was about hope back then. I remember particularly the way Wrigley Field looked—the green grass and the blue sky and just the funkiness of it. I went with friends who lived in the neighborhood. Of course, we sat in the bleachers.

Beer is just part of the experience that has always been. If you go back to the early 1900s when the ballpark first opened, there were all these bars. They were on every corner around Wrigley Field. You had your personal bar. I used to work at a bar that's no longer there. It was called "Extra Innings." You never hang out at the bar you work in, it's poor form. The bar I hung out in was Bernie's.

Bernie's was one of the original bars that was probably the last to change and become yuppified. It was run by Bernie Dillman who had owned it since the last time the Cubs went to the World Series. It was not fancy in any way. It was a little rat-hole of a bar populated all day long by Cubs fans. You see, people who are true Cubs fans don't just like the games and go to the games. They make it their life. They get jobs there as groundskeepers or else the really rabid ones who can't get in as groundskeepers get jobs as vendors. This is their only jobs—they make it their life. All these kinds of people just stand out in front of *their* bar and wait for it to open. They hurry up, "Give me my drink." They're mostly old men who drink shots of straight whiskey. The bar is really dark and grungy and smells of beer. The first thing you do is put on the TV and start talking about the Cubs. These people knew everything about the Cubs—everything—going back all through the fifties. They were amazing to talk to. It really defines your whole life.

Everything revolved around the Cubs season if you lived near Wrigley, which I did. You had to plan your whole life around the Cubs games. The first thing you did was get the Cubs schedule and find out when they were going to be in town because all the people coming to see the Cubs would dictate whether or not you could have people over or have food delivered and things like that because the streets were so crowded.

They fly flags at Wrigley Field to show who's going to play that day and whether the team won or lost. The first thing you did was lean out your window and look at the flags to see if they're in town or out of town or playing the Marlins or whatever. It would determine, too, whether you would decide to go to the bar. If it was a game day, you didn't want to go to a bar, because all of the "fair-weather" Cubs fans were there.

I started college in Chicago and I had to make a living. I wanted to take night classes, but they didn't really have what I needed. In order to take day classes, I started tending bar and that's how I came to work there and got to know all these things.

Like with the Cub fan ruining the Alou catch—everyone was like, "it's the curse." I guess I'm superstitious. The curse might be real. Everybody talks about the curse all the time. Now that the Cubs are winning, there are all these people who claim to be Cubs fans. When I start questioning them, one of the first things I ask them is, "What do you think? Is the curse lifted?" If they say, "What curse?" I know they're fake Cubs fans, and I rule them out right away, and there are a lot of them now. Sometimes, I won't even wear my Cubs hat because I'm afraid I might be mistaken for one of them.

I moved to New York right before 1990. I am a Cubs fan in New York and I still flaunt it. I talk about the Cubs all the time, and I never for a minute change my loyalty or disgrace myself by going to a Yankees game or a Mets game—that would be heresy. All I can say is being a Cubs fan in Chicago is like being a Democrat in Chicago. You know how Democrats of Chicago are linked. You are born a Cubs fan, you die a Cubs fan. You never, ever change loyalty. Same thing if you're a Chicagoan of the old school, you were a Democrat. There was no question about it. It didn't matter where you went. I've always been a Cubs fan. I never even had any temptation whatsoever to change loyalties. In fact, I enjoy being the one to pop up and say, "This is going to be the year for the Cubs." I know everyone is going to laugh at me, but I don't care. Because I know that one year, it will be the year for the Cubs.

There are levels of Cubs fans. There is the level of the fans who make it their life and get a job there in Wrigley Field or sell items in front of it, and then there's a level even more hard-core than them. Those are the Cubs fan groupies. It's like a rock star's groupie. They absolutely latch onto them and follow them everywhere—women mostly, a lot of young girls. They hang out right in front of the entrance to go in. They try and get invited in. It's a really small old park and it's so old that the players still have to come through a door that everybody knows where it is and can stand around it. There's no underground, secret entrances for them.

I wrote a song about these fans. One of them was legendary, and we called her "Loose Linda." I never personally saw any of this happen, but she would wear very provocative outfits. She would hang out with the Cubs, and then later stories would come out that they would invite her into the team rooms.

My worst moment as a Cubs fan is when there's a good game, and you can't get a ticket. Right now, it's a worst moment because I'm in New York, and they're in Chicago. I know that if they ever win and go to the World Series, there's no way I'll be able to afford a ticket. No, my worst moment as a Cubs fan was when Steve Goodman, who was such a Cubs fan, died. He wrote the anthem, "Go, Cubs, Go," which everybody sang. Some of his ashes are buried under home plate. He's a well-known folk-rock singer from Chicago. He wrote "City of New Orleans" and a number of well-known songs. He had leukemia and died in 1984. Everybody loved him.

He wrote this song, "A Dying Cubs Fan's Last Request." When he wrote it, he knew he was dying, but nobody else did. It's all about how if I die, all I want to do is be buried in Wrigley Field, and I want to have an umpire call me out at home plate. When he actually died, he was cremated, and the Cubs loved him so much, that before one of their games, they actually had the ceremony. They did that—they carried his ashes around and buried them under home plate. I was outside the field. I could hear it going on and couldn't get in. That pretty much broke my heart. I really loved him.

I actually dated a security guard who worked at Wrigley Field. He was from the South Side. I suspect that he was truly a White Sox fan, pretending to be a Cubs fan to get the job. He just didn't fit the profile of the Cubs fan. He was a little bit too gritty. The Sox fans are a lot tougher. The South Side and the North Side are very, very different. Cubs fans are happy go lucky, "Let's everybody have a good time, eat a Frosty Malt and have a few laughs." Whereas, on the South Side, that's the City of Big Shoulders. That's where Mayor Daley is from. People are tougher. They just, in general, don't mix.

It's hard for me to pick a favorite. I have to go back a long way to Minnie Minoso. He was a White Sox, but I link him so much with Wrigley Field because that's where he hurt his arm. He wasn't used to playing in a small field like that. So I guess I'll amend my pick and say someone from the eighties—Ryne Sandberg. The first thing I ever wrote when I was in school at Roosevelt University in Chicago, my journalism teacher was a Cuban man who was writing a book on Minnie Minoso. He needed somebody to write the Foreword. He didn't have time. He had me ghost write it. That's how I learned about Minnie Minoso. I became fascinated with him. I loved it that he got hurt in Wrigley Field, actually.

Cubs fans are really resilient. I don't remember much about that loss in '84 to San Diego. I know there was steely-eyed resignation. Cubs fans are used to rejection and take it real well. Cubs fans get angry, "Why did you do this to us again?" But they still love them anyway; they never stop being Cubs fans. It was pretty sad, but I don't remember people crying in the streets or anything. One of the things that attracts me to the Cubs is the optimistic nature of a Cubs fan. They're almost hopelessly optimistic. I pray for the Cubs all the time. Everybody prays for the Cubs. Cubs fans are bold. They don't sneak a radio in anywhere. They'd be more like, "How can you not understand the importance of this?"

I'm very homesick now for Chicago. New York is a wonderful place, but you never stop being a Cubs fan. The Internet is the best thing. You can go right on to the site and go out and visit the bars, your neighborhood on the Wrigleyville cams. Murphy's Bleachers, a bar on the opposite corner from Bernie's, has a web cam. I like to look at them.

The Cubs are particularly important at this point in our history in America. Americans really need a hero right now. They really need to be happy between all the terrible things that happened on September 11, and all the unemployment now, and the strife and uncertainty in our country. The Cub fans are both a symbol of yesterday when things were right, and they're also a symbol of optimism and underdog winning. They tell everybody, "Hey, guys, it's gonna be okay because there's always tomorrow."

HOPE – REALITY = BOTTOM LINE

Cindy Perlmutter

Cindy grew up in a northern suburb of Chicago, Lincolnwood, and now lives in Highland Park, Illinois. She's a 52-year-old homemaker who loves the Cubs.

This past season was the first year that I ever realized that the ivy vines changed colors. Who knew? Why would we know?

Nobody in my house was a spectator sports fan. I had to come to this—being a Cubs fan—by myself. I just loved it. The first color TV show I ever saw, in sixth or seventh grade, was a Cubs game. I loved it. Wrigley Field was so beautiful. When I was a little girl, none of my girlfriends were interested in watching a baseball game, so I was a closet fan. They were all day games, usually at one o'clock, so I couldn't come home from school and watch a game because they would usually be over by then. I would pay attention on the news and read the papers to check their standing. My parents just were not interested so there was no one to discuss it with. Every now and then I'd have a boyfriend who was a Cubs fan. It really wasn't until the late sixties, probably my senior year in high school, that I pieced it all together. I could start to watch games—listen to entire games.

The summer of '69 was an amazing summer. I knew every statistic. I knew every player. I knew when pitchers were going to be pulled. In October of that year, I started going to Halloween parties as number eighteen, Glenn Beckert, Cubs second baseman. I was a Glenn Beckert for years. I wore a Cubs jersey and a hat. I came to admiring him first and then I thought he was the cutest of the Cubs.

When Ernie Banks used to be interviewed, he dropped his esses when naming names—Billy Williams became Billy William. He himself became Ernie Bank. It was a riot. Glenn, before he went to San Diego, was such a good second baseman. He rarely erred. He was not the guy who called attention to himself. In my eyes, he was an unsung hero and was such an integral part of the team—Kessinger to Beckert to Banks. And Santo sliding on his stomach and sometimes coming up short. And then we sang "Jose, can you see…?" for Jose Cardenal. Joe Pepitone came. It was so exciting. They were such characters and were so alive for me.

Some time after college, I had a boyfriend who was a huge Cub fan. I remember two or three years really suffering through those opening days because it was so cold, and raining—and people were so happy to be there! I just couldn't believe it. I'd have been happy to watch it on TV—please, I'm wet; my hair is curling. I would never have dated a White Sox fan. I'm real amazed at how nasty the rivalry can be—how nasty it was this past season.

My child's high school friends would call here when the Cubs would start to lose in the playoff games. They had no interest at all in the game and otherwise they don't call, but they just had to call when the Cubs are losing. My son would just say, "I can't talk now." It's the old story. They have two favorite teams: the White Sox and anyone playing the Cubs. It's so strange. This is our city. I just think you should support your city because there aren't so many winners here. I have a brother-in-law who said he was rooting for the Marlins—he'd rather the Marlins would win—and I was shocked. This is an ordinarily really nice guy so I was speechless. It burned me to the core. He's from the northern suburbs—I don't know where these Sox fans come from. I do honestly think that being a Cub fan is like living in Chicago. It builds character. It's not an easy life. The winters can be hard. It's like the Cubs. They're going to break your heart, but it's so much fun on the way.

I don't know that that this is so extreme but, in the spring of '72, there was a pitcher named Milt Pappas. I was in school at Madison. I listened to a game where he came one pitch short of a perfect game. He went down to the bottom of the ninth, and he walked a guy. I was devastated. I had listened to the entire thing on the radio, sitting outside the student union. Most of my friends couldn't understand why you'd listen on the radio—at least on TV you could see some action.

But, it was the most exciting game I had ever listened to. It was so fun. Brickhouse and **Lou Boudreau** were doing the games.

The high point of my being a Cub fan was the 2003 run. I was able to enjoy it with my kids, too. It was a great season. It came from nowhere, and it was so much fun to watch, and they kept getting better and better and better. Being able to share it with my boys. My oldest boy went off to school in August and we talked to each other as we both watched the games. I don't know if he had trouble studying during this or not—he wouldn't tell me that—it wouldn't be politically correct. The Cubs have taken up all my TV viewing time. I could only watch the West Wing on tape. I can finally get back to a regular TV schedule now.

My husband is a good sport, but he's not a Cubs fan. He grew up in New York, so if anything he was a Met fan, certainly not a Yankee fan. He doesn't understand my passion for the Cubs, but he's accepting. Throughout the last couple of series, he wouldn't change the channel so that was a concession—because usually he's quick with the remote control. He would come upstairs to find the game on in every room. God forbid you have to get up. We have speakers in the bathroom in case you have to get up, you can go and not miss anything. I can be roaming the house, and he'd say, "But I thought you were watching the game." I'd say, "I am." You just can't sit still. It's too nerve-wracking. It's too anxiety-provoking. There's nobody I know who sits through and doesn't move. Everybody gets nervous and has to walk around. Then if they start to win, that's when you can't stop doing whatever it was you were doing at that moment.

Sosa is overrated. It's a shame he got caught doing what he was doing—I guess it's a shame he was doing what he was doing! They

In 1942, the Cleveland Indians paid Lou Boudreau $25,000... $5,000 for playing and $20,000 for managing. That ruse allowed the Indians to adequately compensate their best everyday player without upsetting the other players.

Boudreau's daughter, Sharon, was married to Denny McLain for over 30 years.

could get a couple of good players for Sosa. More often than not, he's not coming through in the clutch. He does well throughout the season, but I don't think he's the reason they're there. I wouldn't think anybody else would pick up his hefty contract.

We miss Harry Caray. He was so distinctive and so much fun. I have such fond memories. I've never gotten to meet any of the Cubs over the years. I have always told my kids, "They're going to break your heart, but it so much fun along the way."

I've been absolutely surprised at how much this all meant to me in 2003. I really thought I had been steeled against hope like this. But, then they were amazing, and then it was so much fun—so much fun. I'm really appreciative for the ride. I shared it with everybody.

What am I going to do now? Watch the Bears! I don't think so.

In 1949, Eddie Waitkus was shot by 19-year-old Ruth Ann Steinhagen, a Chicago typist who had constructed a shrine for the player at the foot of her bed. Steinhagen had never spoken to Waitkus, but she became despondent over his trade from the Chicago Cubs to the Philadelphia Phillies. When he returned to Chicago with the Phillies, she was waiting at the Edgewater Beach Hotel, where the team was staying. She left Waitkus a stack of messages to go to her room. He knocked on her door. When she opened it, she told him, "I have a surprise for you." He entered the room. Steinhagen went to the closet, took out a rifle and shot him. She called the front desk and informed the hotel of the shooting. Waitkus recovered and returned to the Phillies' line-up the following season. Steinhagen spent three years in a mental hospital, then disappeared.

MARK BELLHORN CARDS ARE SELLING LIKE HOT CAKES... $2 A STACK

Ruth Banas

Ruth Banas, 37, is a lifelong Cubs fan from Darien, IL. When it comes to the Cubs, Banas keeps her priorities straight...everything else takes a back seat to her Cubbies.

The fans are always more hurt than the players are when the Cubs lose. My parents are both 80. My mom says, "The players are not what they used to be. We used to be able to walk in the day of, get good seats, sit right in front, get there as early as they opened, watch them take batting practices, get autographs, and talk to them. Now security is everywhere and the players don't want to bother with you, but you still cheer for them."

When I got older, we watched every game when I was home from school. The weekends, the TV or the radio was on...I grew up on WGN. My friends would make fun of me and laugh and say, "Don't you know any FM stations?" I don't know music...I know WGN. I grew up on it and that was our life. My friends would make fun of me because one of my favorite players was Ron Cey. They would ask why I cheered for the nobodies and I would say because someone has to. I always liked the guys that were the nobodies. They were important to the team. I loved the non-names more so than the big popular ones. Sammy Sosa is not my favorite player, let me tell you. My husband got me a jersey of Mark Bellhorn and it became a big joke, then he got traded and I cried. My husband said, "I'm going to get you a shirt next year that has Velcro on it and I'm going to get a bunch of letters so every time they change you can cheer for another player." Next, I started cheering for Randall Simon. We were in Wisconsin when he bought the whole section sausages because he was the one that beat up on their sausage. He donated a thousand sausages and they gave them away to a section in the ballpark. So, when the sausage race came up, they announced this and he got a standing ovation. Listening to his interviews, he's such a nice down to earth person. When you saw him beating up the sausage you're thinking, "Great, a guy with an attitude." Then when he made this gesture of buying the Milwaukee fans sausages it was the greatest thing in the world. We actually stayed at the same place the Cubs were staying and it was such a fun time. I was going up and down the elevators chasing them. My mother who is 80 and has only one lung…she was going up and down the elevators with me and then finds out that she's only two doors away from Steve Stone and next to him was Kerry Wood. She's chasing them around the hallway. It was hysterical. I told Steve Stone, "Listen, she can't hurt ya. She can barely walk, but she wants to talk to ya." So, he talked to her for quite a while.

I remember very little from my first time at Wrigley Field. I remember going in and seeing how big it was because on TV it doesn't look that big, per se. It's a ballpark. You're going in, it's really big, all the people seem big as a little kid. It was just fun not necessarily being able to see the ball. I remember seeing batting practice and wondering where the ball went. On TV, you can see the little things. Even today, I get amazed because I can't follow the ball. It's always awe-inspiring. My husband yells at me all the time because I go in with my radio, my binoculars, and my scorecard. We took several couples once and the girls are wanting to talk to me and I tell them, "Ssshh. I'm at a ball game; don't bother me." My husband is doing something with this one, talking to that one and I'm sitting there with my earphones on and my scorecard, which a lot of people don't do any more, and watching the game. I'm really into the game when I'm there. They think I'm crazy.

I learned to keep score from my father. I'm not really good at it, but I try. There's times I'm not really sure what happened so I'll cheat a little bit. Growing up my aunt was a really big fan too. She'll be almost 90 and she's taught me a lot about what to do. Last year we actually went out to Vegas in November and bought $100 of World Series tickets for the Cubs to win. It was right before Dusty Baker signed, so the odds were 25 to 1. My husband put them in for $10 bets and that's what we gave out for Christmas presents. Right before Game 5 they were so excited about making the money. We would have made a total of $2500.

All hell would break loose if the Cubs won the World Series. Not in a bad sense. I know people did bad things when the Bulls won but I don't think they're going to burn things down. I could see people taking time off and having massive celebrations. We went to the first game of the NLCS. It went into extra innings, and Sosa hit that home run in the ninth inning that tied it up. When we left, it was almost 11 o'clock and the people were just in awe that they were there. They were depressed that we lost but the cops were trying to hold people back and wanted the cars to go by. There're thousands of people walking and the cops just shrugged their shoulders and said, "Forget it. Just let them walk." I could just see the fans taking over. Not in a bad sense, but just let them do what they want to do. Not in a bad way, but just let them close the streets, have a good time, and it will continue for days. It would be a big celebration, whether it be small parties at houses or bigger stuff down town at the ball park. It would be a massive thing…it would be celebrated across the United States as well because the Cubs have a big following.

One time we went to see Shakespeare and I took my headset and was trying to listen to a game during the Shakespeare play, but I had bad reception. It was at Navy Pier, I went outside, and three people chased me down to hear what the score was. My husband told me not to do it, but I had no problem with it…I wanted to know what was going on.

EQUAL RITES

I have come to Ernie Banks Day, Billy Williams Day, Ron Santo Day. And then I was at this recent Santo Day, when they retired his number. Ernie Banks came up in '53; Ron Santo came up in '60. When Ron Santo came up, the first series he ever played with the Cubs was an away series in Pittsburgh, and he told us on WGN Radio, it was the first time he was ever in a major league ballpark. He was 20 years old. He was thrilled. After they finished that series in Pittsburgh, they came home to Chicago. The Cubs used to enter the field in the left field corner, so the day he was playing in his first game, he and Ernie were walking together. He starts telling Ernie Banks about how neat it was to be in the ballpark in Pittsburgh, and Ernie Banks says to him—I almost cry when I tell this story—"Wait until you walk on this field." So he walks out and, he couldn't believe it. They asked him what was his greatest memory, and that was it, the first day he stepped on the field at Wrigley.

———MARY JO DOYLE, 64, North Chicago

We have three arches in front of the Second City, the façade of the theater. Actually, it was the façade of the Garrick Theater, designed by Adler and Sullivan. When they tore the Garrick down, we bought the façade, and we literally carried it piece-by-piece in '67 down the street. We had it pieced together so there are three heads on these arches of famous musicians. We put Cub hats on them and the Clement beards.

For years, the Cubs have been asking me to throw out the first ball, and I've never done it. I would get too nervous walking out to throw the ball. I suggested maybe I could do it like Hillary Clinton—from a box seat. They said I could, but I still never did. So, on my birthday a few years ago, they tricked me. We had breakfast at the Stadium Club. I went out on the Cub Circle, the batting box which is right near the Cubs dugout and took a picture with Jim Riggleman, the manager. He gave me a batting order to make out. What I wrote on the lineup was: Phil Cavarretta, Bill Nicholson....

Jack Brickhouse was a good friend. He used to come to Second City all the time, and the kids loved it. We used to do a scene at Second City of everybody imitating Harry Caray—everybody does Harry Caray. Over the years, Chris Farley did the very best....

My brother had a restaurant in the suburbs of Chicago, and he used to pay the ball players to come out and do an interview. He'd send a limo for them to get back and forth. Pete Rose was the only one who refused to sign autographs for the kids, and I thought that was really rotten. He was very tacky, wearing polyester, perspiring.

———**JOYCE SLOAN**, 73, Producer Emeritus of the renowned Second City

Margie McCartney (left)

We sang "God Bless America" and the "The Star-Spangled Banner" on September 14, 2003 at Wrigley, and Dusty Baker came out and shook our hand. I called Dusty Baker and left a voice message on his phone, later that month, to see if he could speak at a business event I'm putting together next year at Soldier Field. Fifteen minutes later, Dusty Baker himself called back.

I was heartbroken in 2003. Watching the Marlins come into Wrigley Field and beat the Cubs was like watching the Germans march down the Champs Elysees in Paris. Whoever said there's no crying in baseball wasn't sitting in my section. Did you know that the Astros have never won a post-season series and the Marlins have never lost one? During Game 6, when Prior was pitching and the kid interfered with the ball and it was all tied up, I turned to my nephew and I told him, "It's going to be all right. We're going to win this game, Charlie." Then I went to the bathroom and when I came back, they had a big '8' on the scoreboard. And I just thought, "How did this happen? How did this happen?" I had a big sign during Game 6 that said: BRING ON THE AMERICAN LEAGUE. The final night when Wood pitched, we had Wood's three-run-homer and Alou's two-run homer. Then I went to the bathroom, and when I came back the Marlins had scored three. My section told me that I couldn't go to the bathroom anymore.

———MARGIE MCCARTNEY, 42, Chicago

I used to like Bill Buckner. We called him "Hollywood" every time he came up to bat because we could yell at him from our fifth-row seats. He was so full of himself. He was a great player, but he was also one of those guys who knew how handsome he was.

My brother and girlfriend and I followed the Cubs to St. Louis on a five-game road trip. We stayed in the same hotel, and I can't remember how Buckner blew the game, but he blew the game single handedly. The next morning, we were sitting in the coffee shop having coffee and he sat down in a booth that was back-to-back with our booth. He turned around and asked if he could have my newspaper. I was finished with it and had set it on the table. I said, "Yes, you can have it, but you're not going to want to read what's in it." I was snotty back to him which made me feel a little bit better. I wouldn't go as far as to say I had a crush on him, only that he was cute, and I was twenty-one years old. It was the time I might have paid attention to that.

———CISSY GREENSPAN, 48, Ex-Chicago Board of Trade, Homemaker

One thing the Cubs do not do is provide any outdoor toilets. There are all these people who come hours early and stand out in front on Waveland Avenue there and try and catch the fly balls that are hit out, and the groupies are trying to get in to see the Cubs and all the little kids are milling around trying to get autographs. Sooner or later, somebody has to go to the bathroom. Inevitably, and Chicago has alleys, they all sneak up the alley and go to the bathroom behind your house. You can see them. They're right out there. My friends and I used to make sport of terrorizing the other Cubs fans. We would wait until they were already going to the bathroom, and we had a loud speaker answering system, and we'd turn it on and start yelling at them. The baseball bars play really loud music at night and it will keep you up. The Cubs fans would be reveling and be making a lot of noise and you'd get really mad at them and do crazy things to them—like shoot bottle rockets at them from your balcony! Of course, it was all in the spirit of fun. You live there because you're a Cubs fan, and it's the only place to be. It's like moving next door to

Bob Dylan—just to be there—just to be that close to Wrigley Field. You felt it rub off on you.

——RAINY HORVATH, 54, Quincy, Illinois Native

When I was out of town just recently in Florida, the people were very nice, but it was the traffic, and learning a whole new system. When I get to Wrigley, I know which door I go into. Wrigley changed completely when the *Tribune* bought the club. My feelings about Wrigley are now—yes it's home and it's a wonderfully marketed place. I respect what John McDonough in Marketing has done because Wrigley was just a *nice* ballpark before. Now it's a hallowed hall— and it should be. When the *Tribune* bought it, they hired people to make this a business. The neighborhood around it changed. At one time, when I first started going, it was a nice neighborhood. Then it went through years of deterioration, and it was not a nice, safe neighborhood. Then it hit its stride, and now property is very valuable in the area. It's a whole party atmosphere that has a different face than it used to.

That's how it was recently for the playoffs. With the success of the Cubs, they gained temporary fans, not the die-hards who continued the game and the team. When it was sold and they did renovations, the Tribune Company built the Stadium Club. They took one corner, and with leading restaurants, have a private-club for season ticket holders. If you're a season ticket holder, and you pay five hundred dollars—it was less initially—you pay a surcharge and it's a meeting place. For me, before every game, I go to the Stadium Club, and I hang out with the same people all the time. At the end of the game when people are milling in the street, I go to the Stadium Club. With or without a cocktail, with or without food—it's a bar and restaurant—it's really very, very comfortable.

——CAROL HADDON, 56, Glencoe, Illinois

…It didn't take long on Waveland to find out what had happened, there were TVs everywhere. Once everything started to go wrong, it became dead silent, it was almost eerie. Since the day after Game 7, I have had a blue and a red band on my right wrist where it will stay until the first pitch of 2004. It was a great season, a little more exciting than some before, but no matter the outcome one thing is always the same: Cubs fans will be Cubs fans, there are no greater fans in the history of sports.

I still remember the days of Dunston, Sandberg, and Grace… even earlier, when we never really expected to go to the post-season. I loved the Cubs then, I still love them now, Arizona isn't so far away.

——AMANDA JUNTUNEN, Lafayette, Indiana

In 2002 I had box seats to the Cubs-Cardinals game the day Darryl Kile died. There was a couple, Jackie and John from St. Louis, who had never been to Wrigley Field. They were sitting next to us, and we were waiting for the game to start, waiting for the game to start… Then people starting talking on their cell phones, and the lady behind me said, "One of the pitchers on St. Louis died." I turned to the couple from St. Louis and said, "What are you going to do today?" They didn't know. So I told them, "I've got a balcony, I've got a grill. Let's have a party!" So they came home with me and we had a party and we've been friends ever since. I hate it when I see fighting in the stands. I try to always buy the person next to me a beer, because when people leave I want them to leave Chicago saying, "Wow! The people from Chicago sure are nice."

——MARGIE MCCARTNEY, 42, Chicago

For me, the Cubs are all about spending time with my father at Wrigley Field. We had season tickets, so in the summer whenever we were going, I would say, "Daddy, do you want to go?" If the weather was OK, not too hot, he would go. We'd get the tickets at will call. He'd come and he'd sit with us, and we would sit in the fresh air. He would watch the people go by, watch the game somewhat…It was more about the experience of just sitting out there with him. He would share hot dogs with my husband, and a cold drink. Comment on this person walking by. Watch the game a little bit. And this went on for many, many summers until recently, when he wasn't well enough to go anymore. This was something we shared with him every summer. The summer 2003 was hard because he died that February. When I looked at the empty seat we had because he was gone, I really missed those days. It was something that was easy for everybody and fun.

When Atlanta played the Marlins in 2003, we were down in Florida and went to a game. This kid in front of us heard us talking about the Cubs, turned around and said, "You're from Chicago? Have you ever been to Wrigley Field?" And I said, "Sure! We go there all the time." And he said, "I've got to tell you, my dad said he would take me anywhere in the world for my 21st birthday. I'm going to Wrigley Field."

I hope Wrigley Field doesn't change. It would be a major loss to the city. Make some improvements, but don't bring it up to the 21st century. We're OK without the big screen TVs. Keep the ivy and the 85-year-old ushers. It has its own reputation. The best part of being a Cubs fan is that your expectations are not terrific. If they win, it's a plus…2003 was such a high, no one thought they would do what they did, and by the time the Marlins series came around, we all thought: maybe, maybe they could pull it out. I think the place is cursed; I really believe that. But I hope they don't change it at all.

In 1973, we lived in a housing complex out in Buffalo Grove. This was before free agency. At that time, about ten of the Cubs were living in this same complex. Rick Monday was there, and both Reuschels. I was pregnant and was walking down the hall one day. Both Reuschels—if you remember both Rick and his brother were very large—came in carrying cases of beer. I could hardly get by the two of them…We had a fellow living next door whose name was Herb Hutson. He was a pitcher called up by the Cubs. He had his entire belongings in a 5x8 trailer. He had a little girl. He had a wife. Anyway, he got called up by the Cubs… This is typical of all good Cubs players: his record was 0-2. He finished by tripping over first base and breaking his toe. I later met Randy Hundley, who was his catcher. I mentioned something to Hundley and he didn't remember anything about him.

———JUDY SMOLLER, 58, Chicago

The band, Pearl Jam, was originally named Mookie Blaylock, after the NBA player, and they recorded their first album, *Ten* under that name. In 1992, the band Mookie Blaylock changed their name to Pearl Jam after a hallucinogenic concoction made by lead singer Eddie Vedder's great-grandmother, Pearl.

Chapter 8

It's Bad Luck to be Superstitious

Broken Mirrors, Broken Bats and Broken Dreams

THERE ARE TWO WAYS TO GET RICH IN LOCAL SPORTS TV: MARRY A RICH GIRL OR WORK HARD FOR 30 YEARS AND THEN MARRY A RICH GIRL

Tom Robison

Tom Robison, 52, grew up in Skokie, Illinois and now lives in Evanston, Illinois. He has been a TV news producer at WLS-TV in Chicago for many years. The ten years he worked in sports TV, Robison considers the best ten years in Chicago sports history.

Growing up, I remember watching Ernie Banks hit his five hundred fourteenth home run on TV and listening to Jack Brickhouse. It was such a kick to work at a Chicago TV station because the station where I worked had that play on tape, and I could watch it over and over again. I did a lot of that this year.

Whenever the Cubs get close, or are in it and have a chance for some type of post-season success, we trot out all the old stuff to do stories on them. It's a good excuse to go back and look at all that good stuff. Especially in 2003, it was really fun going back, even all the way back to 1907-08. We had short clips from then and we had the old pictures of Three-Finger Brown. Three-Finger Brown was a pitcher on the 1908 team. The Chicago Historical Society has an exhibit with a lot of the old pictures. You have to go so far back to find some good stories—in my lifetime, there isn't anything that is a good memory. We did pieces where you go back to every year, and every year ended with this great disappointment—so all your *great* memories are disappointments.

After college, I bounced around some small towns in the Midwest. The Cubs were always my team. In '84, I was working at Channel 7, and I remember the fifth game of that playoff. At that time, it was one of the biggest sports days in Chicago history. The same day, **Walter Payton** was going to break Jim Brown's record. We had these elaborate plans to cover both events, which was really exciting. The convergence of these two major events on the same day was really hard to believe. Going in, we thought that Payton's going to break Jim Brown's record and the Cubs are going to beat the Padres and go to the World Series. It was going to be spectacular. But, it didn't exactly work out that way. Payton did break Jim Brown's record against the Saints, so at least that worked out. Nobody ever speaks of the Bears having a curse.

In the '84 playoffs, the Cubs had won the first two games, and it was pretty comparable to Mark Prior and Kerry Wood in the 2003 NLCS. We had our best pitcher going. Everybody was confident they were going to do it. The Cubs had won two, and the Padres had won two, and this game was on Sunday, and everybody was very confident about our chances. We did an hour show that night, and the show's focus was to have been a celebration of everything. That went out the window. It was just too bad because we had this really terrible ending of the Cubs, and yet Walter Payton broke Jim Brown's record. We had Payton in the studio and had **Jim Brown** live in LA—two football greats talking, and a great event. But then we had the Cubs loss to deal with, so it was just so excruciatingly painful to do that.

When the corked-bat incident happened with Sosa, people weren't surprised. It wasn't like, "Oh, geez, how can this be?" Sosa got hit in

In the last 30 years, the record for the most touchdown passes thrown by a non-quarterback is held by Walter Payton, with eight. In football pileups, Walter Payton used to lie at the bottom and untie his opponents' shoelaces. That's why a lot of defenders put tape over their laces.

The only person to score back-to-back fifty-point games in the history of Long Island High School basketball is Jim Brown, the NFL legend.

the head, and the feeling was that he wasn't the same afterward. His bat wasn't as quick, or he wasn't the same guy after that. When it happened, I wasn't mad about it. I was not surprised. Knowing how competitive he is, I'm not surprised that he may have done this. I actually believe his explanation that this was like a batting-practice bat, because he does make a point of making a big show at batting practice—putting balls out of the ballpark. It's unlikely, but he does do that, and it could be. That could be true.

I'm a contrarian, and because everybody thought they were going to lose, I thought, *They're going to win.* Thinking they were going to lose was a more typical Cub fan reaction, but I personally really thought they were going to win.

When the Cubs lost, I was honestly stunned by it. I felt bad. Oddly enough, I can't really convince my family to be fans. My kids are eight and eleven, and you want to get them excited about it, but the games were at the kids' bedtimes and they had school. My wife tolerates my devotion to the Cubs.

I was so angry at the last out and immediately turned off the TV and went downstairs and jumped into bed and stared at the ceiling for about two hours. That sounds miserable, and it was.

The next day, I just dreaded having to put the story together—to write the headlines and just the idea of having to retell the story. I felt so bad about it, and I didn't want to go back through the curses and the loss. At our TV station, there are a lot of out-of-towners, and there weren't that many people really invested in the Cubs.

A lot of the Cub fans do put on the cynic suits, but, deep down, everybody really, really, really wants them to win. I cannot tell you how deflated everybody was after the playoffs.

VOODOO YOU THINK YOU ARE?

In 2002, they had the Wrigley Field Experience, and I was one of nineteen winners. I was on the field. My son had two inside-the-park home runs; they had the pitching thing there. I couldn't do anything because I'm handicapped. I touched the ivy. I walked around the bases. This was in September. My son got married in November. Guess what? That was more important than his wedding, and that says a lot. To me, that is the highlight.

I have a button at home that says: "New Team. Old Results." Before I went to Game 6 of the NCLS, in 2003, I said, "Uh-oh. Should I take it out?" And then I said, "No. I'm going to take all my positive ones out." I was outside, really doing good, until the crash of the eighth inning, and I swore on the bus, I said, "I'm never going to do this again. I'm never going to come to another Cubs game." I went back for Game 7, when the Marlins clinched and went on to the World Series and won the championship that should have been the Cubs. Once a Cub fan—always a Cub fan.

In 2003, I tried to be reserved. But I was real excited at Game 6, and I was so angry. Of course, I said I was never going to come to another Cub game. I've probably said that a thousand times or more. The problem with Wrigley is that a lot of people are not true fans that are inside there. People like myself, who are true fans, we couldn't afford it. Face value, even, for the tickets is ridiculous. I believe it has become more of a business than it is for the fans: I shouldn't say this, but I am. Right now, at this point, it isn't fan-friendly. It is for the VIPs—well, yeah, they're fair-weather fans, they're on the bandwagon now, they've got tickets. Somebody gave 'em to 'em. Then take people like me, who really want to go inside and can't, because I'm a true fan, it makes it hard. I personally feel that they *blew* the game in Florida *deliberately* to come back and play here. That's just my personal feeling. This is big business. You don't have the fun, the excitement that you used to.

———TRUDY ACHEATEL, 58, Chicago

You have to be superstitious! They've lost for so many years that if they start to do something right, you have to help them. The last two games we won, my husband, Jack, was out walking the dog when the Cubs first started scoring. When he came back, I said, "You have to leave again." He looked at me like I had lost my mind. To the best of my knowledge he did that for me, but I had to keep walking the rest of the house—I couldn't stand still then. Sometimes you can't watch, but you stay within earshot or eyeshot. If you're organizing a cabinet and they start to do good, you have to clean every closet then. Whatever it is, you have to keep doing. They didn't win, so I have to conclude that not everybody was helping—not doing their part. There would have to have been some naysayers. Right this second, I have a very clean house.

Game 6 of the 2003 NLCS was the worst moment in my Cub history. There was such hope. You just have to think, 'That's how they are." Even when the kid touched the ball, I was still optimistic—until the wild pitch, until Prior couldn't hold it together—and then I knew.

After the game, I couldn't go to sleep. I talked to all my Cub-fan friends. I tried to be optimistic. I tried to say, "But, we have another game. It's okay." Most of them were saying, "That's it. It's over. They're done. If they didn't win tonight, they're never going to win." All day, I was talking to my women friends, checking in with everybody, discussing everything—every play, every pitch, unbelievable. It was so much fun. Game 7 was anti-climatic. I had hopes for Kerry Wood, that he could carry it off, but no. No! No! It was really sad. These upstarts! Twice in seven years.

———CINDY PERLMUTTER, 52, Highland Park Homemaker

I'm a mathematician, so I have a rather rational mind—sometimes it conflicts with being a Cub fan. My friend sent me an e-mail the night after Game 6 of the 2003 series against the Marlins. He wrote, "Today, October 14, 2003, the Red Sox were beaten by the Yankees, but the Cubs were beaten by a curse. Is the result of tomorrow's Cubs game a foregone conclusion? Signed, Bob." I wrote him back and said, "Bob, I'm a scientist. I don't believe in curses—except this one." I read an ad one time that expressed my sentiments perfectly going into Game 7. It said, "All Cubs fans have seen this movie before. We know how it's going to end." We went into Game 7, and I thought, "We've got one of the top pitchers in the game going, the game's at home, the players have had 24 hours to recuperate from the heartbreaking Game 6 loss, and the newspaper has them listed as 5-2 favorites—a seventy percent change of winning, roughly speaking. If you're rational, you think the Cubs are probably going to win. Going into the sixth game, most fans thought, *Okay, so we lost to Josh Beckett on Sunday in Game 5—Cubs just got shut down.* There's nothing you can do about that, but they should win in Game 6 and 7. So you go into Game 6 with Prior pitching and everyone thought, *This is our year, the Cubs are going to win.* Well, then in the eighth inning, everything changed. Somehow you knew in your soul, in your heart, that it just wasn't going to happen. What were the odds that the Marlins would end up winning it all?

———JIM FILL, Math Professor at Johns Hopkins University

I went to one of the 2003 Cubs-Braves playoff games. We paid four hundred each for the tickets from a ticket broker. Mark Prior won Game 3 against the Braves, and that was heavenly. After the game, I got to go on the field. I scooped up some grass from the warning track, and my buddy clipped some ivy, and he's trying to grow it—down in Texas. I have the dirt in a cup setting here next to my Sosa-autographed baseball. I'm taking care of that dirt. Everybody knows what it is. It's up high where the kids can't reach it, and I've already sprinkled some on my son's bed. While he was in bed, I sprinkled some on his head and his pillow and his bed. I was telling him a good-night story, and I said, "Here's the really special part of this good-night story." I pulled out the dirt, and I explained to him what it was, and he was very happy that I was sprinkling it on him. He was three at the time.

As soon as the fan, Steve Bartman, touched the ball, I started shaking my head and said, "That's not good. I can't believe we just gave them another out." Then when the next pitch was ball four and went through the catcher's legs for a wild pitch to get first and third and bring Rodriguez up, I went, "Oh s——, here we go." I sat there in stunned disbelief, watching them tie it at 3–3, watching it go 8-3. I was lying down on my couch and didn't even watch the last inning and a half. I was lying there with my face buried in the pillows on the couch. It happened so fast. I was hopeful for Game 7, but at that point—I knew. I have not spoken to my father since Game 5. He has said hello through my mother a few times when she has called, but I have not spoken to him. I was on the phone in constant communication prior to the collapse with good friends from Chicago, Cub fans, who live in California and Texas, Florida, Philadelphia, Virginia. We call each other during games back and forth, back and forth. I had talked to a few of them during the early parts of Game 6. We had been e-mailing about the Cubs for two weeks before, but I haven't spoken to a soul since the fan tipped that ball.

——JIM DEMARET, raised on the North Side until the age of six

Cubs fans expect things to go wrong. They really do. There were so many stories about "the curse" and the "goat of Wrigley Field" that by the middle of the last week of the 2003 season, I couldn't take it anymore. It's annoying to me. People in town who have only experienced the playoffs once or twice grab onto this. The goat is a creation of a guy named Sam Sianis, who runs The Billy Goat Tavern. It's really his doing just to keep it going. Every time he brings the goat out, it's like he opens another restaurant.

I'm not superstitious and don't believe in any of that. But you have to give it its due. They were up 3-1, and they lost three in a row, with Mark Prior and Kerry Wood pitching. I'm not superstitious, but that's just hard to believe. It's stunning.

Under normal circumstances, working and covering the team gets to be routine and you don't really think about it. But this year was a really special time. I was surprised, after having casually watched it these past few years, the amount of baseball I've watched in 2003. Now there's just an empty feeling. It wasn't really a young team that's going to come back and do it again. We do have young pitchers, but they don't really have a core of young players so that we can think they are going to do it every year. I'm surprised at how deflated I am, thinking, *Oh gosh, this isn't going to happen for a while again.* I'm sorry it's over. I just wanted it to keep going.

——TOM ROBISON, 52, TV news producer, WLS-TV, Chicago

There is divine retribution. I went to a 1989 Cubs-Giants playoff game. It was during the High Holidays, I forget which one. I went, and I was taught my lesson for going 'cause the Cubs were killed.

Ordinarily I would say that I am not superstitious, but after things like that and certainly after 2003, you have to wonder. I vowed to myself that I would do nothing whatsoever to acknowledge the fact that the Cubs might end up going to the World Series—not alter anything I did because of it 'cause it would jinx it. But, I made a mistake. The mistake was because I was thinking ahead about possibly going to Chicago for a World Series game. I knew it would be on Tuesday, Wednesday and Thursday. I purposely scheduled patients around those days, just in case I would have to cancel in order to go to the game. As far as I can remember, that's the only thing I did to acknowledge that this was a possibility—and it was clearly too much! So, I blame myself. It's as much my fault as Steve Bartman's.

These things affect people's lives even beyond their sports lives. For me there's a certain discomfort about the Cubs winning. I'm so used to their being a losing team, that it fits in well with my perception of life and how things are supposed to progress in life. I don't identify myself with them as being a loser, it's just that the Cubs, as losers, are just the way the world is supposed to be. It's uncomfortable for me when the Cubs win. It's more expected and comfortable when they lose. Of course, clearly, I do not want them to lose, so I am talking about psychologically. I wouldn't disagree that it's like an abused person who is habituated to loss and sticks with it. I look at what they do.

In my mind, it's not for lack of trying. Cincinnati doesn't try. They don't put out the money to win. But, the Cubs try. They're not being cheap. They've bought the players. They do what they're supposed to do. Their payroll is somewhere in the upper twenty five percent of the league, around eighth or tenth.

It would be interesting to know if Chicago Cubs fans have a lower divorce rate than other people because of their tolerance.

———**DR. ROBERT WACHS**, Palo Alto, California

The 2003 NLCS may be the new all-time worst Cubs fan experience. I, and a lot of other Cub fans, was trying to keep our emotions in check all season long. You just try not to get too excited—just wait. I watched the Braves series at the Bellagio in Las Vegas with an old friend who was also a Cubs fan. We were only there for three days, and we watched the masterful job Kerry Wood did in the first game, and then we suddenly started to think, *maybe they've got the toughness to make it this year.*

And then a few days later, Game 6 of the NLCS, I was sitting after work in my office watching, and in the seventh inning, they score a couple of runs. I call my parents in Indiana and, of course, they're glued to the television set. My father was not a baseball fan for his entire life, and then when he retired, he became an *enormous* Cubs fan. He scheduled his time around Cubs games. He naps before them to make sure he's fresh for the game. He said, "You know, I don't want to jinx this, but I think they look pretty good this year." and we were in agreement—there was something magical about this. But then there was still this, "I don't want to jinx this. I'm off the phone."

And then the whole thing just went down the crapper. When that kid prevented Alou from catching that ball, suddenly there's this emotional tremor that rolled over me. A moment later, when Gonzalcz kickcd that double play grounder, I became awash in that "Oh, no" feeling. It's like the collective negativity of millions of Cubs fans has just coalesced and dropped on your shoulders. I absolutely knew at that point—this is over! I wanted to turn the TV off at that point, because there was not a hint of doubt in my mind that that game was lost. And I absolutely thought they were going to lose Game 7.

I was telling my friends, "I've got to get on one of these online betting services. I've got to put down $200 on the Marlins, because I flat-out guarantee you there isn't a prayer the Cubs can win this." That's how certain I was. I couldn't do it, because there was some sort of 24-hour waiting period. Now, what about the ethics of being a Cubs fan? Here was my thinking, "I'm doing them a favor, because if I go online and bet against them, it may be their best chance to win. I'm going to cover my base emotionally. If I lose $200, that will be the happiest $200 loss of my life. I would be happy to give that for my Cubs to win the pennant. But the Marlins were giving two-to-one odds…

I pray to a higher power up there for the Cubs, "Give 'em a break. Give the deserving fans a break. Cubs fans deserve this. I mean, wouldn't it just be easier to say, "Aw, the heck with it," but I would never consider that for a millisecond.

—JACK WIERS, long-suffering Cubs fan

I sometimes have superstitions about the Cubs with my clothing. Each year my husband buys me something different. I find that the one hat I didn't win with so I got rid of it and he got me a new hat. They won the first couple of games so I thought I could continue wearing the new hat. The jersey, if they've lost a couple of games while I was there while I wore that jersey, I won't wear it any more to a game. I got Cubs socks last year and those were winning socks so we keep wearing those when we go to games. We're in with a group of season ticket holders and we go to about seven or eight games a year. Depending on the weather, I have to wear certain things. Each year we go through the same thing. If I'm at the first couple of games and they lose, we change our outfit totally and wear different Cubs things. I probably have eight or nine shirts now that I can play with. This is really silly, but during the National League Championships when I was wearing Cubs gear, they won. The one day I didn't have it on, they lost. So one day they were playing later on a Sunday night and I already had on my pajamas, but I had my Cubs hat on.

——RUTH BANAS, 37, lifelong Cubs fan from Darien, IL

People say the curse is one thing, but we could easily blow out the Curse. And here's why: all it takes is one guy. The best acquisition the Cubs have made since I can remember. That's Dusty Baker. First place or second in the National League West for ten years in a row. To bring that attitude over and say, "Why not us?" It's huge. To be five outs away from the World Series, this is without us going out and pulling a New York Yankees, or Atlanta Braves, or New York Mets, or anyone who spent that extra money to get over the hump. Unfortunately, our ownership has never been the type to go out and spend the extra money. One of the interesting things that I heard Jim Hendry say in 2003, "With all this extra playoff money this year, we're going to be able to afford an extra 10-15 million on the payroll next year." Well, that remains to be seen.

But I'll tell you what coming up short did this year...It instilled belief: this city deserves a winner. We're way too close to be able to just throw it away. Dusty Baker isn't going to let that happen, number one. Number two, the city isn't going to let that happen, knowing that we didn't really go the extra mile and bring in Pudge Rodriguez, or Gary Sheffield, that extra 10-million-dollar-a-year guy to get us over the hump. We made some smart business acquisitions, and a lot of them were Tribune-type lightning in the bottle acquisitions. We had a closer in Joe Borowski who somehow just got guys out with guts and savvy, not with Mariano Rivera-type stuff.

It's the pressure that's put on the players by the organizations and the media that would have you believe a curse is in order. But the truth is that the organization has never gone out and spent the extra money above and beyond what they went into the year wanting to spend in order to get them over the hump. They may go out and spend a few million to get a Kenny Lofton, or a Randall Simon, but we didn't want to make the killer deal to knock your socks off and go get Juan Gonzalez, or Randy Johnson a couple of years ago… That guy who is going to get you over the hump. We're closer to getting to the Promised Land thanks to Dusty Baker and where he took the team this year. No, I don't believe in curses. The product of your environment and the pressure put upon yourself as a ballplayer and by the media and by other people outside of the organization will lead you to believe there's a curse, but I don't believe there's a curse.

——**DAVID LEWIS**, Owner, Actors Center of Chicago

My friend, Rick, got standing room only tickets to the 1998 playoff game against Atlanta. We were standing on the foul line down left field, so for standing room only, it's the best you can do, because there isn't any obstruction. We were overlooking Waveland Avenue and there's a gate down there that you can only exit; you can't enter. The next day at nine or ten o'clock at night, I'm coming back from the grocery store, riding my bike down Waveland Avenue and I'm going towards the lake. A black cat crosses in front of me and enters through that revolving door gate that we were standing above. There's a full moon to boot. If you know anything about Cubs history, there was a black cat that came out on the field in 1969.

——**JIM "BOO" BRADLEY**, University of Iowa Grad

Chapter 9

Cubbiepalooza

NOW, HERE'S OZZY OSBOURNE FOR THE SEVENTH INNING RETCH

Joe Rios

Joe Rios has the enviable job of coordinating singers for the Cubs' famous seventh-inning "Take Me Out to the Ball Game" tradition. On June 5, 2001, Jack Buck gave a rendition that both Cub and Cardinal fans loved. There's a great photo of Buck singing at Wrigley in the color picture section of this book. Also, the Cardinals play the video of Buck singing at Wrigley during the seventh inning stretch at Busch Stadium. See the appendix of this book for a roster of all the Wrigley Field "singers."

Every aspect of Wrigley Field has its purpose and, in 1998, the singing became a new thing of Wrigley Field. Fans really like this new tradition. You'll hear them say things like "Yeah, I went to the game where Sammy hit his thirty-fifth home run, and by the way Ozzie Smith was singing. It was really cool." They won't remember necessarily whether we won or lost or who pitched, but they remember that Joe Mantegna, a Chicago native, sang on the day of the twenty-strikeout game and that was pretty cool.

We wanted Jack Buck to sing "Take Me Out to the Ball Game" because, he's a legendary broadcaster. He came out and he had the red blazer on. I gave him a hat. I was trying to explain to him exactly what was going on. He said, "Joe, don't worry about it. I've got a good routine down. I know what's going on." It was just amazing that I got the opportunity to sit with him for five or ten minutes and just talk with him. I wasn't around for all his great calls, but his mind was absolutely perfect, in good working order—it was just this disease that he had that was just so—you'd think he'd be down, but he was very happy. When he went out and did that, it blew us all away. It was the greatest thing. We had no idea that the *SportsCenter* would be picking it up that night and they showed it for a couple of days. I saw that he had two hats and just thought I would let him do what he wanted to do. He's Jack Buck. I wasn't about to tell him no. We love it when Bob Uecker sings. He always says, "Root, root, root for the Brewers." Harry Kalas says "the Cubbies," but he's got an agenda behind that because every time he sings, and he says "Cubbies," the Phillies win. He gets a lot of guff from the clubhouse guys, but when he sang, if you noticed, the Phillies players all stood up and just folded their arms and looked up at him to see if he'd say "Phillies" or "Cubbies," and he said, "Cubbies" again and, lo and behold, the Phillies won.

We always give the guest conductor a Cubs cap that has a little engraving on the side that says the year, and 7th inning stretch. It's up to them if they want to wear it or throw it out. We get eighty-one caps made each year. You can't know sizes of who is going to sing so we can't get fitted caps. The cap Jack wore was a fitted cap though. Jack brought the Cardinal cap with him.

We don't have a big Jumbotron so not everybody could see what Jack was wearing. We put the name up and everybody knew it was the legendary Jack Buck when he started singing. He starts off by saying something like "This is the greatest rivalry in sports—the Cubs and the Cards." Then he started singing, wearing a Cubs cap. Halfway through the song he takes off the hat and puts on the Cardinal hat. At the point where you're supposed to say, "root, root, root for the Cubs," he said "… for the Cardinals." That place went wild. We loved it. He has that old-time baseball voice that was just perfect. And then he sat and talked to our broadcasters for a while.

Unfortunately, we didn't have the opportunity to have him do a repeat performance. Stan Musial did it here in 1998 with his harmonica, and he also did it in 2002. We always ask whoever's retiring that year to do it, and we've asked McGwire. We asked Cal Ripken and Tony Gwynn. Maybe after a couple of years, after they're out of the limelight, they'll come back. I was pretty impressed that Carlton Fisk did it, even though he played on the South Side for the White Sox. It's hard to say who has been the best we had. Vin Scully did it and he was wonderful. Our organist feels he's the very best of all time including professional singers.

I don't know how thrilled Mike Ditka is about doing it. He doesn't like to be considered a bad singer. In 2002 he was gonna throw a "Millie Vanilli." He brought in a ringer—the lounge singer at his restaurant who sings Frank Sinatra-style—he wanted him to come out and hide behind the broadcast booth and Mike Ditka would lip sync it without his voice coming through. I said, "You know what—I can't have you do that. People really want to hear you." It would have been super funny, but we finally convinced him to do a duet with his guy so he did that. He did keep it down and let the other guy sing out…. We've had a couple of athletes that were just horrible, absolutely horrible, Nancy Kerrigan comes to mind, she was just horrible, and another ice skater, Nicole Bobeck was absolutely horrible. Looking at some of the baseball players, to tell you the truth a lot of the baseball players sang pretty well—Andre Dawson, Andy Pafko, Bill Buckner sang well. Billy Williams did great. Bruce Sutter did great. **Ernie Banks** always has a great time with it. We had Jody Davis came on, and he didn't sing that well. Ozzie Smith sang very well, Paul Molitor.

For the most part, the baseball players all sang very well. We had the coolest one the other day, Vance Law and his father, Vernon Law. For the first time we had the guest conductor for "Take Me Out to the Ball Game" also sing the National Anthem. It was just incredible. They have the greatest voices. Vance is head baseball coach at BYU and Vernon has just retired. It's just amazing that we have these two guys, former big league players, who sang both songs. Only Wayne Messmer has sung both songs here for us…Susan Hawk was a character on *Survivor*, and she was absolutely horrible…We had some hockey players who were pretty bad. Chris Chelios has gotten much better as the years go by. He's sung it four or five times. Brian Urlacher, the Bears linebacker, he's just absolutely horrible. We had Dan Hampton, who just went into the Hall of Fame, do it.

Ernie Banks and O. J. Simpson are cousins.
Their grandfathers were twin brothers.

WISCONSIN: COME SMELL OUR DAIRY AIR

Mike Haupert

After growing up in Dubuque, Iowa, Mike Haupert graduated from Washington University in St. Louis. He is now a Professor of Economics at the University of Wisconsin-La Crosse.

When I was 12, I went with my dad and two of my cousins for my first trip to Wrigley Field. We were just underneath the overhang of the grandstand. We were behind first base. We were talking about getting a foul ball. I remember my cousin pounding his glove and saying, "If they hit one right here, I'm going to reach out and grab it." All of a sudden we hear this loud *whap* and something landed in his glove. We turned and couldn't believe he had a ball, and then we find out somebody from the upper deck had thrown a donut down.

We were about four hours by car from Wrigley Field. It was a "once in a few years" event. We got cable TV in the early '70s and WGN played all the day games then. I would come home and watch the last three or four innings every day. There were no White Sox fans: either you were a Cubs or Cardinals fan. The Twins were relative newcomers. They had moved into the geographic area only recently, in 1961. Either you had cable and watched the Cubs, or your parents grew up with the Cardinals.

People love the Cubs so much that they're just like being human, you try, you give your best, you're heroic, sometimes you succeed, you get this close to your ultimate goal, and then in the end you fail. That's just life. That's what happens to all of us. Then you find out that nobody can identify with the Yankees, because nobody lives like the Yankees. They win all the time; whenever they want something they buy it. Lots of people *root* for the Yankees, but not many people *identify* with the Yankees.

The Cubs really can't afford to buy better players. They already sell out the stadium on the average day. They approach three million. They routinely draw lots of people, so how much money could they possibly make by spending $20 million on Alex Rodriguez. They could never recoup that investment. The Cubs don't need to spend the money. The fans like the team and the fans have shown that they don't need a winner. The Brewers are the complete opposite. The Brewers are terrible and nobody goes there, even though the new stadium is beautiful. People went the first year to see a bad team in a new stadium; now they probably won't go back again until the Brewers get good again. Fenway Park and Wrigley Field are interesting because they are two parks that you probably wouldn't be able to draw more fans if you replaced them, even if you added capacity. If they tore them down, they could never build a new stadium in the same place. There's not enough room. The Cubs would have to move out to the suburbs. Really important to the new stadiums are the luxury boxes that rent for one hundred fifty to two hundred thousand dollars a year. Now the Cubs' problem is that if they move into a new stadium, they're going to *have* to field a winning team to draw as many people as they draw to Wrigley as it already is. There's a lot of risk there: I don't think it's a good business decision. In economic parlance, we say that if they don't demand a winner, don't give them one. Year in, year out, we find that what the fans really like is watching the Cubs at Wrigley Field—not winning. The marginal Cubs fans like to hop on the bandwagon and see a winning team. But a large base of people come whether they win or whether they lose. The people at the *Chicago Tribune* realize that. They're smart people. I should say I don't demand a winner either: I support the Cubs regardless. I have to admit that if I were an owner, I probably don't spend the money to appease the fan who says, "Here's my twenty dollars. I would like a winner, but here's my money anyway."

The Cubs don't sign a lot free agents. Except for middle-of-the-road guys like Mike Remlinger and Dave Veres who weren't going to go anywhere else anyway. Sammy Sosa is very well paid, so he's happy where he is. A lot of the other players are younger and haven't had a chance to leave yet. Some guys came over in trades in the summer of 2003, so they're still under contract. But they didn't get Greg Maddux to come back. They let Mark Grace go, because they didn't want to pay him. When Alex Rodriguez was on the market, the Cubs were never mentioned. The third biggest market in the country, and the Cubs were never mentioned as a contender. They weren't a contender for Randy Johnson or Tom Glavine when they were available.

I don't agree that the primary driving factor when free agents decide where they're going to play is whether they're going to a winner. A much bigger factor is how much money they're going to get paid. That may change later in their careers, when they've already accumulated 700 million, and then they say, "OK, I'm willing to trade off a little bit of that income to win." But you wouldn't be able to explain why Alex Rodriguez went to Texas, or why *every* free agent doesn't sign with the Braves or the Yankees. If a guy can get a salary from a team that isn't doing so well, two things are going through their mind: "One, that's a bigger paycheck, and that's worth something. *I'll be the King of the Hill*; two, there's probably a sense of ego—*Hey, they're not very good now, but wait 'til I get there."*

I use the Cubs a lot in class, when I talk about averages and marginal differences. We teach a class here called Economics of the Sports and Entertainment Industry. I use as an example the question, "Why can't the Cubs go out and sign marquee free agents?" If I'm going to talk about stadiums, I talk about the Brewers and Twins. The kids know I'm a big Cubs fan. One kid came up to me during the 2003 NLCS and explained that he wasn't going to be in class on the day of Game 7, and *promised* me that he would give me a foul ball if he caught one. Yeah, sure. Kids in class the day after Game 6 yelled out, "How 'bout them Marlins?" I told them, "I can't figure out who it was that said that, but if I do, you flunk."

In 2003, I was in a funk for a couple of days. When they lost Game 6, I knew it was all over. I was watching the game in the living room with my twelve-year-old son. They got the first out in the eighth inning, and we were jumping around in the family room celebrating, "We're going to the World Series!" We've got our best pitcher out there. Even after the fan grabbed the ball, we weren't disheartened. Then there was another hit, then there was the shortstop error, and then the Marlins took the lead, and then I realized: "They're not going to win this game." And when they lost, I knew they were going to lose Game 7. My son is still trying to get over it. He ripped up the paper the next day, he was so upset. He was crying. I told him, "I know how you feel." I told him about 1984, but I was about 22 then. I had to explain to him that this is what it is to be a Cubs fan: they're always going to let you down. I was disappointed. But I wasn't going to go kill a cat…again. Just kidding.

I haven't figured out the mathematical possibility of the Cubs winning a World Series in my lifetime. Practically, it has to be near zero. I really thought 2003 was the year. I was sure they were going to win the division, and they did. I was sure they were going to beat the Braves, and they did. I really thought it was their year of destiny. I look at what happened and I say, "If that wasn't it, it will never be."

The Cubs are like a sunny day. They're so exciting; they're so bright. But every night they go away. They burn you if you get too close to them.

Avid cub fans Donald and Nelda Danz of Palatine, IL in front of Murphy's Sports Bar, across from Wrigley Field.

EMIL VERBAN MIGHT HAVE BEEN SLOW, BUT HE HAD BAD HANDS

Bruce Ladd

Bruce Ladd lives in Chapel Hill, N.C. Originally from Chicago's South Side, he is the founder of the famed Emil Verban Society.

Photo by Grant Halverson

I founded the society in 1975, and I am its leader, for lack of a better word. Somebody had sent me a book review of Leo Durocher's new book, *Nice Guys Finish Last*, and I thought, *well, that's cute. I'll send this book out to some of these other Cubs fans in Washington, with whom I periodically get together, and they'll get a kick out of it.* So I did, I sent it out to about half a dozen people. In doing that, I said, "To the members of the Cubs fan club..." Well, that didn't ring. "To the um..." Well, all of a sudden Emil Verban's name jumped into my head. Emil was a very steady, reliable, and in some cases excellent, second baseman for seven years in the majors, including three years with the Cubs, '48, '49, '50. So I wrote: "To the members of the Emil Verban Society." Then I decided to put "memorial" in there. I didn't know if he was alive or dead. One of the six people I sent this out to, incidentally, was Dick Cheney.

The next thing I know, these fellas are saying, "Hey, that was great. When do we get memo number two?" A month later the Cubs got beat 23-2 by the Pittsburgh Pirates, and I pulled that clip out of the *Washington Post*, and I sent it out to them again. And it just grew, and they recommended other people, and we capped the membership at 700 about ten years ago.

Members do nothing. And that's why everybody wants into it. We have no dues, no offices, no committees, no obligations of membership whatsoever. Periodically, every 60 days or so, they will get a memorandum from the Historian, that's me. That's as close as we come to having an officer. Every two years since 1980, we have had a biennial lunch, which attracts some 500 people, at 50 bucks a piece, to the ballroom of the Capitol Hilton. We bring in half a dozen former Cubs ballplayers or broadcasters, like Harry Caray, and we've had commissioners of baseball and we've had the President of the Cubs. We've had all kinds of great people come to be our guests.

That was up until I retired down here to North Carolina, from Washington several years ago. After that, we changed the mix a little bit. In 2002, we went out to Chicago for what we called, "Wrigley Weekend," and did back-to-back day games and had a nice banquet at Harry Caray's restaurant. In 2004, we're going to the Hall of Fame, where one of our members is president. In between, something may come up. The Cubs played in Baltimore in 2003, and we bought a block of tickets and a bunch of us went up to the ball game. Otherwise, it's a really room-temperature IQ kind of an organization.

Besides Dick Cheney, the society includes: Ronald Reagan; Hillary Clinton; Scott Turow, the author; Tom Bosley the actor; Ray Floyd the golfer; George Will; Bob Novak...The list goes on and on. Harry Caray was a unique fellow. As was Jack Brickhouse, who was one of our most active and ardent members. Jack was a fellow who said about the Cubs: "Hey, anybody can have a bad century." It's only been 95 years.

When you live at 8200 South, and you go all the way to Wrigley Field on the North Side, that's an effort right there. And that's what we had to do. Why, you may ask, would you become a Cubs fan living on the South Side? Dumb luck. My den mother in Cub Scouts said to us: "Boys. Next week bring some spending money. We're going to a baseball game." And for some unknown reason, we got into her Mercury sedan and went all the way across town to Wrigley Field. That was 1946. It was awesome. And it's awesome every time I go in there. Management has done a tremendous job of keeping that place almost a shrine. People wonder why Cubs fans are so dedicated and die-hard. In large measure, it's because of Wrigley Field, and the fact that it's the one constant in people's lives. I've talked to people in their 90s who still talk reverently about the first time their dad took them to Wrigley Field.

I was hooked right away. It was a non-fatal but incurable disease. As a kid at home, prior to college, you got out to the games as much as you could. When I was growing up, there was no television yet, so radio was very important. You could always remember Bert Wilson, a Cubs radio announcer who would always comment that it was a beautiful day in Chicago and the Cubs were about to play.

Bob Michel, former minority leader of the U.S. House, will tell you about being in a foxhole in WWII in Europe and getting newspapers from his mother about a month or two old telling him news about the Cubs, and he would sit there in the foxhole and read every single word. He is no less enthusiastic today than he was then.

My favorite player was Andy Pafko, #48. Lives in Mount Prospect, Illinois, today. Great guy. Still in super health. Cubs love him. He threw out the first ball at one of the 2003 playoff games at Wrigley Field. He was a center fielder with a bullet arm. Andy was the epitome of a Midwestern guy who tried to do everything right. He played right on the field and lived right off the field. He had the strongest work ethic you could imagine. He was just one of those people who you can easily relate to. He's a good friend and a member of the Society. There are only two living members of the '45 Cubs team. He's one of them. Phil Cavarretta is the other one. He won the batting title in the National League in 1945.

If you look at the state of Illinois, you'll see St. Louis way down at the bottom. And then Chicago is up at the top. You draw a line through the middle of Illinois and the people to the south of that line relate to the Cardinals, and the people to the north relate to the Cubs. People like the White Sox less than they like the Cardinals. Now that was a rivalry, because you're right in the same town. Particularly when you've got Sox fans living in your neighborhood. Rivalries develop. We used to call them the "White Sux" and other such names.

I collect Cubs memorabilia: you name it, I've got something. But I'm an amateur. I've got a friend who is the most die-hard Cubs fan I've ever met. He's not married—his entire apartment is a shrine. It's actually called "The Shrine." This place is museum-quality. No wife would ever let a guy get away with that, but he doesn't have to worry about that.

I'll tell you who gets devastated about the Cubs losing in 2003: recent recruits to Cub fandom. Those of us who have been fans for a few years have a certain equanimity about us. We realize that the record doesn't show that they're going to be awful good, so don't expect. Just enjoy the game of baseball, enjoy the players, enjoy Wrigley Field, and don't sink or swim on the basis of whether they win a pennant or a World Series.

The Emil Verban Fan Club has three awards. One of them is the Brock-for-Broglio Judgment Award, which is given out every two years. The most recent hanging on my wall went to number 43, George W. Bush. The award goes to the person who we deem exercised the worst judgment of the previous two years. It's gone to Saddam Hussein. George W. Bush got it a couple of years ago because he's the guy who gave away Sammy Sosa to the White Sox. The Sox then made the mistake of shipping him off to the Cubs. Award No. 2 is what we call the Ernie Banks Positivism Trophy. It's a huge, beautiful trophy. It goes to the person who has—over the past two years—shown the most positive, can-do attitude toward life in general and the importance of helping other people. Ron Reagan got that one year, as did others who the society deemed appropriate. The third award is called the Hack Wilson Look-Alike Award. He was about 5'9" and must have weighed about 230 pounds. That award goes annually to the member of the society who has put on the most weight. And it's a big disincentive to our members: they do not want to get the Hack Wilson Look-Alike Award. The awards are chosen by a phantom committee. It's called the "Phantom Committee." It disposes of matters in wondrous ways. You don't just join the Society; you have to be nominated by a member. That recommendation is made to me, and I turn it over to the Phantom Committee, and it disposes and advises me, and then whatever they say, we do.

The teams from the '50s were terrible. You just prayed that they would make it into seventh place. I remember Chuck Connors, *The Rifleman*. Chuck was absolutely terrible. He fought it out with Dee

Fondy for first base. There was a contest, I'll tell you. And Chuck lost. He was an actor, not a ballplayer. Connors was righthanded; Fondy was lefthanded, which is more conducive to playing first. Fondy, though, could also hit for something resembling **.250**. Fondy even approached .300 in a couple of seasons, and was also a pretty slick fielder, which Connors wasn't.

Joe Pepitone is bald as a billiard ball. And he wears this ugly, cheap wig. One day we had lunch with Joe Garagiola, and Joe Pepitone was among the guests. I said to Pepitone, "When you come, make sure to bring your extra ugly wig. When Garagiola goes up to the podium, I want you to get up and go put that extra wig right on him." So he did. And we got great pictures. At least he didn't reach over and take Pepitone's off his head. We first met Pepitone in 1991 when we went to a Cubs fantasy camp.

There is a very big nostalgia factor. When you start to analyze why all these people are so devoted to this terrible team, it comes down to Wrigley Field and a paternalistic ownership. The team recognizes that fans are important, and you don't get that in some places. In 2003, the Cubs filed suit against the owners of the buildings on Waveland and Sheffield that sell their rooftops to watch the games. It's been quite a bitter feud. I can't say who is right or wrong, but I think it flies in the face of the way the Cubs have always treated their fans. It seems to be out of pattern.

Many days, I was at the Union League Club downtown. I would get on the same "L," get off at the same Addison Street stop, walk the same number of feet, walk up to the same door, and come in to what appears to be the same stadium. You've got to get a little dewy-eyed over that. Because nothing is the same. But this *is* the same. In baseball, there's a kind of reverence. There's a much deeper feeling about baseball than there is about any of the other sports. Maybe in the next hundred years, the others will catch up to this, but they're going to have to work hard to do it.

The difference between a .250 and a .300 hitter is one base hit per week.

In Case You're Ever on Jeopardy

Between walks and strikeouts, Mickey Mantle went the equivalent of seven full seasons without putting the bat on the ball.

Phil Rizzuto is the only baseball person to earn a Gold Record...his game calling was in the background of Meat Loaf's *Paradise by the Dashboard Lights*.

In 1916, the Giants had a 26-game winning streak. When they started the streak they were in fourth place and when they finally lost, they were still in fourth place.

When Jim Bunning, currently the U.S. Senator from Kentucky, retired in 1971, Walter Johnson was the only pitcher in baseball history with more strikeouts.

The last major leaguer to lose playing time during a season due to military service was Nolan Ryan of the New York Mets.

When Knute Rockne was killed in a 1931 plane crash, where seven other people perished, it was the largest disaster in U. S. aviation history up until that time.

When Don Shula retired, he had more victories than over half the NFL teams.

Phil Mickelson has never won a golf "major," yet he once held the record for the lowest four-round total in the PGA Championship. A few minutes later, David Toms broke Mickelson's record and won the 2001 PGA Championship.

PEPSI NOT ONLY HITS THE SPOT, IT REMOVES IT TOO!

David Lewis

David Lewis spent his early youth on the West Coast, his college years on the East Coast, and his best years at Wrigley Field. He was in a memorable Pepsi commercial with Sammy Sosa and Ken Griffey, Jr.

David Lewis and Sammy Sosa

One of my acting gigs was a non-speaking role where I sat next to Sammy in the dugout of that infamous Pepsi commercial, during the All-Star game a couple of years ago. It also featured Ken Griffey, Jr., and, as luck would have it, Miguel Cabrera of the Marlins, back when he was eighteen years old. The entire day was spent sitting around ninety percent of the time and actually acting or doing work ten percent of the time. Over the course of an entire day, we got to hang out and talk baseball with Sammy, Griffey, and the other guys.

Sammy was just the greatest guy. You could understand how a superstar could be standoffish when it comes to autographs, but here he is hanging around guys who love baseball, talking nothing but baseball, not really asking for much. At the end of the day, he was gracious enough to give everyone autographs on baseballs and shirts, and he offered tons of photograph opportunities. I've got a picture of us hanging out in the dugout that he eventually signed. It was a unique experience, because Sammy had already been the league MVP in 1998, and obviously was quite the star at the time of this commercial. It was great to dispel the rumors about how big Sammy was and how he must have hit all these home runs "on the juice." This was obviously before the corked bat incident, but here I am, I'm 6'1", 205 pounds, and sitting next to Sammy all day without the extra shirts on underneath his jersey. You look at him and the guy doesn't look like he weighs 200 pounds. Standing next to each other in the photo, it looks like I dwarf the guy. Certainly, he has built up his strength and he's much stronger than I am, but by no means would I say he was "on the juice."

It's unique whenever you shoot a film or commercial to see what's scripted, what happens, and what actually sticks in the final cut. There was a scene there where the question was, "What is Griffey thinking while he's waiting on a 90 mph fastball?" and as this fastball is coming in, Griffey's mindset slows it down and he sees Sosa in the dugout reaching for his Pepsi. What happens is when Griffey looks up and supposedly sprays this foul ball into the dugout; the producers actually throw a Wiffle Ball into the dugout at Sammy. Sammy is supposed to dive out of the way onto this pad. The first two or three times they did it, Sammy had a stand-in to do it, but Sammy decided to do it himself. And so Sammy would dive and the ball kept coming at odd times, or would bounce off the wall and come and hit him in the back of the head…they eventually got the stand-in to do it.

One thing that was not part of the script was they were sitting in the dugout and screwing around. Sammy was reaching out for the Pepsi, and Griffey reaches out and slaps his hand. Griffey's a funny guy— the media makes him out to be a sourpuss, but he's a really nice guy. Sammy was really going to take a sip of it, not realizing that the cameras were rolling. Griffey actually smacks him and Sammy put his hands down like a sulking little kid. That made the final cut. I would like to say Sammy surprised me with his acting, but really there wasn't a lot of acting for Sammy in the commercial. He never actually spoke in the commercial: it was Griffey's inner monologue.

As a season ticket holder in the bleachers, sticking with these players through thick and thin, we go there and see the players every day. You get a lot of favorite players who are quiet, off the cuff, do their job, and then you get the other guys. Sammy tends to be an easy guy to pick on because he's a superstar and he makes millions, but I challenge you to find another superstar who hustles like Sammy does, and who plays the game on the field the way Sammy does. Now we don't know what kind of a guy he is in the clubhouse, and we don't know what kind of a guy he is outside of the baseball world, back home or with his other friends. But we do know that he gives 110% on the field. The guy puts on a happy face and does his job every day. As a die-hard Cubs fan, I also love the guys like Thad Bosley, or like Glenallen Hill, who come in and do their jobs in a limited capacity, but were still fan-friendly and left it all out on the field.

When I grew up in California, we had a Die-Hard Cubs Fan Club of Los Angeles. My mom would drive me about an hour and a half once a month to go to these meetings. There would be a lot of ex-Chicagoans, die-hard Cubs fans. We would all get together at a Chicago-style pizza place, and talk Cubs, and share memorabilia, and just get together like any club might. One time we were able to get Ernie Banks and his wife Marjorie to come out and say hello to all the die-hard Cubs fans of LA. This was in 1986. We got to hang around and talk baseball with Ernie. He took pictures with us, he gave autographs—he did the thing as a parent that you would expect a superstar athlete to tell your kid: "Stay in school. Work hard." Every summer, I would come out to Chicago to visit my dad for a few weeks, and I would always schedule my trips around Cubs home stands so that I could see as many games as possible. When I did that, I would always ask if it were possible if I could be a Cubs batboy next time I came to visit. Well my mom asked Ernie Banks, and he said, "I'll check on it." Ernie wound up calling my mom a few weeks later and said, "Listen. Usually they have their own bat boys at home, but the visiting teams don't really travel their bat boys." So, he said that if I wanted to come out, they would let me be batboy for the Phillies for a game. I was 16 years old. I was the first guy in the stadium. I was the first guy in the clubhouse. I took my camera in the Phillies dugout, and during the game I'm snapping photos face to face with guys like Mike Schmidt, Juan Samuel, and rookies like **Jeff Stone**. On the field for the Cubs, the Sarge was still on that team, Ryno was on the team. Ed Lynch was pitching for the Cubs, funny enough. Glen Wilson hit a line drive right off of his leg and broke his bat.

> In 1994, six months after the Nancy Kerrigan assault, Tonya Harding's husband, Jeff Gillooly, legally changed his name to Jeff Stone.

Afterwards, Glen Wilson gave me his bat and autographed it. Here I am dressed in a Phillies uniform, going out to home plate and having to give these guys low fives after a home run when I pick up a bat. Inside my guts are getting torn out because the Cubs are losing.

My first game at Wrigley Field, the crowd was just electric. Everything was really green. Then I lived in California for a long while. By that time I was about ten years old. I came back and got reunited with my father for the first time. I really didn't remember much about Wrigley except for what I'd seen on TV, you know the ivy, the greenery. So the first time walking out from the tunnels and onto the concourse at Wrigley was like walking out into this Mecca, that you only see on TV, and remembering, "Gosh. When I was two years old this really *did* exist. This is how it was." Our first game we went out there, and Fergie Jenkins was out on the mound for the Cubs in his second stint. Bobby Bonds actually hit two home runs in the game in what was one of his last games in baseball. This was 1980 and the first time I had come back to visit my dad. At that point, I said, "I'm coming back every summer and I'm going to sit in the bleachers every game." And I did. I would come back for three weeks. I would go sometimes with my dad, but most of the time I would take the train and the bus to get to every single game by myself, and spend the $3.50 to sit in the bleachers by myself, and get autographs and take pictures and just hang out. That's kind of what turned me on to it. After growing up in California and going to college on the East Coast, my goal was to move back to Chicago and move as close to Wrigley Field as possible. I ended up living on Kenmore Avenue a block over the left field wall. I live in a loft now a little further away, but I still have season tickets to the bleachers.

We have a nice little family that sits in the left field section right before the family section. A lot of these guys have been there since the early '70s. It's a nice community because we always have a few people who show up right when the gates get opened, and they'll go up there and save seats for the regulars. The nicest part about being a regular is that the Cubbies see you and recognize you as loyal fans when they're out at batting practice. You're not out there for the beer drinking, party-atmosphere. You're not there as a fair-weather fan because the Cubs are doing well, you're out there because you love the Cubbies, you love the atmosphere, you love the team, and you want to come out and support the team and be a part of it. The greatest part of seeing those people who aren't regulars is seeing the guy who walks into Wrigley Field for the first time, who has been a fan, but has lived in Iowa his entire life, or some other part of the country, and you see him walk out onto the ramp and his eyes light up like he's some little kid who is seeing Santa Claus for the first time. It's priceless. Or the guy who walks up with the girlfriend who knows nothing about baseball. He's in tears, and he says: "You just don't understand." It reminds me about coming back to Wrigley for the first time in 1980, and it makes you feel good, being part of this great team and this beautiful neighborhood: it reminds you why you're a season ticket-holder. Seeing someone out there for the first time, whether they're six or sixty: everyone is like a kid the first time they come out to Wrigley. It's great to be able to see that on a day-to-day basis.

I don't know if there's a Die-Hard Cubs Fan Club in Chicago. There is a Die-Hard Cub Fan Club that I have been a member of since I was nine years old. I still have my membership card. I haven't heard much about it since the early '80s, and I haven't run into anyone from the club since.

I have caught three home run balls in left field in my time. Two of them, amazingly, were Sosa and McGwire balls. In 1998, early in the season, at a Cardinal-Cub game at Wrigley, McGwire hit a home run in the ninth inning off of Rod Beck. It was the 399th of his career and only his twelfth of the year—who knew that he would go on to break Maris' record and hit 70 for the year? This was the first home run I had ever caught. The crowd was packed. Waveland Avenue was exactly like the playoffs in 2003, waiting for a home run from Sosa or McGwire. Sure enough, this meaningless home run in the ninth inning is bouncing around in the left field bleachers. I wind up with it. I was so excited. I knew, "As soon as I catch a home run ball, if it's not the Cubbies, I'm throwing it back." Because I wanted to be part of that lore. And so I stuck my foot up on the wall and I launched this thing all the way to the infield grass on the fly. Most people didn't believe that, but I still play baseball, so my arm's in great shape. And the entire thing was captured on camera. So as soon as I let go of this ball, I raise my arms up in victory. And as the ball is halfway there, right about the same time, I realize that I just threw a potential Hall-of-Famer's home run ball away. As a left field regular, we're trained to maybe keep the "special ball" and let go of a throwback or batting practice ball. As soon as I let go of it, I had fifteen Cardinals fans come up offering me big money for that ball. And this was before he went on to break the record.

Kind of in justification, early in 2003, Sammy launched a home run into the back of left field bleachers right near where I was sitting, and the ball bounced right out of the hands of a guy on my left. I got it. It was home run number 512 of Sammy's career, tying him with Ernie Banks for ninth on the list of all-time home runs.

When I was ten years old, Dave Kingman was my hero. He always got a bad rap in the media and was never big on autographs. I sent him a letter from California saying that he was my favorite player, that I hoped he never got traded, and hopefully the Cubs will win the World Series. An assistant for the Cubs called my mom and said, "Dave Kingman doesn't usually respond to fan mail, but he's really impressed with your son's letter. We'd like to send out an 8x10." On Christmas in 1980, I unwrapped a picture and there it was, an auto-graphed picture from Dave Kingman, and it said: "Dear David: I appreciated your letter. Keep up the good work. Maybe one day, you can be a pro, too."

Someday I hope to run into Dave Kingman and have him sign it again.

Fittingly, Rick Monday will be remembered long after the names of the fans who made headlines on April 25, 1976. The Chicago Cub was on his way out to center field for the fourth inning in Dodger Stadium. "I saw the creeps run on the field from somewhere down the left field line," Monday recalled. "One of the idiots had something rolled up in his arm. It was a flag. They unfurled it on the grass, like a picnic blanket. One of the idiots took a shiny can out of his pocket. I thought he was dousing it with a flammable liquid, which was the case. The other person whipped out a book of matches. The wind blew the first match out." Monday raced to the scene, snatched the flag and ran away. "The guy threw the can of lighter fluid at me. It missed. I took the flag into foul territory. Doug Rau, a left-handed pitcher with the Dodgers, came out of the dugout and I gave the flag to him." The Dodgers' scoreboard flashed, "Rick Monday…You made a great play." The crowd began singing "God Bless America." The fans—William Thomas of Eldon, Mo., and his 11-year-old son—were protesting the treatment of American Indians during the Bicentennial year. Each was fined $800 and put on probation for two years.

CUBBIEPALOOZA

BITS AND BITES,
BEGGED AND BORROWED

There are fewer suicides among Cub fans than any other fandom in the world. It's because every day when we get out of bed, we say, "This might be the year—you know, this might be the year the Cubs win the World Series." Now, you want to be around for that! My biggest fear is that if the Cubs win the World Series, the following day, some twenty thousand people will leap off the top of the Tribune Tower.

——**TOM DREESEN**, America's Sports Comedian

My best moment as a Cubs fan was 1989 when the Cubs clinched, beating the Pirates on the road. I was at the Cubbie Bear with my roommate at the time. We were watching the game at home, and it got to the seventh inning and we said we had to get out of there and go to the Cubbie Bear. It's only about a five block walk from the apartment, but we decided it was taking too long so we grabbed a cab for the last three and a half blocks just to get there a little faster. We got there with a bunch of total strangers, and the Cubs won. They got the last out in the bottom of the ninth inning, and we're jumping up and down, and we're cheering and hugging people. I'm hugging this guy, and I have no idea who he is. All of a sudden we both realized we didn't know who we were hugging, and we paused for a split second and then it was like we said, "Who cares?" and we kept hugging and jumping up and down. The whole party spilled out into the street. We were right in front of Wrigley Field and there were people everywhere.

——**JIM DEMARET**, 37, trader, Chicago Stock Exchange

During the playoffs there was a pool on the commodities trading floor for two lower deck tickets to a playoff game. For twenty bucks you got to put your name in one of 100 squares. I'm not sure how it worked but a winning square was drawn, with the guy who won getting the tickets and three-hundred bucks. I just heard of another guy who had two tickets right behind the Cubs' dugout for the three World Series games that would have been played at Wrigley if the

Cubs had won the LCS that sold for thirty grand—five thousand a ticket for the three games at Wrigley. He sold them to a ticket broker. The ticket brokers were going nuts. This broker resold them for seventy-five hundred. He then called this guy back and said, "Just because these are such great tickets, I'm going to give you two other tickets for all the games somewhere else in the park."

——**PETE ALDWORTH**, Hinsdale, Illinois

Everyone compares the Red Sox and the Cubs—both being cursed. I don't buy that. The Red Sox sold Babe Ruth, so I believe they're cursed because they gave away the best player of the time. They have at least gotten back in The Show. They've been to the World Series, although they've always lost since then—and they have had some good teams. The Cubs, though, have just had bad teams. Ever since 1945, they just suck. Then you've got Pudge Rodriguez as a free agent. Why don't we sign him? He goes and signs with Florida for about 50 bucks. Dusty Baker is bad. When Kerry Wood hits a home run, how can you not win the game?

——**RICHARD DRAKE**, 29, Chicago

A lot of out-of-town players would call and make arrangements to come and see the Second City show since all the games were during the afternoon. Harry Caray used to come on a fairly regular basis, too. Harry used to live in Palm Springs during the off-season. I went to a restaurant, and Harry was there. You always knew when he was there because he talked so loud, and the room just changed when he walked in. Then the waitress showed up with a couple of Budweisers from Mr. Caray. He was a spokesperson for Budweiser, so it made sense. The waitress said, "He wants to know if you're an ex-ballplayer." I told her, "No. You can go ahead and tell Mr. Caray thank you for the beers, but I'm not an ex-ballplayer. He probably remembers me from Second City in Chicago." The waitress went back and relayed the information. Then we heard him say, "Second City? Holy Cow!" from across the room. On the way out, we thanked him for the beers. It was nice to be recognized, especially by Harry Caray in Palm Springs.

I remember looking for my first apartment in California. We were looking at this one place, and it was nice, and we were thinking about taking it. I asked the guy if it had cable, and he said it did. I asked if it had WGN, and he says, "No." I said to my wife, "Well, let's go." He couldn't believe it. The guy asked my wife, "He won't live in an apartment that doesn't have WGN?" She told him, "No. Absolutely not." So we wound up taking a pass on that apartment for a place where we could watch the games.

During the 2003 NLCS, I had other actors over to my house to watch the games. There's a small band of us originally from Chicago, and we like to get together. Some people prefer to watch the games alone, though. It's hard to watch the games because every pitch is excruciating, and, as a Cubs fan, you're always waiting for the other shoe to drop. The people you have over to watch a game have to be your close allies—ones that can see you in your uglier moments. At the end of the series, it was like everyone had the wind taken out of them.

——**MIKE HAGERTY**, 49, movie and TV actor, *Friends*, *ER*, *Cheers*, etc.

When Harry Caray came to Chicago, he had a deal where he got so much money for selling season tickets. He calls me up and says, "Look, I know you've got tickets for the Sox. I'm going to start up this thing called Restaurant Row, and it's going to be in the upper deck just beneath me. We're going to have a lot of fun with it, and I'm going to give you guys a bunch of mentions. I'd like you guys to get rid of your tickets and buy new ones up there. About eighty of us moved up to the upper deck. We used to sit behind the dugout, and now, because of Harry, we're in the upper deck. Opening Day, 1974, it was freezing cold and the place is sold out. Harry is having a lot of fun, telling people about Restaurant Row. Then he lowers the microphone so you can hear everybody sing. We were the idiots sitting there singing. That's when you got the "Take Me Out to the Ball Game" with the fans singing.

Now a second day comes. Opening Day was a Monday—Tuesday got cancelled so Wednesday is the second game. The attendance for that day was about 12,000, so they didn't open up the upper deck. We went up the ramp to go to our seats, and the gate is closed. We went up and told Harry about it. About ten minutes later, up the ramp—not in the elevator—comes old one-legged Bill Veeck. He's got a wad of keys and an usher. He says, "Oh, we're so sorry, guys. You're the only upper deck season tickets we've got." He opens it up, brings us in, sits us down in our seats, and he tells the usher, "You are here *every game* for these guys. You run down and get their drinks, get their hot dogs, anything else. If they're here, you're here. I don't care what anyone else tells you. That's your job." So we had our own private usher running back and forth. All year long, whenever the upper deck was closed, he was there waiting for us. He would run and get us a hot dog, get us a beer, get us some mixed drinks in the Poodle Room. We had VIP service. That's how he thought about us.

Although 2003 was a heartbreak, Dusty's back, our pitchers are back—it's going to be a beautiful summer in 2004!

——**JIM RITTENBERG**, 56, Famed Chicago Restaurateur

I know everybody who's not a Cubs or Red Sox fan wants a Cubs-Red Sox World Series, but real Cubs fans want to play the Yankees.

This character thing goes really deep. Being a Cubs fan tells you how to deal with adversity, stay positive, look for the good. Mets fans say the same thing, but it's not the same. The Mets were world champions seven years after the franchise started. It's really not the same thing. Mets fans are just spoiled by comparison to Yankee fans. As franchises go, they've done relatively well over the years. They're greedy and they expect to win every year. They've been in the World Series several times. For people who aren't Cubs fans, or if they're Johnny-come-lately Cubs fans, fair-weather Cubs fans, they can't understand what it's like to say, "Wait till next year," every single year.

Nobody ever stops being a Cubs fan because they lose, and that's why Cubs fans are superior to Mets fans and superior to fans of any other baseball team within miles because they understand what loyalty is and understand what fidelity is. I'm sure that Cubs fans make the best husbands, and wives, in the world. It teaches you most of the right values. The only thing it doesn't teach you is that "nothing succeeds like success."

Like that great tee shirt that says, "Any Team Can Have a Bad Century." There's a great shirt that has, *The Last Request of a Dying Cubs Fan*.

One of the things that is annoying to me is that there is a latter-day Cubs fan—somebody who maybe came from a Midwestern state, maybe listened to three Cub games on the radio when they were kids, and now it's trendy for them to be Cubs fans. For somebody who grew up in the shadow of the ballpark, that's ever so slightly annoying.

——**JONATHAN ALTER**, journalist, *Newsweek*

A couple of years ago, the Cubs were playing Atlanta, and we were in the bleachers because we're bleacher fans. The Atlanta players were in the outfield. We were all trying to get to Greg Maddux, an old Cubbie, who was starting for Atlanta that day and was in the bullpen to warm up, to just throw us an old practice ball. We tried for about 20 or 30 minutes, but he wouldn't do it. Finally, when he was getting ready to head back to the dugout, he looks back at me and throws me a ball. No sooner did I catch it, than I whipped it back at him and said, "We don't want your ——ing ball, Maddux". The whole bleachers went crazy, and he lost that game, too!

——**DEBORAH STANTON**, 40, Newport, Indiana

In 1984, when the Cubs were really doing well, me and my best buddy in high school wanted to sneak into a local parade in Silvis, Illinois. There was an old white car way in the back of the yard, and I didn't know whose car it was. We painted it up in Cub colors. We spray painted "Cubs Win, Harry Caray" on it, and we tried to sneak this car into this parade behind some horses. As we were trying to sneak in, a police officer pulled us over. This old car just barely ran, one of our back tires was low, a lot of smoke was coming out of the back end, and the muffler was very loud. A week before this, I had lost my driver's license. The police officer went through the whole ritual and asked us what we were trying to do. I told him we were Cub fans. He asked for my license. I told him I had lost it. He asked for the registration, and we looked in the glove box, and there was a big hole in it. He asked me whose car it was. I told him I had no idea and that my brother had just brought it to this farm we live on, and we decided to fix it up that day and run it in the parade. The cop said, "Let me get this straight. You have no identification, no registration, no license, and you don't know whose car it is?" Well, it turns out that he was a huge Cubs fan, too, so he let us go. If he'd been a Cardinal fan, we'd still be toast in Silvis.

——**TYRONE WILLIAMS**, 39, Moline, Illinois

Maybe we Cub fans are selfish. How about a little love for the long-suffering people of Miami. You have to remember that these fans have not seen the Marlins win the Series since 1997, six long years ago. It almost brings me to tears when I think of a guy like Cliff Floyd, suffering through the championship drought of 1998-2002, battling bravely with a bruised pinky, subsisting on a mere $2.5 million per year just to be draped in teal. For old Cliffy, it wasn't about the money, it was for the love of the game. "Let's play two," he was fond of saying.

This one was for the die-hard fans, those who routinely fill historic Pro Player Stadium to nearly a quarter of its capacity. Some of these fans, five years old or younger, had never seen the Marlins win the World Series. I'm sure they thought, as they played with their friends in kindergarten, that they might never see the Marlins get to the World Series in their lifetime. Now they have, even if they get hit by the school bus tomorrow.

———GARY COHEN, 36, Los Angeles

That Maddux trade was the maddest the Cubs ever made me. I was living in New York at the time so I couldn't boycott the games. It was just so stupid, so unnecessary. It was just a matter of "my ego's bigger than his ego." We need a pitcher more than we need a general manager.

On two different occasions, I have gone on a bus tour of different ballparks. This group of fifty people get together and drives around to the different parks. Both trips started out at Shea Stadium and ended up going to Yankee Stadium, Baltimore, Pittsburgh, Cleveland, Chicago, Toronto, Montreal, Boston. You stop off at each city and see the games there. On one of those, I got to see the Cubs play against Atlanta, and Maddux pitched against us as part of a doubleheader. We won one game, but he beat us the second game. he pitched sixty-two pitches for the whole game. He was fabulous. It was the fewest pitches he'd ever had in his whole life. He just sat us right down very, very quickly. I've been fortunate in the games I've gone to. I can say that I've seen home runs hit the same year by McGwire, Sosa and Bonds. I saw Jose Jiminez pitch a no-hitter for the Cardinals against Arizona, which I guess was the highlight of my baseball-watching life.

———DR. JERRY WACHS, New Jersey Cub Fanatic

Every year at spring training in Mesa, Arizona, someone brings a tape of Lee Elia's tirade. Every spring training, it's played in the hotel room, just in case someone might have missed it after all these years.

In those days, the Cubs didn't draw two million people, and so there were people who were very, very mad, but the hype didn't get quite as far; although, obviously you're well aware of it. People were certainly mad and thought that he should be out of his job. But it was passed over like a lot of irrational things.

When I first started going to spring training, I went by myself and it was my time away from younger children and my husband. Being in a baseball environment, I was comfortable as opposed to going off by myself to some spa.

The first time I ever went, I took my friend Halvie O'Connell. It was her first air flight ever. She had never had the nerve to fly, and she cried when we took off. Ever since then, I've been going back, and I stay in the same Best Western facility, which was once Cub headquarters. For the last twelve years or so, they've held the same room for me, and I have season tickets out there as well—first row behind the screen. The Hohokam people, the organization that monitors the ballpark is a not-for-profit group of men, and they are so nice. The gentleman who was at that time—don't laugh— "Big Ho," Fernando Guerrero, has a son Fernando Guerrero, Jr. is a Big-Ho-to-be—he's now like second and dad is a "good old boy" now. They have included me for the last several years in a few of the things usually available for players and their families only. I get invited to the wives' luncheon. It's very nice. I get invited to the barbecue steak fry that they have. This is only because I've watched their organization grow and watched the ballpark grow. I've been included very nicely by them. They're that way to all the people.

——CAROL HADDON, Glencoe, 20-Year Spring training Vet

I've done some pretty interesting Cubs tattoos in the past. Pretty much the most die-hard Cubs fan I know of is a good friend of mine. I did a tattoo on. It was a broken heart with a Cubs symbol in it, and underneath it there was a banner that said, "When" with a question mark. He had it tattooed on his leg, just above his ankle. He said, "The only thing that's ever made me cry were the Cubs in '84." And, that was his story. That's why he got it.

As for Cubs tattoos, I've probably done a dozen of them in 2003. I did a Cubs logo with an angel wing, another with a Cubs logo and a halo…things like that. People get nostalgic and want some older Cubs stuff from the '60s.

——NICK COLELLA, 28, Chicago, tattoo artist

I became friendly with Ernie Banks back in the early 1960s. He was my son's hero as well as mine. Ernie told me to bring Richard, my son, to a Dodger game about an hour before game time so he could meet him in the Chicago dugout—give him a ball and a bat.

When we arrived, I told Ernie that Richard knew everything about him. "Like what?" asked Ernie. "1-31-31," answered the twelve-year-old Richard. "1-31-31?" asked Ernie, puzzled. Since Richard had memorized every statistic from his baseball card, he replied—"The date of your birth on top of the card—1-31-31!" Ernie and I have met each other on rare occasions at golf tournaments, airports, and other places—and "1-31-31" has become our password.

Recently, I made an appearance at Wrigley Field to throw out the first pitch. When I arrived at the park, I asked if Ernie was on the premises. I hadn't seen him for several years. Yes, he was in the dining room. "Go over to him," I advised a young man, "and whisper 1-31-31 in his ear." In two minutes, my old friend and I were embracing. He knew the password.

And, he still thinks it's a great day to play two!

——MONTY HALL, Host of *Let's Make a Deal* from 1963–1986

I've played on a softball team in Glenview for many years, and Ron Santo is the neighbor of a friend of mine. When he retired from the White Sox, the following summer he played on our team. A lot of people came out to watch us play, and even one of the local TV stations did a story on us. Meeting him was neat. Then, about fifteen years later, through work, I met him at spring training and he remembered the team and remembered me. There was a kid who was really sick, a good friend of my family, and he gave us a bat and signed it. After having watched him as I was growing up, it was just a real treat to actually say, "I played with Ron Santo."

——TOM ROBISON, 52, TV news producer, WLS-TV, Chicago

The great thing about driving the rickshaw is that every day is a new adventure. You never know who is going to be in the back, what they're going to be like, from what walk of life, or what not. We had a woman who traveled from Alaska for her first Cubs game, she was 100 years old, and three guys had to lift her into the rickshaw 'cause she's a little dainty, you know, not a lot of muscle left in her legs.

John Maholm and Bill Murray.

I took Bill Murray during the All-Star game. He was subdued. I wish the ride would have been longer. He's a good tipper: he gave me fifty bucks for a five dollar ride, so that was nice. Brett Hull was good for a hundo. I took Jeff Garland and his wife and his son around the parking lot when he was here for the seventh inning stretch. He's a local Chicago guy who plays Larry David's agent on "Curb Your Enthusiasm." It was against my better judgment, but I took Ronnie "Woo Woo" and five people. We don't like to do six; it's more of a two-seater. But if people want to lap it up, I tell them, "Boys on bottom, girls on top. I take you to your very stop."

—— JOHN MAHOLM, Wrigley Field Rickshaw Driver

Chug-Chug, The Comeback Clown actually originated through the *Heckler*. They were looking for a promotional way to promote the newspaper and bring something new to Chicago. The idea came from that stupid rally monkey that the freakin Anaheim Angels used to have. The idea came after a brain session over a thirty-case. The idea, you know what, why don't we have the Comeback Clown? They call us lovable losers. Why not the Comeback Clown? And of course every Cubs fan drinks to chase away those losing blues, so we thought why not Chug-Chug, the Comeback Clown. The idea stuck and they actually had tryouts for it. I was the only gentleman that showed up for the tryouts. I intimidated everybody and shooed them off. I had the physique for it. I'm about 5'10" 265-270, so I'm short and stocky, which is perfect for the part. I wasn't just some idiot that they hired just to go and walk around the park and try to do my part to try to reverse the curse of the goat, or anything else. The costume started out as an old blue and white baseball shirt that said *The Heckler* on the front. I had a pair of softball shorts with home **pinstripes**

> The Yankees' pin-striped uniforms were designed by owner Colonel Jacob Ruppert to make Babe Ruth look skinnier.

on it, and then I ended up wearing my Sammy Sosa Cubs jersey—with Chuck Taylor All-Stars, eye black under my eyes to get the baseball effect, and then I had a red wig that was bald on top, and then I had a Cubs fishing hat, with ivy growing out of the sides. In 2003, I made a lot of friends with the security people, the crowd control, the ushers, the vendors... I've made some great friends with all those people. Then some of the famous people who I've met out there, from politicians, to sports athletes outside of the baseball realm, to just actors. John Elway was a heck of a fan. He shook my hand, was willing to take pictures with me, complimented me on the get-up. Roger, the ex-governor of Illinois, was a great, great gentleman. He actually reads *The Heckler*, which is amazing, that a man who was the Governor of Illinois would not only read it, but also endorse it and take pictures with a gentleman such as me in a clown outfit, standing out in front of Wrigley Field during the playoffs.

Baseball is for all ages. Clowns are for all ages.

——JASON YURECHKO, 25, Chug-Chug, the Comeback Clown

The Cubs had a manager named Lee Elia, and it was another frustrating year. After a bad loss, he just unloaded. Somebody asked him something, and he just went into this profanity-laden tirade. I was working in the sports department at WLS and one of the other stations in town got the tirade on tape. The Cubs were playing the Dodgers that day. It was particularly frustrating to us because our station also had a camera in the locker room, but they were working for a Los Angeles TV station. They heard some screaming going on up in the manager's office and didn't think to go in and check it out, so we did not get the tirade on tape like the other station. There was only one station, Chet Coppock on WMAQ-TV, that got it. He got the interview and one of the other sports guys in town, Johnny Morris, demanded that Chet give him the interview—that he owed it to him to share it with him. Chet told him, "Forget it."

Anyway, this profanity-laden tirade was played on radio and cassettes of it started surfacing all over town. Getting a copy of that became great Cubs memorabilia. The general reaction was, "Boy, that guy's going to get fired." He blasted the fans, too. I remember thinking it was funny. I agreed with him and probably what he said was true, but I did think the whole thing was funny.

——TOM ROBISON, 52, TV news producer, WLS-TV, Chicago

During batting practice before a Mets game a few years ago none of the Mets were throwin' up any balls into the bleachers. The only guy to hit a few out was Piazza. It's getting really late into batting practice and I'm getting upset that the players haven't been feeding the bleacher bums any baseballs. So, I yell out at the top of my lungs, "Hey, we're dying out here!" I'm in the front row wearing my Cubs stuff. Mookie, my friend, is dressed in all his Mets stuff and he's standing on the second row of the bleachers. He's maybe 5'8 or 5'9; I'm a few inches taller than him. The Mets player turns around and throws a ball into the bleachers. I reach out my glove and catch it, but I was like, "Holy Cow, this is a World Series ball from the Subway Series, Mets-Yankees in 2000." I wasn't even aware that they had special balls that they used for the World Series. I turned to him and go, "When the Cubs make the World Series and I get a Cubs World Series ball, you can have this. I'll hang on to it until then."

——JIM BRADLEY aka "BOO", 35, Wrigleyville, Software QA Engineer

I wrote to Bob Costas and he wrote me a little post card saying thank you very much. That was good enough for me. How many people would take the time to ever write back? Wrigley Field and the day games make me feel young, like being a kid again. Like you were family. When you got out of school you run home and you couldn't wait to see how the Cubs were doing for the day games and to hear Jack Brickhouse. And then, at night or just like I said watching my uncle at the kitchen table with the radio on listening to Lou Boudreau and Vince Lloyd, they were great, reading the sports section. Just so typical urban Chicago, Italian neighborhood, Polish neighborhood, I loved it. And when I see a Cubs day game, sun shining, blue sky, it just brings back those memories and I feel youthful. That's why I'm so bitter about all these night games for the full season. They ruined the whole experience. Even when you were young, passing all the homes in the neighborhoods and seeing all the signs in the windows, "Go Cubs" and all that. When I went back last year I actually walked around all the neighborhoods to get a feel, the trees, the breeze. You can't do that at Comiskey. You can't do that at Bank One Ballpark. Wrigley Field is in a neighborhood, part of the community. Look at San Diego; it's nothing but a black top parking lot all around it. Big deal.

I want to see some real baseball stuff. There was an article in our paper about how people wanted to have the Cubs and Red Sox play a "Consolation World Series." Why don't they ask and see if they could use Fenway and Wrigley Field? They would get all their money. Do a consolation series between the Red Sox and Cubs. They have that stupid Pro Bowl thing in Hawaii that no one gives a rat's ass about.

—————JOE HUTCHINSON, 50, Arizona resident since '67

Ronald Reagan loved to see those guys and they loved to see him. It was kind of like a big love fest. You go in with Al Kaline, Harmon Killebrew, Ernie Banks, just wonderful players. And you stand in the Oval Office, and everybody shakes hands, and the next thing you know, Ron Reagan starts to talk and everybody shuts up. He stands there for what was supposed to be a ten-minute photo-op. Pretty soon the staff is coming in and putting the time out sign on him and what have you, and Ronald Reagan just kept going. He has a very active baseball background, not just in announcing. The Cubs sent him to California, that's how he got on the map. He was broadcasting in Iowa in Des Moines and talked his way into having them send him out there to cover the Cubs in spring training. And while he was out there, he met some guy who said, "Let's go to a casting call." And that's how it all started. He talked about all of this. When he finally finished, the staff has finally pried us out of there, you go out, they open the door of the Oval Office, and here's half the White House staff standing there with pencil and paper because they want autographs from the players. I told some of the players in the limousine, "Now look. We don't ask the President for an autograph, all right?" Well then, I'd have to almost search them to make sure they weren't carrying baseballs. They were. Now he would have signed them, that's not the point. You're darn right I told them not to bring those baseballs in there.

—————BRUCE LADD, Founder, Emil Verban Society

I attended the game where Sammy Sosa broke his bat and had the cork in it. That was probably the most unusual game I've ever been to, because the crowd was large and very vocal up until that time and then it was like a pall came over the stadium—whispering and buzz—until the end of the game. I was pretty anti-Sosa for a few weeks, and I thought it was a dishonest thing to do. It lowered his esteem in my eyes.

———JOHN LAMARE, 50, Analyst, City of Chicago

I wasn't a big fan of the lights when they put them in. But I really do believe that playing eighty-one day games a year at home hurt the Cubs' chances in the past of winning the division. The players get hot and tired, and when they have played away the night before and fly in at one or two in the morning, they have to be ready to play a game at one the next day and don't get the rest they need. Overall, I would come in on the positive side for lights. I wasn't in favor or putting them in, but I was living in the city at the time about a mile away from the park, and I rode my bike over to the park just to soak in the excitement and feel the electricity that was there that night. I thought it looked really beautiful and that it was cool. During the eight years that I lived in the city, I always made it a point never to live farther than a mile away from Wrigley so I could either walk or bike there. I would probably average going to about ten or twelve games a year.

———DANNY SCHUMAN, Wilmette, Ad Copywriter

From the time I was ten years old, I was a Cub fan. My all-time hero was Hank Sauer. I could tell you his batting average, the days he hit homers, and then he got traded to the St. Louis Cardinals. Because of that, I quit the Cubs for a number of years, then came back years later in 1969. When I was 52, I was with the government in St. Louis, Missouri, and they had a baseball show. Hank Sauer was there and Bobby Shantz was there—they were the Most Valuable Players of the 1952 season. I took my youngest son, Andy, and there was no line to see these guys so I got to visit, with my son, with Hank Sauer for about forty-five minutes. When he signed an autograph picture, he addressed it to "Andy and Mike" and I said to my son, "He was my boyhood hero, and he named you first." Then two years ago at the Cubs' Convention, my son got to meet his all-time hero, Dave Kingman. I was with my son when Dave Kingman went to autograph the baseball, and I said, "Excuse me Dave, could you sign it to Mike and Andy?" He did! Payback is tough.

It was the 1987 World Series, Minnesota Twinkies and the St. Louis Cardinals. I was with the FBI office in St. Louis, and we had field privileges. I was talking to the Commissioner of Baseball's

Director of Security, and I said, "Who's that older coach out at second base?" He said, "That's Wayne Terwilliger." I said, "You're kidding! Wayne Terwilliger?" He said, "Yeah." I said, "How old is he?" He said, "Oh, he's in his seventies." I said, "I had a baseball card of Wayne Terwilliger when I was a kid about eleven years old. On the back of the card, it told of how Wayne Terwilliger ran for twelve miles in one of the islands to take a wounded Yank away from the Japanese." The Director of Security said, "We've got to go tell that to him." He takes me out behind second base, introduces me, I tell the story to Mr. Terwilliger. He's got tears in his eyes hearing it, and all of a sudden, we're looking around, and there are only three of us out there because the Twins had gone off the field. But I then said to Wayne Terwilliger, "Sir, it's an honor to meet you." I said, "My all-time hero besides you was Hank Sauer." He said, "Yeah, the big guy really hit them, didn't he?"

———MIKE KEGEBEIN, 62, Geneva, Illinois

When the Tribune Company bought the Cubs and bought Wrigley, they changed the concourse décor. Above the concession stands, when you first enter the park at the main entrance on Clark and Addison, there used to be a large circular Cub logo and on each side were several large photos of the then-current team. I was able to purchase the large Cub logo and a few of those pictures. That's the centerpiece of my collection, which includes team-autographed balls. I get one Cub autographed ball each year since the early seventies. Then I have other autographed balls. We have a very large basement so one whole wall consists of about thirty Pete Rose photos and things signed to me personally by him. Over the years I have a collection of many things which, to me, are valuable.

———CAROL HADDON, 56, Glencoe, Illinois

One of my favorite Cub characters is Don Zimmer who was the manager of the Cubs in '89. He used to do a manager's show and come on and talk about the plays and talk baseball. Guys like Don Zimmer— all they know is baseball. He won't talk about anything else. He'll talk your ear off about baseball, but ask him about politics, and it's blank—their life is all baseball. He's such a great character. He's from three generations ago where his wife packed all his clothes. He can't even tie a tie. He needed to wear a tie on the show, so his wife tied them for him. So, we bought him clip-on ties, and if he forgot to bring his tie, I'd have a clip-on tie in the drawer for him. He was an encyclopedia of baseball and had so many baseball stories…but he'll never make it on the senior boxing circuit.

When Jim Frey was manager, we had a "Second-Guessers Hotline." Fans would call in and say, "What about…?" Jim Frey absolutely hated that. He went along with it but he didn't like doing it. He, too, had a lot of baseball stories and did a good show.

———TOM ROBISON, 52, TV news producer, WLS-TV, Chicago

It's a great job; I've been out here sometimes like three-four hours before the game because people just want to be out and about, want to be part of history. The downside is being outside and listening on the radio and hearing the peoples' reaction.

I've got a lot of lines: "Hey, hey, what do you say, how bout a rickshaw ride today?" "It's Wednesday night, let's do it up right." "Roses are red, our rickshaws are blue; I'm sitting here and I'd love to transport you." "Step right up, do not be shy, give the rickshaw ride a try." "Come on up, sit right down, ride the best rickshaw ride in town."

———JOHN MAHOLM, Wrigley Field Rickshaw Driver

The Cubs…I wish I could explain to you what it is about the Cubs…is like a sick relationship. It's one of those relationships where, if the Cubs were a guy, you would have dumped him a long time ago. Because, you just can't keep doing this to somebody. I can't be mad at the Cubs. I can't be mad at the uniform. It's frustrating, but it's something that for forty years I've lived with. I'm used to it. I said to a friend of mine, who's a sportswriter, "If the Cubs ever do make it, I don't know how I will feel not being a lovable loser because that's how I've grown up with this team." I think a lot of people feel that way in life, too.

I told my son the morning after the Marlins beat us and ended our hope of going to the World Series, "Now you have really been indoctrinated into being a real Cubs fan. You have heard about '69. You've heard about '84, when they lost three to San Diego. I know you've felt the pain of the Cubs the last couple of years. But now, you have officially been inaugurated into the Cub-fan life. You knew that Mark Prior and Kerry Wood had not lost a game, ever, back-to-back.

You knew that they were going to go to the World Series. Well, welcome to the world of the Cubs."

The night that Mark Prior was pitching against the Marlins, my son said, "Mother, there's no way." I said, "They're the Cubs. Don't get overconfident." He wouldn't listen to me. Now he knows. It's a whole new generation of Cub fans, aged twenty or less, who know this new heartbreak and won't be so stunned next time it happens, because it happens all the time.

——BONNY BECKERMAN, North Shore, Businesswoman

I never got to go to Wrigley Field until 1990. Sometimes the game of the week would be from Wrigley Field. I would read all the sports magazines I could find about baseball and was always reading about how wonderful Wrigley Field is. I could see it in the '84 playoffs between the Cubs and the Padres, but the first time I went was, of all things, the All-Star Game.

I'll never forget when I went in and sat down—I was in the grandstand, back of first base. I got there as early as I could. When I sat down and started looking out over those ivy-covered walls and at all the houses and businesses across the street that had those flat roofs with people up on them looking over into the park, I said to myself, "I am sitting in the middle of a Norman Rockwell painting." I'd seen at least one of his paintings where he had painted from inside Wrigley Field. My sitting there just made me feel like I was part of that painting. It was just exactly everything I ever thought it would be and more. Since then, I've been very fortunate and been back up to Wrigley Field ten times.

——GENE BROCK, 66, Brevard County, Florida

Here I am nearly fifty-years-old, a confirmed humanist, and for the sixth game of the 2003 playoffs, I would not leave a four-foot area of my couch—this was when they were winning—only five outs away from winning. It's not rational, but this very powerful belief takes hold, and it makes no sense—are the Cubs gonna lose if I walk three feet over to the chair? Of course, they're not. But it's so important, you just don't want to jinx it—don't want to take a chance. One of my favorite tee shirts to sleep in is a Marlin shirt I bought several years ago—I liked the feel of it and the fit. I can't wear it now. My wife couldn't understand and asked if I liked it now. I said, "I do, but you just don't understand." Steve Goodman, the folk singer, has a song, *The Dying Cub Fan's Last Request,* on one of his albums. It's a wonderful song. He was a Chicagoan who died fairly young of cancer. He did the song, and it was this great tribute. In the song, he said he wanted his casket carried by the Cubs. He wanted his ashes distributed by the prevailing westerly winds. He wanted Keith Moreland to drop a routine fly. Basically, it was about what we, Cub fans, usually talked about—all the mistakes the Cubs made. We are rooted in history. I think there's something about connecting to the game that causes me to go back and to know about these teams. And I'm glad my son is learning that too.

Pat Piper was the P.A. announcer of the Cubs for decades. He would start out every game with, "Ladies and gentlemen, boys and girls get your scorecards ready." It's that voice that I would love to hear again. He wasn't like Jack Brickhouse and didn't do color commentary. He introduced everybody at the beginning of the game. It just made my heart thump. It is true what Billy Crystal described in the movie *City Slickers.* Wrigley's one of those fields where you walk through a tunnel, and you walk up into this park, and it's beautiful—the green—and I just loved being there. And I still do.

——MITCHELL SNAY, 49, Granville, Ohio

TO BE CONTINUED!

LAST CALL

Cub Fans　　　　**Notre Dame Fans**
Bear Fans　　　　**Packer Fans**

It may not be too late to get your story into *For Notre Dame Fans Only, For Bear Fans Only, For Packer Fans Only*, or next year's edition of *For Cubs Fans Only*. You can e-mail it to printedpage@cox.net (put "Notre Dame/Bears/Packers/Cubs Fan" in the Subject line...pick one) or call the author directly at 602-738-5889.

For information on ordering more copies of *For Cubs Fans Only,* as well as any of the author's other best-selling books, go to www.fandemonium.net.

APPENDIX

Kurt Warner had his appendix removed on May 16, 2000 at Missouri Baptist Medical Center in St. Louis, MO.

Chicago Cubs All-Time Seventh Inning Stretch Guest Conductors 1998-2003

Actors/Actresses

Ann-Margret	2001
Tom Arnold	2002
Bea Arthur	2001
James Belushi	1999, 2003
Jack Black	2003
Tom Bosley	2000
Kyle Chandler	1999
Russel Crowe & Band	2003
Joan Cusack	1998
John Cusack	1999, 2003
Barbara Eden	2000
Jeff Foxworthy	1998
Dennis Franz	1998
Jeff Garlin	2003
Mel Gibson	2000
Cuba Gooding, Jr.	1999
David Alan Grier	1999
Bonnie Hunt	1999
John Leguizamo	2002
Jay Leno	1998
Jonathan Lipnicki	2000
Bernie Mac	2002
John Mahoney	1999
Joe Mantegna	1998, 2002
Jackie Mason	2003
Jerry Mathers	1998
Laurie Metcalf	1999
Bill Murray	1998
Frank Nicotero	2002
Chris O'Donnell	1998
William Petersen	2003
Bronson Pinchot	2001
Harold Ramis	1999
Mickey Rooney	2001
Marion Ross	2000
Alan Ruck	2001
Gary Sandy	2001
Horation Sanz	2003
Jane Seymour	2003
Gary Sinise	2000
Vince Vaughn	1999
Dawn Wells	2002
George Wendt	2002

Billy Dee Williams	2003
Robert Wuhl	2000

Music

Trace Adkins	2003
Bill Anderson	2002
Frankie Avalon	1998
The B-52s	2000
Lance Bass, 'N SYNC	2001
Chuck Berry	2001
Big Head Todd & the Monsters	2002
The Buckinghams	2000
Michael Bolton	2000
Meredith Brooks	2002
Jimmy Buffett	1998, 1999
Peter Cetera	2003
Cheap Trick	1998
Chicago	1999
Billy Corgan, Smashing Pumpkins	1998
Deborah Cox	1999
Charlie Daniels	2000
Dennis DeYoung, Styx	2000
Joey Fatone, 'N SYNC	2001
Faze 4	2001
Peter Frampton	2002
The Grand Ole Opry	2000
Andy Griggs	2002
Buddy Guy	1998, 1999
Mickey Hart, Grateful Dead	2000
Hootie and the Blowfish	1999
KC & The Sunshine Band	2000
Kid Rock	2003
Cyndi Lauper	1999
Richard Marx	1999, 2003
Martina McBride	1998
Oak Ridge Boys	2003
Tony Orlando	2000, 2002
Radio City Rockettes	2000
Kenny Rogers	1999
Shania Twain	2003
Koko Taylor	1998
Eddie Vedder, Pearl Jam	1998, 2003
Mary Wilson—Supremes	2001

Well-Known Faces

Barney the Dinosaur	2001
Bozo the Clown	2001
Budweiser Whassup Guys	2000
Dick Clark	2000, 2001
David Copperfield	2000
Mark Cuban	2002
Tom Dreesen	2002
Roger Ebert	2001
Susan Hawk, Survivor I	2001
Bill Kurtis	2000, 2002, 2003
Bill O'Reilly, The O'Reilly Factor	2001
Sharon and Ozzy Osbourne	2003
Pat Sajak	1999
Cael Sanderson	2002
Macho Man Randy Savage	1999
Donald Trump	2000
Governor Jesse Ventura	2000
Vanna White	2002
George Will	2002

Olympians

Bonnie Blair	1998
Nicole Bobek	2000
Josh Davis	2000
Jennifer Gutierrez	2000
Bruce Jenner	2003
Nancy Kerrigan	1999
Karch Kiraly	1999
Frank Klopas	1999

Hockey

Chicago Wolves	2000
Chris Chelios	1998, 2000, 2001, 2002, 2003
Keith Magnuson	1998
Steve Maltais	2000
Stan Mikita	1998
Loren Molleken	1999
Ed Olczyk	2000
Dennis Savard	2001
Alpo Suhonen	2000
Brian Sutter	2001
Doug Wilson	2002

Baseball

Ernie Banks	1998, 1999, 2000, 2001, 2002, 2003
Glenn Beckert	1999, 2001, 2003
Mike Bielecki	2000, 2001
Bill Buckner	2002
Don Cardwell	2002

Joe Carter	2001
Jody Davis	2001, 2003
Andre Dawson	1998, 1999, 2000
Bobby Dernier	2000, 2003
Carlton Fisk	2000
Gary Gaetti	2001
Glenallen Hill	2003
Ken Holtzman	2001, 2002
Randy Hundley	1998
Fergie Jenkins	2001, 2003
Dave Kingman	2003
Tommy Lasorda	1999, 2002, 2003
Vance Law	2001, 2002, 2003
Vernon Law	2002
Bill Madlock	2000, 2003
Wayne Messmer	2003
Minnie Minoso	1998
Paul Molitor	1999
Mickey Morandini	2001
Keith Moreland	2002
Joe Morgan	1998
Stan Musial	1998, 2000
Andy Pafko	2000, 2003
Milt Pappas	2002
Tony Perez	2000
Jimmy Piersall	1998
Rick Reuschel	2002
Ryne Sandberg	1998, 1999, 2000, 2001, 2003
Scott Sanderson	1998
Ron Santo	1998, 1999, 2000, 2001, 2002, 2003
Lee Smith	2002, 2003
Ozzie Smith	1999
Tim Stoddard	2001
Steve Stone	1998, 1999, 2000, 2003
Rick Sutcliffe	1998, 2000, 2001, 2002, 2003
Bruce Sutter	2001
Billy Williams	1998, 2002, 2003

Basketball

Elton Brand	2000
Cory Carr	1999
Tyson Chandler	2001, 2003
Terry Cummings	2000
Eddy Curry	2001
Bryce Drew	2001
Michael Finley	1999
Ron Harper	1999
Johnny "Red" Kerr	2002
Steve Kerr	1998

Frank Layden	2002
Bob Love	1998
Corey Maggette	1999
Tracy McGrady	2000
Brad Miller	2003
Scottie Pippen	1998
Jalen Rose	2002
Norm Van Lier	2001
Dwyane Wade	2003
Antoine Walker	2001
Bill Wennington	1999

Basketball Coaches
Steve Alford (Iowa)	2001
Geno Auriemma (UConn)	2002
Mike Brey (Notre Dame)	2001, 2003
Jim Calhoun (UConn)	1999
Jimmy Collins (UIC)	1998
Tom Crean (Marquette)	2002, 2003
Larry Farmer (Loyola)	2003
Pat Kennedy (DePaul)	1999
Lon Krueger (Illinois)	1999
Mike Krzyzewski (Duke)	1998
Dave Leitao (DePaul)	2002
Jim Les (Bradley)	2002
Rick Majerus (Utah)	1999
Ray Meyer (DePaul)	1999
Porter Moses (ISU)	2003
Robin Pingeton	2003
Bill Self (Illinois)	2001
Bruce Weber (Illinois)	2003

Boxing
Muhammad Ali	1999
George Foreman	1999
Joe Frazier	2000

Football
Damien Anderson	2001
Drew Brees	2000
Marty Booker	2003
Derrick Brooks	2003
Dick Butkus	2000
Kevin Butler	2002
Marc Colombo	2002
Roosevelt Colvin	2002
Antwaan Randle El	2003
Gary Fencik	2000
Jim Flanigan	1999
Dan Hampton	1999, 2002
Paul Hornung	2001, 2002
Erik Kramer	1999
Jim McMahon	1998

Steve McMichael	2001
Cade McNown	2000
R. W. McQuarters	2002
Walter Payton	1999
Jake Plummer	2000
Simeon Rice	2001
Marcus Robinson	2000, 2001
Mike Singletary	1999
Roger Staubach	2000
Kordell Stewart	2003
David Terrell	2002
Anthony Thomas	2002
Jim Tressel	2003
Brian Urlacher	2000, 2001
Tom Waddle	1998
Otis Wilson	1999

Football Coaches
Barry Alvarez (Wisconsin)	1999
Gary Barnett (Northwestern)	1998
Mike Ditka (Bears)	1998, 1999, 2000, 2002, 2003
Dick Jauron (Bears)	1999, 2000
Marv Levy (Bills)	1998, 2001
Bob Stoops (Oklahoma)	2002
Hank Stram	2000
Joe Tiller (Purdue)	2001
Ron Turner (Illinois)	1999, 2002, 2003
Randy Walker (Northwestern)	2002
Tyrone Willingham (Notre Dame)	2002

Special Guests
American Girl Theater Actresses (American Girl Day)	2002, 2003
Darren Baker (Dusty Baker's 4-year-old son)	2003
Barbie	1999
Beth Bauer (LPGA)	2003
Governor Rod Blagojevich	2003
Tae Bo's Billy Blanks	1999
Dutchie Caray	2000, 2003
Ryan Clifford	2000
Private Jeremy Crandall	2001
Gil de Ferran (2003Indianapolis 500 Champion	2003
Amy Dikinson (Advice Columnist)	2003
Downers Grove South HS Football Champs	2002
Comedian Tom Dreesen	1998, 2001, 2003
Elgin Children's Chorus	1999
Francis Cardinal George	1998
Bob Grimm (IL Teacher of the year)	2002

Natalie Gulbis (LPGA)	2003
Arne Harris Family	2002
Hinsdale Central HS Girls Basketball Champs	2002
Ken Hubbs' Family	2002
Illinois Barber Shop Quartet	1999
Astronaut Dr. Mae Jemison	2000
Deloris Jordan	1999
Cristie Kerr (LPGA)	2003
Astronaut Captain James A. Lovell	1999
Maine South HS Football Champs	2001
The Roger Maris Family	1998
Wayne Messmer	1998, 1999, 2000, 2002
Mount Carmel HS Class 7A Football Champs	2003
Naperville Central HS Girls Basketball Champs	2003
New Trier HS Baseball Champs	2000
New Trier HS Ice Hockey Champs	2000, 2002
New Trier HS Soccer Champs	2000
Connie Payton	2000
Peoria HS Baskeball Champs	2003
Pleasant Plains HS Baseball Champs	2000
Organist Gary Pressy	1999
Prospect HS Football Champs	2003
Rent Cast Members	1999
The Second City Cast	2003
Kate Shindle, Miss America	1998
Frank Sinatra Jr.	2003
Scott Turow	2002
Paul Vallas	2000
Pete Vonachen	1998
West Aurora HS Boys Basketball Champs	2000
Westinghouse HS Boys Basketball Champs	2002
Westlawn Little League Baseball Champs	1999
Ronnie "Woo Woo" Wickers	2001
Wrigley Field Ground Crew	2000, 2002

Broadcasters & Journalists

Chris Berman (ESPN)	1999
Steve Blass (Pirates)	2003
Lou Boudreau (Cubs)	1998
Marty Brennaman (Reds)	2003
Thom Brennaman (Diamondbacks)	2000
Jack Brickhouse (Cubs)	1999
Jack Buck (Cardinals)	2001
John Callaway (WTTW)	1999

Chip Caray (Cubs)	1998, 1999, 2000, 2001, 2002, 2003
Steve Cochran	2003
Rob Dibble (ESPN)	2000
John Drury (ABC-7)	2002
Gail Fisher (Fox Sports Net)	2000
Pat Foley (Blackhawks)	2000, 2002
Eric Goodman (Fox Sports Net)	2000
Arne Harris (WGN Sports)	1998, 2000
Arne Harris Family	2002
Ernie Harwell (Tigers)	1998
Jerome Holtzman (*Chicago Tribune*)	1998
Pat Hughes (Cubs)	1998, 1999, 2000, 2002, 2003
Walter Jacobson (Fox-32)	1999
Harry Kalas (Phillies)	1999, 2002
Dave Kaplan (WGN)	1998
Kathy & Judy (WGN)	2000
Vince Lloyd (Cubs)	2000
Steve Lyons (Fox)	1998
Jon Miller (ESPN)	1999
Bobby Murcer (Cubs, Yankees)	2003
Joe Nuxhall (Reds)	1998
Spike O'Dell (WGN-Radio)	1999
Dave Otto (Cubs)	2000, 2001
Dan Patrick (ESPN)	1999, 2000, 2001
Allison Payne (WGN-TV)	1998
Digger Phelps (ESPN)	1998, 1999, 2000, 2001, 2002, 2003
Dean Richards (WGN)	2003
Dan Roan (WGN-TV)	1998
John Rooney (ESPN-1000)	2002
Steve Sanders (WGN-TV)	1998
Stuart Scott (ESPN)	1999
Vin Scully (Dodgers)	1998
Bob Sirott (Fox-32)	1999
Tom Skilling (WGN-TV)	1999
Dewayne Staats (Devil Rays)	2003
Bob Uecker (Brewers)	1998, 1999, 2000, 2001
Dick Vitale (ABC/ESPN)	1998
WGN Morning Crew	2000
WGN Morning News	2003
Bruce Wolfe (WFLD)	2002

HOW DO CUBS FANS STACK UP?

Sample Excerpts from Other Fan Books

Somehow, my dad arranged for me to shake hands with Ted Williams. I had poison ivy at that time. Ted Williams' huge paw was around my hand. He was not wearing a tie. He wore a checkered sports jacket with flyaway collar. He was like John Wayne…on the way back in the car, I became very anxious and concerned that I may have given Ted Williams poison ivy. Even though I was a Yankee fan, I had a lot of respect for Ted Williams. I said, "What if he gets poison ivy and can't hold a bat? Can they trace it back to me?" I knew I was in big trouble.

—— **JIM COPACINO**, 53, Yankee fan, Torrington, CT

I was about a sixth grader when I saw a Mickey Mantle card that I wanted badly. In the schoolyard, some kids were flipping cards, and the cards were scattered all over the asphalt. I took a piece of bubble gum, which you weren't allowed to chew, and I stuck it on the bottom of my shoe. Then I walked past their game, and in a moment of confusion when an argument was ensuing, I stepped on the card and it attached itself to the bottom of my shoe. Basically, I illegally acquired a Mickey Mantle card. I had coveted it, but it was only a venial sin, not a mortal sin because I couldn't help myself. The power of the Mick, the desire to possess him was too great. I didn't invent this way of stealing cards. There was a wave of this kind of petty crime…

——**ROY PETER CLARK**, 54, St. Petersburg, FL

It was so strange when The Mick died. There's a radio in the bathroom, and I always turn it on. I hit CBS at the top of the hour, and the first thing I heard was that Mick had died. I sat on my bed and…I'm crying now, because I was crying like a baby that night. You feel attached to these people. It's hard to explain. I'm not part of their life, but, for sure, they were part of mine.

——**MARK ROLLINSON**, 52, Yonkers, NY

On my eighth birthday, Dad took me to a Yankee game. As we were ready to go, Dad said, "Jimmy, come on inside with me for a minute." He picked up the phone and called Western Union. He said, "Operator, I want to send a telegram. I want to send it to Mr. Mickey Mantle, Yankee Stadium." I'm sitting there with my mouth open. My dad dictated the telegram, "Dear Mickey, I'll be at the game today. Please hit a home run for me. Jimmy Copacino." I was stunned that my father had this power, this ability, to send telegrams to gods! I knew that my father must be a very important man if he could do this. Now, Mickey Mantle struck out three times that day and popped up. He didn't hit a home run. Dad said, "He must not have gotten the telegram…"

———JIM COPACINO, 53, Waterbury, CT

I left the Stadium with my mom and dad. Before we even got to the parking lot, kids approached me, asking for my autograph. I signed about ten and then I said, "Okay, I've got to go. I'm gonna have dinner with my parents now. I'll sign more tomorrow." Mom said, "No, you don't. You stay right here and you sign every one of these autographs. We'll wait." I spent twenty minutes signing an autograph for every single kid because my mom said I had to.

———JIM BOUTON, Ex-Yankee Ace

My wife, Linda, is a huge Red Sox fan. She's a big believer in the Curse of the Bambino mythology. A couple of years ago, she set up a shrine in our kitchen. It consisted of a photograph of Babe in a Red Sox uniform. Underneath she set a little candle and every Friday she would light the candle. Every Friday she would also go buy the Babe a cigar. These weren't cheap cigars either. After about six months, I told her that the Babe had been dead for over half a century, and I really didn't feel like spending five bucks a week on cigars for him anymore.

———MARK JURKOWITZ, Yankee Fan

I want my ashes to be put in the dumpster in the bleachers with all the other garbage the cleaning crew filters on the day I die. It would be a fitting end to my love of the Red Sox. But I'll never feel like my time has been wasted, because it is about the process, not about the product. It's about the love of the game. You just think about the crowd and sharing times with people you love….Whether we ever win doesn't matter because I'm going to follow the Red Sox until I die.

——SHAUN KELLY, Wellesley, MA

Any big game feels like history the minute you walk up. You feel the buzz, you feel the energy—everything is different. I sat in the bleachers all my life. We "know" when the bat hits the ball. You listen and you know what's going to happen ahead of time. Your heart is ahead of even seeing the end of the play. There's something about the smell of the park, the ambiance of it. It makes it feel like home.

——DALE SCOTT, Raymond, NH

A lot of my love for the Red Sox—and I get emotional when I think about it—is that I love Fenway Park. It is one of the most beautiful places in the world. When you walk up, it's so dirty and so old, but so pure…the way it looks, the way it smells, the way it feels.

——ROBERTA MOCKENSTURM, Clearwater, FL

Rico Petrocelli we loved. We used to see Rico in church. My sister and I would try to cut in front of people in communion line so we could stand near Rico. We got in big trouble for that.…I used to pray that I could meet Yaz and marry him. I did not do that in church, just in bed at night.

——LAUREN DOMBROWSKI, Lynnfield, MA

Every year I bring my oldest boys with me and a couple of friends and we go on a road trip to a different ballpark. We were at Fenway for the first time. They have these old urinals there that are just troughs. I turned around and there was my seven-year-old son trying to wash his hands in it. He had never seen one before. "Wow, look at this big sink!" he said. I said, "Sean, don't." Too late! That's my Fenway memory.

——PATRICK HOGAN, Brooklyn, NY, Yankee fan

…Bucky Dent. By then, I'm 28 years old and had gone through my share of heartbreak with females. But you don't know what heartbreak is until you are sitting in my living room with friends watching that game unfold…

——ANDY CORNBLATT, Washington, DC

Lugging duffel bags and bats and an autographed newspaper article on Hendrick, we made our way up the stairs. My mind raced. We could turn right at the main corridor and walk out the stadium door. I knew it was likely we would not find our way back in for the game. Because we had no tickets, that would be the honest thing to do. Or, we could turn left and illegally enter the area behind the box seats. Though we would not have a place to sit, we'd be inside the stadium and could watch the game in the standing-room-only area. What should be done in front of impressionable youngsters? Well, there is a time to be honorable and to do what is right in the eyes of the law. But there is also a time to get into the World Series any way you can.

————GRADY JIM ROBINSON, 52, Cardinal fan

Sammy Sosa was aided by far more official at-bats, the short porches at Wrigley Field, the prevailing winds coming off Lake Michigan and better hitters surrounding him. If Sammy Sosa played at Busch Stadium, he wouldn't hit forty home runs if he batted from second base using a corked fungo bat.

On the other hand, in my book, all baseball statistics became meaningless the day Brady Anderson hit his fiftieth home run. If Brady Anderson walked in here right now and sat down, even with the sideburns, we wouldn't recognize him. That was the end of baseball as we know it.

————DICK FOX, 61, Cardinal Fan, Lost Nation, Iowa

I still remember the excitement in Boston with the 1967 World Series. Then, you were into it immediately. There weren't all these playoffs. I remember when they had the red, white, and blue banners all around Fenway. It looked different. It was so great. Just recently I saw a highlight on ESPN of the '67 Series. It was so much fun to see it again. I remember how close Jim Lonborg came to pitching a no-hitter. I remember a cartoon in the paper of a little kid writing on a fence, because Julian Javier got the hit to break up the no-hitter. And he wrote, "Julian Javier is a herk."

————BILL BRAUDIS, 46, Dorcester, Mass. from *For Red Sox Fans Only*